W9-BGN-477

TECHNOLOGY ASSESSMENT IN EDUCATION AND TRAINING

TECHNOLOGY ASSESSMENT IN EDUCATION AND TRAINING

Edited by
EVA L. BAKER
University of California, Los Angeles
HAROLD F. O'NEIL, JR.
University of Southern California

LAWRENCE ERLBAUM ASSOCIATES, PUBLISHERS
1994 Hillsdale, New Jersey Hove, UK

Lawrence Erlbaum Associates, Inc., Publishers
365 Broadway
Hillsdale, New Jersey 07642

Library of Congress Cataloging-in-Publication Data

Technology assessment in education and training / edited by Eva L. Baker, Harold F. O'Neil, Jr.
p. cm.
Includes bibliographical references and indexes.
ISBN 0-8058-1246-6 (v. 1 : cloth : acid-free paper). — ISBN 0-8058-1247-4 (v. 1 : paper : acid-free paper)
1. Educational technology—Evaluation. 2. Computer-assisted instruction—Evaluation. 3. Intelligent tutoring systems—Evaluation. 4. Educational tests and measurements—Evaluation. I. Baker, Eva L. II. O'Neil, Harold F., 1943– .
LB1028.3.T3967 1994
371.2'6—dc20 94-20927
CIP

Books published by Lawrence Erlbaum Associates are printed on acid-free paper, and their bindings are chosen for strength and durability.

Printed in the United States of America
10 9 8 7 6 5 4 3 2 1

Contents

Preface

This is the first book of a two-volume set on technology assessment (see also O'Neil & Baker, 1994). Our intention is to capture the best evidence to date of the useful strategies to judge the future utility of technology. As the reader will see, some of the chapters straddle the boundary between evaluating a particular case of technology and broader conceptions of assessment. In chapters that report the evaluation of particular developments, the view to the future is often vague and left to the reader to infer in greater detail. For other chapters, however, there is a clear effort to present and review particular methods by which technologies in general may be evaluated. Three different approaches are taken by authors: analytic models, empirical summaries, and reports of development and evaluation.

It becomes obvious that it is almost impossible to meet the day-to-day demands of deadlines, software glitches, resource development, and empirical research, and to keep one's eye on the future of the field's progress. Conceptual bifocals are needed. Nonetheless, the authors in this volume represent a selection of the very best thinkers and actors in the practice of technology research, development, and evaluation. Trained as psychologists, their particular areas of expertise differ substantially and include cognitive, developmental, instructional, psychometric, and educational specialties. Most have decided to work in a particular environment—postgraduate, military, elementary, or secondary school. Together they present a wide array of approaches, from deep qualitative analysis, to classroom observation, performance assessment, or controlled experimentation. Evidence of validity is presented by some in tight frameworks and by others in freewheeling empiricism.

From their efforts we can learn our status in a representative set of important educational technologies, the strategies for evaluation and assessment that may help shape our analytic and empirical efforts, and, perhaps, how we can better affect the future.

ACKNOWLEDGMENTS

The vast majority of support for this project was provided by a contract from the Defense Advanced Research Projects Agency (DARPA) in conjunction with supervision by the Office of Naval Research. Dr. Craig Fields, former DARPA director, encouraged the exploration of technology assessment ideas. It was his support that made our efforts possible. His sage advice to us in times of trouble was "Optimize." Dr. Susan Chipman of the Office of Naval Research provided operational oversight of our efforts. She facilitated the inclusion of a broad range of technologies, both civilian and military, in our studies and the conference on which the major portion of these companion books is based.

We would also like to thank Hollis Heimbouch, our editor at LEA, for her perseverance and support. Great assistance in this project was provided by Frances Butler and Elaine Lindheim, who were staff at the time at the UCLA Center. We also are grateful to Katharine Fry for her efforts in manuscript preparation and for the keen eye she puts to all our work.

This research was supported in part by a contract (N00014-86-K-0395) from the Defense Advanced Research Projects Agency (DARPA), administered by the Office of Naval Research (ONR), to the UCLA Center for the Study of Evaluation/Center for Technology Assessment. However, the findings and opinions expressed do not necessarily reflect the positions of DARPA or ONR, and no official endorsement by these two organizations should be inferred. This research also was supported in part under the Educational Research and Development Center Program cooperative agreement R117G10027 and CFDA catalog number 84.117G as administered by the Office of Educational Research and Improvement, U.S. Department of Education. The findings and opinions expressed do not reflect the position or policies of the Office of Educational Research and Improvement or the U.S. Department of Education.

REFERENCES

O'Neil, H.F., Jr., & Baker, E. L. (Eds.). (1994). *Technology assessment in software applications*. Hillsdale, NJ: Lawrence Erlbaum Associates.

Introduction

Eva L. Baker
CRESST/University of California, Los Angeles

Harold F. O'Neil, Jr.
University of Southern California/CRESST

Technology continues to transform education and training but usually in ways unforeseen by its inventors. Who would have predicted the effects of the printing press or of the automobile on the way we transmit knowledge and organize schools? Yet, unlike other periods, where any thought of educational applications lagged well behind other technologies, today an explicit set of expectations about educational and training applications and vaunted improvements accompany each new technological advance. As new options or discernible progress occur in computer-based technology, almost simultaneously their potential educational applications are heralded. Whether marketing strategy or sincere prediction, this promotion of educational uses by computer designers has led to a continuing and growing set of expectations. News magazines portentously announce almost monthly that we stand on the brink of a new information era, where the capacity promised by computers will be realized in dramatic reductions in the cost of education, or in the unfettered expansion of students' accomplishments. To some of us, it feels like the longest brink in history. For, despite the hoopla, not much has happened yet. In fact, since educational technology applications have appeared as a market—about 30 years ago—with the exception of texts and tests, no major technological application has made a significant impact in education.

Technology's role has been marginal at best. Remember the flurry of predictions when mechanical teaching machines and programmed instruction were developed? Recall the planned classroom applications of broadcast, interactive, cable, or taped television? And, more recently, each wave of computer technology has been accompanied by visions and claims, whether mainframe, mini, micro, laptop or hand-held, whether time-sharing, networking, artificially intelligent, or virtually real. For the most part, these promises have been unfulfilled.

The contribution of technology to educational training functions to date is an add-on or a fill-in—its hyphenated state underscoring its tentative role. Why?

Reasons for the current trivial effects of educational technology can be assigned to three major sources. They reside in (a) the structure of the educational system; (b) the backgrounds and predilections of technology developers; and (c) the nature of research, development, and evaluation in education. Let's consider each explanation source in turn.

EDUCATIONAL ORGANIZATION AS A BARRIER TO TECHNOLOGY

Educational structure and organization, in its grossest sense, has not changed in hundreds of years. Students are brought together for their early years to learn subject matter, to acquire modes of behavior, to develop friends, and to stay out of the work force. Students are guided and led by adult teachers. As schools have survived as the only consistent social institution for transmitting content and values, they have, so the critique goes, been terribly strained by the burdens placed on them. No longer focused on teaching language and mathematics, they struggle with drug education, work preparation, civics, health, parenting, interracial tolerance, and a full range of other laudable topics systematically addressed nowhere else in society. Without families, religious institutions, or other positive social groups to serve these goals, and in the face of urgent needs, the schools have been all that we have had.

Traditional school organizations, underscored by legal constraints, high teacher–student ratios, administrative timidity, unrealistic teacher union expectations, and even the physical arrangement of classrooms, have created barriers to technology that have yet to be overcome. Added to these constraints are the precarious role of public schools in our total educational system and their resulting difficulty in attracting and retaining highly qualified, inventive teachers. Thus, technologies have not been embraced and pulled by real needs of the system because institutional focus has been on maintenance of existing goals. A real market for technology—in the sense of demand for innovative applications by teachers, administrators, and curriculum developers—has not developed. Instead, new technology has had to fit into existing niches, where it cannot seriously threaten existing organizations and staffing structures. Technology is acceptable if it does not upset or supplant functions served by people in the system. In fact, one group (The Edison Project) is creating a network of private schools, organized to facilitate the implementation. But for the great proportion of schools, educational technology finds a role only if it can augment instruction a bit, or add a little fun or novelty to the student day. Given the practice of school-based technology, it is not surprising that its effects, however rarely evaluated, have almost always been unremarkable. Save a few dreamers and marketeers, educational technology has created no particular constituency for its expansion.

INVENTORS AND DEVELOPERS OF TECHNOLOGY AS PARADOXICAL BARRIERS TO ITS USE

Who are the inventors and what do they know about the education and training market? Typically most advances have been developed by scientists and engineers. Often academics, their goals are to demonstrate a theory, document an approach, or design a prototype. Business and industry create products for widespread distribution or for highly structured markets (niches), and most of all for markets that are easy to penetrate and can be sustained. Schools as institutions, suffering economic disaster after disaster, have not been attractive as healthy markets, notwithstanding the disincentives caused by their structure and organization. With few exceptions, inhibited by their own short-term expectations for profit, serious commercial developers have not targeted education.

Even in those instances where school-age students have been the focus of special software development, lack of knowledge about important educational goals, students' developmental templates, or productive instructional strategies have, in the end, deflected technology away from student learning and how to improve it, toward kid entertainment and how to prolong it. This entertainment focus is generally true of implementations designed for schools, for home, or for other noninstitutional use. One set of developers of software has been grown from the hardware side of the business—computer scientists, software designers with little background in teaching, students, or subject matter. They aim to make the implementation run and to date have exhibited almost no interest in or at least very unsophisticated approaches to finding out if their system has results on student learning. Another set of developers come from education—teachers or individuals who want to use the technology to teach particular skills, provide new opportunities, or even to transform the educational environment. Unexpectedly, developers from the education side similarly have demonstrated little interest in external validation of the quality of their efforts. They inspect the organization of the subject matter, analyze the ideas conveyed in an implementation, and also assume that because the implementation "runs," it is meeting its goals. Neither group of developers has had more than casual interest in demonstrating that their implementations contribute to good education for students. Certainly business goals have mitigated against investment in research and development on student learning or on the evaluation and assessment of technology. Ironically, it would seem likely that good documentation of real educational effects in our struggling schools could have an enormous market impact, even overcoming the limits imposed by school organizations.

ORGANIZED EDUCATIONAL RESEARCH AND DEVELOPMENT AS A BARRIER TO TECHNOLOGY USE

One would expect educational research and development (R&D) to foster the ideal use of educational technology—to improve children's learning and to make schools more efficient and productive—but to date, such effects have not occurred. Why? Real technology development takes resources, and no funding sources have materialized with financial backing both substantial enough and sufficiently sustained to create serious, academically based R&D in educational technology. Because of these limits in support, educational R&D has evolved into a project-oriented rather than program-focused enterprise. Projects typically have very constrained, modest foci and limited goals: a math program for junior high school, a writing program for college students, or a new technology option for testing. Larger images for technology use are in short supply. Outside of the military, very few technology development efforts have been formulated with aspirations to affect all students, most subject matters, many age ranges, and so on.

The staffing patterns of the project focus have a side effect, as well, with implications for technology development. Projects are developed by relatively few individuals, people with unique experiences and training. Small projects draw people of like minds and training. If we look across projects, we discover very little overlap in perspective, background, and development pattern. Different projects rarely share a knowledge base, disciplinary orientation, or even general goals. Even at their most abstract level, it is difficult to see integration. Lack of integration reduces the chance of the emergence of generally useful principles of technology design; these are the principles that might form the core of the new visions for technology. Consequently, technology development is fractionated, piecemeal, and noncumulative.

Without a larger programmatic base, either directed to goals, principles of design, or shared theory, it is hard to see how technology development in education will make rapid progress.

TECHNOLOGY ASSESSMENT: HOW DOES IT FIT?

This book (and its companion, O'Neil & Baker, 1994) is devoted to the topic of technology assessment. Why should we think hard about assessing weak, partial interventions? The argument we make is that the assessment process itself should impact technology design. We have no doubt that the promises for technology applications will ultimately come to pass, at least insofar as barriers on resources and to the ease of design will be reduced. Our interest is not simply on the goal of having many technology options. Rather, we wish to encourage the design of educational technology that will most help students learn, most advantage teachers, most transform schools into truly valued, productive communities.

We argue for two levels of knowledge about implementations: (a) the effects of the implementation for its designed and other purposes and (b) the estimate of the utility of the technology for wider applications. The first level—on effects—should sound very much like evaluation; the second pushes us more directly into broader predictions about technology applications.

EVALUATING EFFECTS OF SINGLE PROJECTS

Evaluation of technology requires dual-level thinking. First, we must address whether the technological innovation accomplishes its intended purpose. If, for example, we are evaluating a reading program delivered on computer systems, we ultimately wish to know whether children who have been exposed to the program actually learn to read. Stepping back from that goal, we need to determine whether we can attribute their reading performance to interaction with the system, and we can use experiments to compare children who have and who have not been assigned to participate in the program. This simple example faces us squarely with many of the problems of technology evaluation. First, if technology projects are designed to achieve goals that take a considerable amount of time to accomplish—for instance, a reading program for primary grade students—we are quickly beset by a number of problems. Just for starters, we have the difficulty of (a) documenting program delivery, (b) keeping track of students who enter and leave the program, and (c) describing "control" or alternative treatment groups in which nonparticipating students engage (if we can find a group willing to be subjected to "control group" status). Furthermore, any new technology is likely to suffer from ills related to its novelty, its integration into existing systems, resistance from users, and its high initial costs. Thus, when any evaluation counterposes a technological intervention with almost any existing practice, and includes cost as a criterion, the technology will probably come out second best. Technology is provided as an option usually on grounds other than efficiency—because it may help attain new goals, it may have attitudinal effects, or because it may free time for other important outcomes. To be fair, any evaluation of technology must consequently emphasize outcomes beyond the instructional or other nominal purposes of the technology itself. This requirement leads to the creation of evaluation detection approaches, where clues are carefully followed to determine the other outcomes, both positive and negative, of the technology use. Even so, the results of many technology evaluations are not positive.

A second level of information is what has been termed *technology assessment* (Baker, 1991; Muraida, Spector, O'Neil, & Marlino, 1993), where the intent is to place given studies within a broad interpretative context. The goal of technology assessment is to provide good and evolving bases for estimating the utility of particular technology approaches for general goal categories. One technique, used by Kulik (chap. 1) involves the reporting in aggregate of the findings of many individual evaluations. The question of technology effects is answered, on average, across a wide range of implementations and settings. Complaints about the methodology—its need to collapse in summary relevant detail—have been made, but such meta-analyses, as they are termed, provide a readily accessible set of information about the impact of technology. A second type of technology assessment occurs when individual evaluation studies, either serially or in parallel designs, attempt to provide coordinated information. These studies may be conceived as natural experiments, where differences in setting, innovation, and subjects happily occur in logical ways. They may be contracted by a supporting agency or funding group, which will look across individually designed studies with a larger purpose and potential set of inferences in mind. Technology assessment studies attempt to make predictions about use to a broad class of potential users and settings, and to inform policymakers' future technology investment strategies.

ABOUT THIS BOOK

For the most part, this volume presents a mix of overall assessments of technology and individual descriptions of work-in-progress. These efforts have been supported by private funders, such as Apple Computer; by nonprofit organizations, such as the Educational Testing Service; by government agencies, including the Departments of Education and Defense and the National Science Foundation; and by a variety of other sources. They address education programs focused on specific subject matter, like mathematics or trouble shooting, of school-based learning using computers. They also focus on classes of technology such as intelligent systems, distance learning, and hypertext. When taken together, they portray the range of strategies through which we can begin to understand the impact of educational technology in the future. They also rather nicely illustrate different approaches presently adopted by technology designers to place and explain their work in a larger context.

Kulik's (chap. 1) meta-analysis of computer-based instruction starts us with a broad summary of our sources in technology and simultaneously illustrates a popular strategy for integrating findings from disparate settings. His work is grounded in the evidence in the field. Z. Peled, E. Peled, and Alexander (chap. 2) provide a more top-down analysis, offering a compelling logic that is intended to guide decision processes in the design, implementation, and adoption of information technology. Their approach is far more deductive in style and provides a framework into which other studies can fit to enable a true assessment of technology potentials. Clark (chap. 3) reviews the status of distance learning technology, giving us both framework and examples by which to make our judgment. Regian and Shute's (chap. 4) description of intelligent tutoring systems also suggests a structure for future design of these systems as well as gives guidance for information needs of developers. Nizamuddin and O'Neil (chap. 6) use a particular intelligent intervention as a vehicle to conduct controlled experiments about the power of certain instructional strategies in intelligent systems. Their efforts have great potential for influencing design of many future systems. Lesgold (chap. 5) takes a different slice at the intelligent training system problem, focusing in depth on his team's experience in designing and evaluating a particularly important training system.

Like the Lesgold effort, the remaining chapters are very much focused on the "project" in which they were embedded, although the boundaries for some projects were very elastic. Three chapters—Gearhart, Herman, Baker, Novak, and Whittaker; Baker, Gearhart, and Herman; and Baker, Niemi, and Herl—derive from multiyear studies of the Apple Classrooms of Tomorrow^{SM}. Baker, Gearhart, and Herman (chap. 9) write of the strategy and details of determining the broad level impacts of a project in which technology was encouraged to be the mainstay of instruction and of classroom organization at a number of school sites. Two spin-offs of this project are described. Gearhart et al. (chap. 8) describe the development of a classroom observation technique designed to measure the instructional processes of teachers as they learned to incorporate technology in their classrooms. Baker, Niemi, and Herl (chap. 7) illustrate the adaptation of existing software, a hypertext system, for the purpose of evaluating students' knowledge of subject matter. This work shares at least some common ground with Braun's (chap. 11) application of hypertext systems for the certification testing of professional architects. Goldman, Pellegrino, and Bransford (chap. 10) describe an evolving set of developments intended to combine in multimedia interventions deep knowledge from cognitive psychology and the learning of subject matter.

Each of the chapters presents a different point of entry on the technology assessment problem. Even those nominally focused on a single implementation, like testing or teacher observation, demonstrate the clear interest by their authors in the larger implications of their work.

We hope this volume, focusing on educational and training applications, and its companion, focusing on software applications, will encourage reflection on technology design and result in greater payoff for students. We look forward to the creation of different approaches to the assessment of technology and a growing acceptance of a need to plan as much of our educational future as rationally as we can.

ACKNOWLEDGMENTS

This research was supported by contract No. N00014-86-K-0395 from the Defense Advanced Research Projects Agency (DARPA), administered by the Office of Naval Research (ONR), to the UCLA Center for the Study of Evaluation/Center for Technology Assessment. However, the opinions expressed do not necessarily reflect the positions of DARPA or ONR, and no official endorsement by either organization should be inferred. This research also was supported in part under the Educational Research and Development Center Program cooperative agreement R117G10027 and CFDA catalog number 84.117G as administered by the Office of Educational Research and Improvement, U.S. Department of Education. The findings and opinions expressed in this report do not reflect the position or policies of the Office of Educational Research and Improvement or the U.S. Department of Education.

REFERENCES

Baker, E. L. (1991). Technology assessment: Policy and methodological issues for training. In H. Burns, J. W. Parlett, & C. L. Redfield (Eds.), *Intelligent tutoring systems: Evolutions in design* (pp. 243–263). Hillsdale, NJ: Lawrence Erlbaum Associates.

Muraida, D. J., Spector, J. M., O'Neil, H. F., Jr., & Marlino, M. R. (1993). Evaluation. In J. M. Spector, M. C. Polson, & D. J. Muraida (Eds.), *Automating instructional design* (pp. 293–321). Hillsdale, NJ: Lawrence Erlbaum Associates.

O'Neil, H. F., Jr., & Baker, E. L. (Eds.). (1994). *Technology assessment in software applications.* Hillsdale, NJ: Lawrence Erlbaum Associates.

1 Meta-Analytic Studies of Findings on Computer-Based Instruction

James A. Kulik
University of Michigan

What do evaluation studies say about computer-based instruction? It is not easy to give a simple answer to the question. The term *computer-based instruction* has been applied to too many different programs, and the term *evaluation* has been used in too many different ways. Nonetheless, the question of what the research says cannot be ignored. Researchers want to know the answer, school administrators need to know, and the public deserves to know. How well has computer-based instruction worked?

Reviewers handle such questions in two different ways. Some reviewers are selective in their approach to evidence. They hold that evaluation questions are best answered by key experiments, and so they sift through piles of reports to find the studies with the most convincing results. These studies become the focus of their reviews. Other reviewers feel that evaluation results are inherently variable and that evaluation questions are seldom decided by the results of an experiment or two. Such reviewers put together a composite picture of all the findings on a topic, and they use statistical methods to identify representative results. Both approaches are valuable. The first shows what researchers and developers can accomplish in extraordinary circumstances; the second shows what is likely to be accomplished under typical conditions. We need both types of reviews in the area of computer-based instruction.

All of my reviews on the topic of computer-based instruction, however, have been of the second type. For more than 10 years, my colleagues and I have been organizing and summarizing the evaluation literature on computer-based instruction and trying to identify representative results. I believe that comprehensive reviews like ours provide a good context for discussing the more exceptional results in the area. Our reviews provide a background. They make discussions of exceptional results more meaningful because they put them into perspective.

In this chapter, I focus on three aspects of evaluation findings on computer-based instruction. First, I describe the methods my colleagues and I have used to create a composite picture of findings on computer-based instruction. Second, I present a broad overview of reviewer conclusions, based on nine separate syntheses of the evaluation findings. Third, I take a closer look at a set of nearly 100 evaluations of computer-based instruction in an attempt to reach some more precise conclusions about its effectiveness.

METHOD

The review method that we use is called *meta-analysis,* and it was given its name by Gene Glass in 1976 in a classic synthesis of the literature on the effects of psychotherapy. Glass used *meta-analysis* to refer to the statistical analysis of a large collection of results from individual studies for the purpose of integrating the findings (Glass, McGaw, & Smith, 1981). Reviewers who carry out meta-analyses first locate studies of an issue by clearly specified procedures. They then characterize the outcomes and features of the studies in quantitative or quasi-quantitative terms. Finally, meta-analysts use multivariate techniques to relate characteristics of the studies to outcomes.

One of Glass' major innovations was his use of measures of *effect size* in research reviews. Researchers had used effect sizes in designing studies long before meta-analysis was developed, but they failed to see the contribution that effect sizes could make to research reviews. Glass saw that results from a variety of different studies could be expressed on a common scale of effect size and that with this transformation reviewers could carry out statistical analyses as sophisticated as those carried out by experimenters.

Size of effect can be measured in several ways, but the measure of effect size most often used is the standardized mean difference. Sometimes called Glass' effect size, this index gives the number of standard deviation units that separates outcome scores of experimental and control groups. It is calculated by subtracting the average score of the control group from the average score of the experimental group and then dividing the remainder by the standard deviation of the measure. For example, if a group that receives computer-based coaching on the Scholastic Aptitude Test (SAT) obtains an average score of 550 on the test, whereas a group that receives conventional teaching averages 500, the effect size for the coaching treatment is .5 because the standard deviation on the SAT is 100.

Methodologists have written at least five books on meta-analytic methods in recent years (Glass et al., 1981; Hedges & Olkin, 1985; Hunter, Schmidt, & Jackson, 1982; Rosenthal, 1984; Wolf, 1986), and reviewers have conducted numerous meta-analyses of research findings. In a recent monograph, for example, we described results from more than 100 meta-analytic reports in education alone (J. A. Kulik & C.-L. C. Kulik, 1989). In addition, meta-analytic methodology has also been used extensively in psychology and the health sciences. Reviewers have used it to draw general conclusions on such diverse subjects as the effects of gender on learning and the effectiveness of coronary bypass surgery.

OVERVIEW

At least a dozen separate meta-analyses have been carried out to answer questions about the effectiveness of computer-based instruction (Table 1.1). The analyses were conducted independently by research teams at eight different research centers. The research teams focused on different uses of the computer with different populations, and they also differed in the methods they used to find studies and analyze study results. Nonetheless, each of the analyses yielded the conclusion that programs of computer-based instruction have a positive record in the evaluation literature.

The following are the major points emerging from these meta-analyses:

1. Students usually learn more in classes in which they receive computer-based instruction. The analyses produced slightly different estimates of the magnitude of the computer effect, but all the estimates were positive. At the low end of the estimates was an average effect size of .22 in 18 studies conducted in elementary and high school science courses (Willett, Yamashita, & Anderson, 1983). At the other end of the scale, Schmidt, Weinstein, Niemiec, and Walberg (1985) found an average effect size of .57 in 18 studies conducted in special education classes. The weighted average effect size in the 12 meta-analyses was .35. This means the average effect of computer-based instruction was to raise examination scores by .35 standard deviations, or from the 50th to the 64th percentile.

2. Students learn their lessons in less time with computer-based instruction. The average reduction in instructional time was 34% in 17 studies of college instruction, and 24% in 15 studies in adult education (C.-L. C. Kulik & J. A. Kulik, 1991).

3. Students also like their classes more when they receive computer help in them. The average effect of computer-based instruction in 22 studies was to raise attitude-toward-instruction scores by .28 standard deviations (C.-L. C. Kulik & J. A. Kulik, 1991).

4. Students develop more positive attitudes toward computers when they receive help from them in school. The average effect size in 19 studies on attitude toward computers was .34 (C.-L. C. Kulik & J. A. Kulik, 1991).

TABLE 1.1
Findings From 12 Meta-Analyses on Computer-Based Instruction

Meta-Analysis	*Instructional level*	*Type of Application*	*Number of Studies Analyzed*	*Average Effect Size*
Bangert-Drowns, J. Kulik, & C Kulik (1985)[a]	Secondary	CAI, CMI, CEI	51	.25
Burns & Bozeman (1981)	Elementary & secondary school	Drill & Tutorial	44	.36
Cohen & Dacanay (1991)	Health professions education	CAI, CMI, CEI	38	.46
Hartley (1978)	Elementary & secondary math	Drill & tutorial	33	.41
Fletcher (1990)	Higher education & adult training	Computer-based interactive video	28	.50
C. Kulik & J. Kulik (1986)[a]	College	CAI, CMI, CEI	119	.29
C. Kulik, J. Kulik, & Shwalb (1986)[a]	Adult education	CAI, CMI, CEI	30	.38
J. Kulik, C. Kulik, & Bangert-Drowns (1985)[a]	Elementary	CAI, CMI, CEI	44	.40
Niemiec & Walbert (1985)	Elementary	Drill, tutorial, CMI, problem solving	48	.37
Roblyer (1988)	Elementary to adult education	CAI, CMI, CEI	82	.31
Schmidt, Weinstein, Niemiec, & Walberg (1985)	Special education	Drill, tutorial, & CMI	18	.57
Willett, Yamashita, & Anderson (1983)	Precollege science	CAT, CMI, CSI	11	.22

Note. CAI = computer-assisted instruction; CEI = computer-enriched instruction; CMI = computer-managed instruction; CSI = computer-simulation in instruction.

[a]based on updated analysis in C. Kulik and J. Kulik (1981).

5. Computers do not, however, have positive effects in every area in which they were studied. The average effect of computer-based instruction in 34 studies of attitude toward subject matter was near zero (C.-L. C. Kulik & J. A. Kulik, 1991).

This brief review shows that there is a good deal of agreement among meta-analysts on the basic facts about computer-based instruction. All the meta-analyses that I have been able to locate show that adding computer-based instruction to a school program, on the average, improves the results of the program. But the meta-analyses differ somewhat on the size of the gains to be expected. We need to look more closely at the studies to determine which factors might cause variation in meta-analytic results.

SPECIFIC FINDINGS

The computer was used in conceptually and procedurally different ways in studies examined in these meta-analyses. Did all the approaches produce the same result? It seems unlikely. It is more reasonable to expect different results from different approaches. A plausible hypothesis is that some computer approaches produce better than average results, whereas other approaches produce below-average results.

To examine this hypothesis, I used a set of 97 studies that were carried out in elementary school and high schools (Table 1.2). Each of the studies was a controlled quantitative study, in which outcomes in a class taught with computer-based instruction were compared to outcomes in a class taught without computer-based instruction. Most of the 97 studies were included in earlier meta-analytic reports on the effectiveness of computer-based instruction (Bangert-Drowns, J. A. Kulik, & C.-L. C. Kulik, 1985, C.-L. C. Kulik & J. A. Kulik, 1991; J. A. Kulik, C.-L. C. Kulik, & R. L. Bangert-Drowns, 1985).

There are a number of ways of dividing these studies into groups by computer use. Early taxonomies often distinguished between four uses of the computer in teaching: drill-and-practice, tutorial, dialogue, and management (e.g., Atkinson, 1969). Recent taxonomies collapse some of these categories and add others. Taylor (1980), for example, distinguished between three uses of the computer in schools: tutor, tool, and tutee. First, as a *tutor,* the computer presents material, evaluates student responses, determines what to present next, and keeps records of student progress. Most computer uses described in earlier taxonomies fall under this heading in Taylor's scheme. Second, the computer serves as a *tool* when students use it for statistical analysis, calculation, or word processing. Third, the computer serves as a *tutee* when students give it directions in a programming language that it understands, such as Basic or Logo.

Slavin (1989) advocated a different way of looking at instructional innova-

TABLE 1.2
Major Features and Achievement Effect Sizes in 96 Studies of Computer-Based Instruction

						Effect Size	
Study	*Type of Publication*	*Place*	*Grade*	*Course Content*	*Weeks of Instruction*	*Local*	*Commercial*
			Tutoring with Stanford-CCC Materials				
Atkinson, 1969	Journal	California	1	Reading	25		—
Cranford, 1976	Dissertation	Mississippi	5-6	Math	12		0.64
Crawford, 1970	Journal	California	7	Math	8		0.10
Davies, 1972	Dissertation	California	3-6	Math	16		0.34
Delon, 1970	Journal	Mississippi	1	Math	36		1.08
Fletcher & Atkinson, 1972	Journal	California	1	Reading	22	.85	0.79
Jamison, Fletcher, Suppes, & Atkinson, 1976	Journal	—	—	Math	8		0.40
Levy, 1985	Dissertation	New York	5	Reading & Math	36		0.22
Litman, 1977	Dissertation	Illinois	4-6	Reading	36		0.23
Mendelsohn, 1972	Journal	New York	2-6	Math	20		0.49
Metric Associates, 1981							
Study I	Report	Massachusetts	1-6	Reading, math, & language arts	36		0.32
Study II	Report	Massachusetts	7-9	Language arts	36		0.56
Miller, 1984	Dissertation	Oregon	5-8	Math	36		0.38
Mravetz, 1980	Dissertation	Ohio	7-8	Reading	12		0.15
Palmer, 1973	Report	California	4-6	Math	16		0.36
Porinchak, 1984	Disertation	New York	9-12	Reading	28		0.19
Prince, 1969	Journal	Mississippi	1-6	Math	36		0.64
Ragosta, 1983	Journal	California	1-6	Reading, math, & language arts	108		0.30
Smith, 1980	Dissertation	Washington, DC	10	Reading & math	34		0.33
Suppes & Morningstar, 1969	Journal	California	1-6	Math	22		0.28
Thompson, 1973	Dissertation	Texas	4-6	Language arts	36		0.11
Vincent, 1977	Dissertation	Ohio	9-12	Math	10		0.34

Tutoring With Other Materials

Alberta Dept. of Education, 1983	Report	Canada	3	Reading	20	0.60	0.92
Al-Hareky, 1983	Dissertation	Saudi Arabia	4	Math	4		0.56
Anderson, 1984	Dissertation	Nebraska	3-4	Keyboard skills	4	0.38	
Bostrom, Cole, Hartley, Lovell, & Tait, 1982	Report	England	8	Math	3	0.16	
Chiang, Stauffer, & Cannara, 1978	Report	California		Reading, math, & language arts	35		0.19
Cole, 1971	Dissertation	Michigan	10-12	Math	16	0.53	0.11
Confer, 1971	Dissertation	Pennsylvania	—	Math	6		0.07
Cooperman, 1985	Dissertation	Delaware	2-4	Reading	36		0.04
Diamond, 1969	Report	Pennsylvania	8-10	Reading & biology	36		0.42
Diamond, 1986	Dissertation	Utah	K	Keyboard skills	8	-0.07	
Dunn, 1974							
Study I	Report	Maryland	4	Math	11		0.45
Study II	Report	Maryland	6	Math	30	0.34	0.53
Study III	Report	Maryland	10	Math	36		0.64
Durward, 1973	Report	Canada	6-7	Math	6	0.19	
Easterling, 1982	Dissertation	Texas	5	Reading & math	16		0.02
Easterling, 1969	Journal	Indiana	4	Math	4	0.80	
Feldhausen, 1986	Dissertation	Nebraska	9-12	History	2	0.10	
Gershman & Sakamoto, 1981	Journal	Canada	7-10	Math	18	0.29	
Grocke, 1982	Report	Australia	1-6	Reading	4		0.82
Haberman, 1977	Dissertation	Pennsylvania	4-6	Math	8		0.57
Henderson, Landesman, & Kachuk, 1983	Report	California	9-12	Math	12	0.88	
MacLean, 1974	Report	Pennsylvania	3-5	Math	3	0.62	
McEwen & Robinson, 1976	Report	Canada	10	French	10		—
Mitzel, 1971	Report	Pennsylvania	9	Math	36	0.56	0.08
Morgan, Sangston, & Porkas, 1977	Report	Maryland	3-6	Math	60	0.23	
O'Connell, 1973	Dissertation	New York	9	Math	2	0.37	
Pachter, 1979	Dissertation	New York	10-11	Math	2	1.44	
Summerlin & Gardner, 1973	Journal	Florida	11	Chemistry	3	-0.38	
Todd, 1986	Dissertation	Texas	4	Reading & math	28		0.25
Turner, 1986	Dissertation	Arizona	3-4	Math	13		0.26
Wainwright, 1985	Dissertation	Minnesota	9-12	Chemistry	3	-0.42	

Warner, 1979	Report	Ohio	6	Math	36		1.31
Way, 1984	Report	Kansas	8-9	Math	24		0.08
Wilson & Fitzgibbon, 1970	Journal	Michigan	4-5	Language arts	16		0.40
Wilson, 1982	Report	—	10-12	Math	18		0.60
			Managing				
Adams et al., 1983	Report	Oregon	2-8	Reading & math	32		0.18
Beck & Chamberlain, 1983	Report	Ohio	9	Reading	28		0.16
Broderick et al., 1973	Report	England	—	Biology	7	0.28	
Chamberlain, Beck, & Johnson, 1983	Report	Ohio	4-8	Reading	25		-0.15
Coffman & Olsen, 1980	Report	Louisiana	3-4	Reading & math	72		-0.01
Fisher, 1973	Report	Maryland	10	Geometry	36		-0.26
Larrea-Peterson, 1985	Dissertation	Utah	2-6	Reading & math	24		0.60
Nabors, 1974	Dissertation	Missouri	5-6	Problem solving	36		0.36
Roberts, 1982	Dissertation	Utah	3-6	Reading	108		-0.18
Staniskis, 1977	Dissertation	Pennsylvania	9-12	Biology	36		0.39
			Simulation				
Hughes, 1974	Dissertation	Ohio	12	Physics	8	0.11	-0.46
Jones, 1974	Dissertation	Iowa	11-12	Physics & chemistry	18	-0.10	
Lang, 1976	Dissertation	Nebraska	11-12	Physics	4	-0.09	
Lunetta, 1972	Dissertation	Massachusetts & Connecticut	11-12	Physics	2	0.69	
Melnik, 1986	Dissertation	Illinois	5	Problem solving	10		0.30
Sperry, 1977	Dissertation	Utah	10-12	Biology	14		-0.04
			Enrichment				
Ash, 1986	Dissertation	Alabama	5	Math	36		0.48
Boyd, 1973	Dissertation	Illinois	9	Math	14	-0.44	-0.22
Clements, 1986	Journal	Ohio	1 & 3	Reading & math	22		-0.29
Coomes, 1986	Dissertation	Texas	4	Reading	36		-0.14
Ferrell, 1985	Report	Texas	6	Math	36		0.39

			Programming				
Foster, 1973	Dissertation	Minneapolis	8	Algebra	12	0.39	
Hatfield, 1970	Dissertation	Minnesota	7	Math	36	0.16	0.18
Jhin, 1971	Dissertation	Alabama	11	Algebra	12		0.19
Johnson, 1971	Dissertation	Minneapolis	7	Math	8		-0.60
Katz, 1971	Dissertation	Pennsylvania	11	Algebra	36	-0.01	-0.39
Kieren, 1969	Dissertation	Minnesota	11	Math	36	0.06	0.28
Krull, 1980	Dissertation	Missouri	7	Math	10	0.68	
Mandelbaum, 1974	Dissertation	Pennsylvania	10	Math	20		0.04
Ronan, 1971	Dissertation	Michigan	11	Math	19	0.40	0.20
			Logo				
Clements, 1986	Journal	Ohio	1 & 3	Problem solving	22	1.00	
Degelman, Free, Scarlato, Blackburn, & Golden, 1986	Journal	—	K	Problem solving	5	1.20	
Horner & Maddux, 1985	Journal	Texas	Jr. high	Problem solving	6		0.05
Horton & Ryba, 1986	Journal	New Zealand	7	Problem solving	7	0.15	0.46
Odom, 1984	Dissertation	Arkansas	5-6	Problem solving	8		0.29
Reimer, 1985	Journal	Canada	K	Problem solving	4	0.75	
Reiber, 1987	Journal	Pennsylvania	2	Problem solving	12	1.52	
Rodefer, 1986	Dissertation	Pennsylvania	4-5	Problem solving	8		0.06
Shaw, 1986	Journal	Alaska	5	Problem solving	7		0.13

tions. He believed that innovations can be defined with different degrees of precision. At Level I, innovations are defined vaguely. According to Slavin, such grab-bag categories as open education and whole-language instruction suggest only fuzzy models for instructional practice. The terms are used for a variety of procedures that do not have a distinct conceptual basis. Level II innovations are more clearly specified. They usually have a conceptual basis that is easy to describe, but in practice Level II approaches are implemented in different ways. Slavin's examples are cooperative learning, direct instruction, mastery learning, and individualized instruction. Level III approaches are precisely defincd. They include specific instructional materials, well-developed training procedures for teachers, and detailed prescriptive manuals. Slavin's examples are DISTAR and Man a Course of Study.

Computer-based instruction should probably be thought of as a Level I, or loose, category. The term refers to a variety of procedures with a variety of conceptual bases. It is a chapter heading rather than a technical term. Under this heading, however, fall several well-defined categories of computer use, which can be thought of as Level II categories. An important one is computer-based tutoring. Most programs of computer tutoring derive their basic form from Skinner's work in programmed instruction. Skinner's model emphasized (a) division of instructional material into a sequence of small steps, or instructional frames; (b) learner responses at each step; and (c) immediate feedback after each response. Level III innovations include common instructional materials, training procedures, and so on. One example is the computer-based material developed under the direction of Suppes and Atkinson at Stanford and later disseminated through the Computer Curriculum Corporation.

It seems reasonable to suppose that results will be least consistent for the loose category of Level I innovations and results will be most consistent for Level II and Level III innovations. To examine this hypothesis, I carried out three separate analyses of the 97 studies of computer-based instruction in elementary and high schools. I first examined the effects in all 97 studies. This Level I analysis was broad; it made no concession to the different uses of the computer in different studies. Next, I examined subgroups of studies, grouping the studies by major types of computer use. This analysis was of Level II categories of innovation. Finally, I examined effects in an especially homogeneous subgroup of studies. Each of the studies in this subgroup used similar materials in a similar way. This final analysis focused on a Level III category of innovation.

Level I Analysis

The distribution of the effect sizes is nearly normal in shape (Fig. 1.1). The median of the effect sizes is slightly lower than the mean, however, indicating a slight degree of positive skew in the distribution. This skew is produced by several studies with unusually high effect sizes. Some analysts feel that unusually

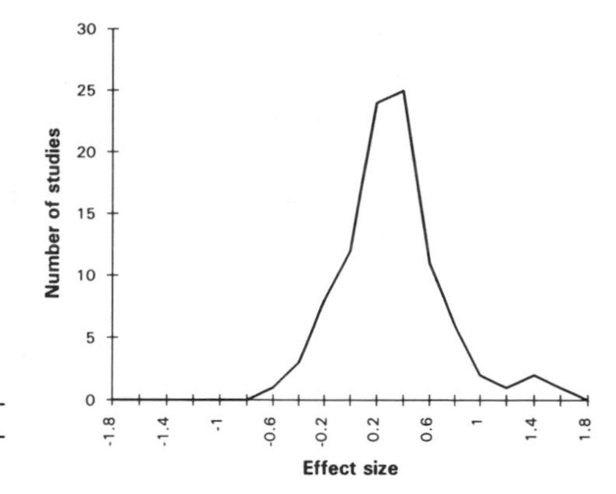

FIG. 1.1. Effects of computer-based instruction on examinations in 97 studies.

high and low values are "outliers" that should be eliminated from a distribution. Others believe that extraordinary results merit careful scrutiny because they may provide valuable clues about improving instructional treatments.

The average effect size in the total group of 97 studies, however, is .32. This implies that the average student receiving computer-based instruction performed at the 63rd percentile, whereas the average student in a conventional class was at the 50th percentile. Effect sizes can also be interpreted in terms of months on a grade-equivalent scale. Pupils in elementary schools gain approximately .1 standard deviations per month in their scores on most standardized tests. An effect size of .32 can thus be thought of as equivalent to a gain of about 3 months on a grade-equivalent scale.

The standard deviation of the distribution of effect sizes is .39. This implies that approximately two thirds of all studies found effects between −.1 and .7 and that 95% of all results fell between −.4 and 1.1. Thus, there is a good deal of uncertainty about the effects of computer-based instruction in a specific setting. Effects of computer-based instruction may be generally positive but they are not totally predictable.

Level II Analysis

The 97 studies can be classified by computer-use into six types:

1. *Tutoring:* The computer presents material, evaluates responses, determines what to present next, and keeps records of progress. Computer uses classified as drill-and-practice and tutorial instruction in earlier taxonomies are covered by this term. The category is therefore similar to Taylor's (1980) category of computer-as-tutor.
2. *Managing:* The computer evaluates students either on-line or off-line, guides students to appropriate instructional resources, and keeps records.

3. *Simulation:* The computer generates data that meets student specifications and presents it numerically or graphically to illustrate relations in models of social or physical reality.
4. *Enrichment:* The computer provides relatively unstructured exercises of various types—games, simulations, tutoring, and so on—to enrich the classroom experience and stimulate and motivate students.
5. *Programming:* Students write short programs in such languages as Basic and Algol to solve mathematics problems. The expectation is that this experience in programming will have positive effects on students' problem-solving abilities and conceptual understanding of mathematics.
6. *Logo:* Students give the computer Logo instructions and observe the results on computer screens. From this experience students are expected to gain in ability to solve problems, plan, foresee consequences, and so on.

Table 1.3 gives the means and standard deviations of effect sizes for studies in each of these categories. The table shows that effect sizes differ as a function of category of computer use. Results for three categories of computer use are especially noteworthy: results for computer tutoring, results for Logo programming, and other results.

Tutoring. The distribution of effect sizes for studies of tutoring is normal in shape (Fig. 1.2). The average effect size is .38; the median effect is .36; and the standard deviation is .34. Comparing this distribution to the distribution for all studies yields some potentially important information. The mean of the distribution for tutoring studies is slightly higher than the mean of the total distribution, and the standard deviation is slightly lower. Thus, if we know that a school system is employing its computers for tutoring, we would predict better than average results for a computer-based program, and we would also know that our

TABLE 1.3
Effect Sizes for Six Categories of Computer-Based Instruction

		Effect Size	
Application	*Number of Studies*	*M*	*SE*
Tutoring	58	.38	.34
Managing	10	.14	.28
Simulation	6	.10	.34
Enrichment	5	.14	.35
Programming	9	.09	.38
Logo	9	.58	.56

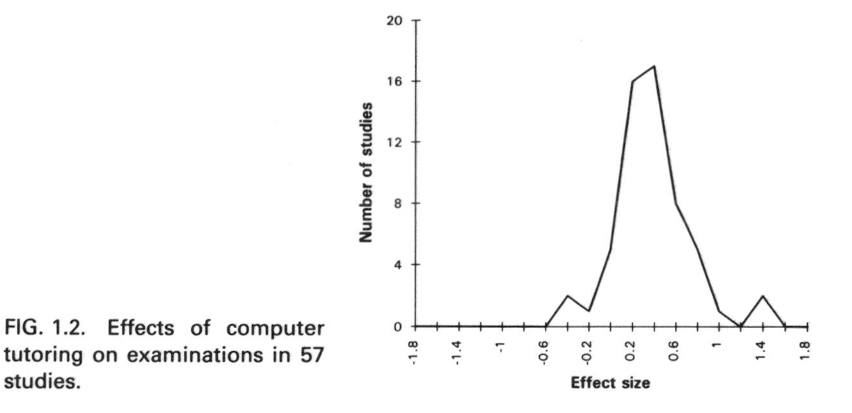

FIG. 1.2. Effects of computer tutoring on examinations in 57 studies.

predictions would be slightly more accurate than predictions that did not take program type into account.

Logo. The results for Logo programming are especially striking. The average effect size is high for the whole set of studies, but what is even more notable is the inconsistency in results. Some of the highest effect sizes in Table 1.2, for example, are associated with use of Logo. In a study by Rieber (1987), the scores on measures of problem solving of children who learned with Logo were 1.5 standard deviations higher than the scores of children who were taught by conventional procedures. But not all studies produce such positive results. Most studies, in fact, report very small effects from Logo programs.

One difference between Logo studies reporting strong positive results and those reporting small effects is method of criterion measurement. In all the studies with strong positive results, the criterion test was individually administered. In all studies with weak results, criterion tests were group administered. These facts raise questions about the meaning of the average effect for Logo studies. The strong positive results may have been produced by unusual evaluator rapport with Logo students during testing or even by unconscious bias in administering and recording responses of the Logo group. The fact is that Logo does not measure up on group tests, and these were the tests that were used in virtually all other studies of computer-based instruction. The case for strong benefits from Logo therefore seems unproven at this point.

Other Uses of the Computer. The record is also unimpressive for other approaches to computer-based instruction. Computer-managed instruction, for example, seldom produces significant positive gains in elementary and high schools. Its record of effectiveness seems similar to the record compiled by diagnostic and prescriptive systems that use only paper-and-pencil and printed materials in instructional delivery (Bangert, J. A. Kulik, & C.-L. C. Kulik,

1983). Programming in Basic or Algol does not usually have positive effects on student learning in mathematics courses. Learning of basic mathematical concepts, in fact, sometimes suffers with the introduction of computer programming into mathematics courses. Use of computer simulations in science courses also seems to have little effect on science learning in elementary and high school courses. More and better simulations may be needed to influence student examination performance.

Level III Analysis

The Stanford-CCC program was evaluated in nearly two dozen controlled experiments during the past two decades. No other program of computer-based instruction has been the object of so much scrutiny. The accumulated studies on the Stanford-CCC programs are a unique resource in the evaluation of computer-based programs. We can use the studies to gauge the consistency of results from a Level III program. It is only natural to expect these results to be less variable than those we have already reviewed. But is the reduction in variability large or small?

The distribution of effect sizes from evaluations of the Stanford-CCC program is nearly normal in shape (Fig. 1.3). The average effect size is .40; the median is .39; and the standard deviation is .23. The mean value is slightly higher and the dispersion is clearly smaller in this distribution than in the distributions in Figs. 1.1 and 1.2. Thus, knowledge that a school is using the Stanford-CCC materials allows us to make clear and accurate predictions about what to expect. Gains of 1.4 years on a grade-equivalent scale are likely with a year-long program, whereas students who are conventionally instructed would gain only 1.0 year on the same scale. Gains of nearly 2.0 years are also quite possible, whereas gains of less than 1.0 years are highly unlikely.

Summary

The previous analyses show that it is possible to make Level I generalizations about computer-based instruction. One such generalization is that computer-based instruction is usually effective instruction. But such a generalization is too gross. There are too many exceptions to the rule. Our analyses also show that some types of computer-based instruction work better than others. Statements about generic computer-based instruction are therefore of limited value. We need to go beyond generic conclusions and make statements about the effectiveness of specific types of computer-based instruction.

Ideally, reviewers would like to be able to form Level III generalizations about specific programs. If numerous evaluations were available on each specific program of computer-based instruction, then reviewers would be able to state with confidence the effectiveness of each approach. But only one or two studies are available on most programs. Only the Stanford-CCC program has been evaluated

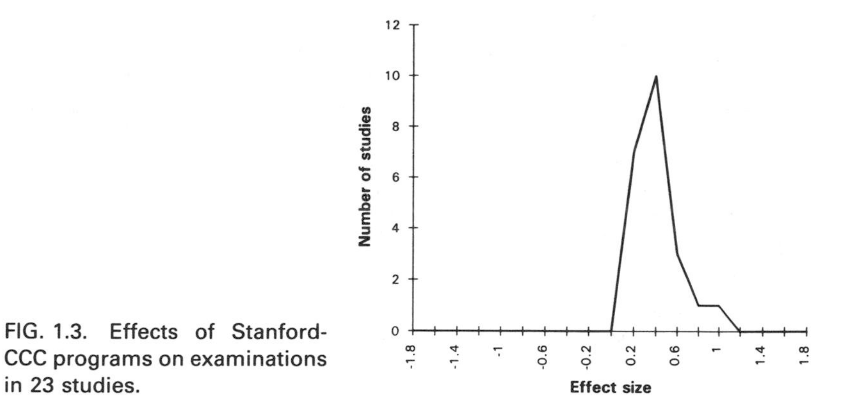

FIG. 1.3. Effects of Stanford-CCC programs on examinations in 23 studies.

frequently enough to warrant separate consideration in a Level III analysis. Based on the evaluation findings, we can state with confidence that this program produces positive results. It will probably be a long time before we can state with equal confidence that other specific programs work equally well.

Until that time we will probably have to content ourselves with Level II generalizations. If not so precise as Level III conclusions, they are nevertheless superior to the gross statements that result from a Level I analysis. Level II conclusions provide a better guide to both practitioners and researchers. They are an important step on the way to understanding the effects of specific programs.

OTHER INSTRUCTIONAL INNOVATIONS

The most important Level II conclusion emerging from our analysis was on computer-based tutoring. Results from school programs that included such tutoring were better, on the average, than results from programs without tutoring. But how important is the gain from computer tutoring? Is it as large as the gain from other innovative programs? Or do other innovations produce equally impressive or even better results?

To answer the question, I compared results from computer-based tutoring to results from other instructional innovations (Table 1.4). The results in Table 1.4 come from meta-analyses carried out at the University of Michigan (Bangert et al., 1983; Cohen, J. A. Kulik, & C.-L. C. Kulik, 1982; C.-L. C. Kulik, J. A. Kulik, & Bangert-Drowns, 1990; C.-L. C. Kulik, Shwalb, & J. A. Kulik, 1982; J. A. Kulik & C.-L. C. Kulik, 1984). Listed are eight instructional areas and the number of studies in each area. Also given is the average unadjusted effect size for each area. This is the average increase in examination scores that is produced by use of the innovation, where the increase is measured in standard deviation units.

TABLE 1.4
Unadjusted Effect Sizes for Computer Tutoring and Other Innovations

Innovation	*Number of Studies*	*Unadjusted Average Effect Size*
Accelerated classes	13	.88
Mastery learning	17	.46
Peer and cross-age tutoring	52	.40
Computer tutoring	58	.38
Classes for gifted	29	.37
Group	80	.13
Learning packages	47	.10
Programmed instruction	47	.07

Computer-based tutoring seems to be in the midrange of instructional effectiveness. Higher effect sizes are associated with programs of accelerated instruction and mastery learning. Smaller effects are associated with the use of programmed texts and learning activity packages. Computer tutoring programs produce effects that are equivalent in size to those produced by programs of peer- and cross-age tutoring and by classes for gifted and talented students.

There is at least one major problem with these kinds of comparison. They ignore certain factors that affect evaluation results, including the types of examinations and experimental designs used in the studies. Because the average effect sizes listed in the table do not take into account evaluation styles in the different areas, the effect sizes given here are labeled *unadjusted effect sizes*.

An important thing to notice about evaluation studies is their source. Findings in dissertations are almost always weaker than those reported in other sources (e.g., journal articles, books, and ERIC reports; Table 1.5). In our meta-analyses on precollege teaching, we did not find a single exception to this rule. It is not certain which set of findings—those from dissertations or those from other sources—are the more trustworthy. On the one hand, dissertation studies may be untrustworthy because they are the work of amateurs, whereas studies found in journals are more likely to be the work of professionals. On the other hand, journal studies may be untrustworthy because they have been carefully screened for statistical significance by editorial gatekeepers. Whatever the reason for the difference in dissertation and other results, it complicates comparison of studies from different areas; in some areas most studies are carried out by graduate students as dissertation research, whereas in other areas most studies are found in journals.

A second factor that seems to influence the outcomes of evaluations at the precollege level is the type of examination used as a criterion measure. Findings on evaluator-designed local measures are usually clearer than findings on standardized measures of school achievement (Table 1.5). It may be that evaluator-designed measures are unconsciously biased toward the experimental treatments,

TABLE 1.5
Effect Sizes for Computer Tutoring and Other Innovations by Study Features

	Source of Documents				Study Duration				Criterion Test			
	Dissertation		Other		Short		Long		Local		Standardized	
Method	*N*	*M*	*N*	*M*	*N*	*M*	*N*	*M*	*N*	*M*	*N*	*M*
Accelerated classes	3	0.72	10	0.93	0	—	13	0.88	0	—	13	0.88
Computer tutoring	24	0.31	33	0.45	11	0.40	46	0.39	20	0.36	37	0.40
Classes for the gifted	17	0.28	12	0.50	0	—	29	0.37	0	—	28	0.39
Grouping	28	0.04	52	0.17	0	—	80	0.13	6	-0.13	72	0.15
Learning packages	36	0.06	13	0.22	0	—	45	0.12	5	0.17	43	0.11
Mastery learning	4	0.40	13	0.49	3	0.46	14	0.47	12	0.63	5	0.08
Programmed instruction	27	0.02	20	0.18	15	0.19	32	0.03	20	0.17	27	0.02
Peer and cross-age tutoring	30	0.27	22	0.58	6	0.95	44	0.34	12	0.84	40	0.27

TABLE 1.6
Adjusted Effect Sizes for Computer Tutoring and Other Innovations

Innovation	*Number of Studies*	*Adjusted Average Effect Size*
Accelerated classes	13	.93
Classes for gifted	29	.50
Computer tutoring	58	.48
Peer and cross-age tutoring	52	.38
Grouping	80	.19
Learning packages	47	.19
Mastery learning	17	.10
Programmed instruction	47	.07

or it may be that standardized tests are too global to use to evaluate specific curricula. Whatever the case, it seems unfair to compare effects from different areas when evaluation studies in some areas rely heavily on local tests and evaluation studies in other areas rely largely on standardized tests.

A third factor that affects the outcomes of precollege studies is their duration. Short studies—where short is defined as a duration of less than 4 weeks—often produce stronger findings than do long studies (Table 1.5). Again, it is hard to say which sort of study we should trust. Short studies may be better controlled, but long studies are certainly more ecologically valid. The problem is that short studies are common in some evaluation areas and rare in others.

Table 1.6 also shows adjusted effect sizes for the eight areas. These are the average effect sizes that we would expect if all the studies in each area were of the same type. I used multiple regression techniques to make the adjustments. The adjusted effect sizes are the best estimates of effects for studies that (a) are reported in journal articles or technical reports, (b) use standardized tests as the criterion measures, and (c) are at least 1 month in duration.

I think these adjusted results are clearer than the unadjusted results. The table suggests that innovations that make the biggest difference involve curricular change for high-achieving individuals. Schools can dramatically improve the achievement of their high-aptitude learners by giving them school programs that provide greater challenge. The next most potent innovations involve individual tutoring by computers or by other students. At this point, computer tutoring seems to be slightly more effective than peer- and cross-age tutoring. Instructional technologies that rely on paper and pencil are at the bottom of the scale of effectiveness.

CONCLUSIONS

Meta-analysts have demonstrated repeatedly that programs of computer-based instruction usually have positive effects on student learning. This conclusion has emerged from too many separate meta-analyses to be considered controversial.

Nonetheless, results are not the same in every study of computer-based instruction. No meta-analyst has reported that all types of computer-based instruction increase student achievement in all types of settings. Study results are not that consistent, nor would we want them to be. Computer-based instruction is a loose category of innovations. It covers some practices that usually work and other programs that have little to offer.

Breaking studies of computer-based instruction into conventional categories clarifies the evaluation results. One kind of computer application that usually produces positive results in elementary and high school classes is computer tutoring. Students usually learn more in classes that include computer tutoring. On the other hand, precollege results are unimpressive for several other computer applications: managing, simulations, enrichment, and programming. Results of Logo evaluations are variable. Logo evaluations that measure gains on individual tests report highly positive results. Logo evaluations that employ group tests report indifferent results.

The overall findings on computer tutoring compare favorably with findings on other innovations. Few innovations in precollege teaching have effects as large as those of computer tutorials. Effects are especially large and consistent in well-designed programs such as the Stanford-CCC program. Programs of curricular change that provide more challenge for high-aptitude students may have produced more dramatic effects in evaluation studies, but such programs affect only a limited part of the school population. The effects of computer tutoring are as great as those of peer- and cross-age tutoring, and they are clearly greater than the gains produced by instructional technologies that rely on print materials.

ACKNOWLEDGMENTS

The research reported in this chapter was supported in part by a contract from the Defense Advanced Research Projects Agency (DARPA), administered by the Office of Naval Research (ONR), to the UCLA Center for the Study of Evaluation/Center for Technology Assessment. However, the opinions expressed do not necessarily reflect the positions of DARPA or ONR, and no official endorsement by either organization should be inferred.

REFERENCES

Adams, M., Ingebo, G., Leitner, D., Miller, S., Mollanen, C., & Peters, L. (1983). *Computer use in the Portland public schools, an evaluation: Computer-based instruction, computer literacy programs, computer management*. Portland, OR: Portland Public Schools, Evaluation Department. (ERIC Document Reproduction Service No. ED 240 158)

Alberta Department of Education. (1983). *Using the computer to teach language arts*. Alberta: Planning Services Branch. Edmonton Public Schools. (ERIC Document Reproduction Service No. ED 252 861)

Al-Hareky, S. M. (1984). A study of the effectiveness of modern educational technology on the mathematics performance of elementary students in Saudi Arabia. *Dissertation Abstracts International, 45,* 734A. (University Microfilms No. 84-19, 010)

Anderson, T. E. (1984). Traditional method versus computer-aided instruction in teaching keyboarding skills to elementary school-age children. *Dissertation Abstracts International, 45,* 388A. (University Microfilms No. 84-12, 292)

Ash, R. C. (1986). Analysis of the cost-effectiveness of a computer-assisted instruction program. *Dissertation Abstracts International, 46,* 2137. (University Microfilms No. 85-23, 784)

Atkinson, R. C. (1969). Computerized instruction and the learning process. In R. C. Atkinson & H. A. Wilson (Eds.), *Computer-assisted instruction: A book of readings* (pp. 143–165). New York: Academic Press.

Bangert, R. L., Kulik, J. A., & Kulik, C.-L. C. (1983). Individualized systems of instruction in secondary schools. *Review of Educational Research, 53,* 143–158.

Bangert-Drowns, R. L., Kulik, J. A., & Kulik, C.-L. C. (1985). Effectiveness of computer-based education in secondary schools. *Journal of Computer-Based Instruction, 12,* 59–68.

Beck, D., & Chamberlain, E. (1983). *Language development component, secondary developmental reading program. Final Evaluation Report.* Columbus, OH: Columbus Public Schools, Department of Evaluation Services. (ERIC Document Reproduction Service No. ED 249 252)

Bostrom, K., Cole, A. J., Hartley, J. R., Lovell, K., & Tait, R. (1982). *An evaluative study of the effects and effectiveness of microcomputer based teaching in schools.* London: Social Science Research Council.

Boyd, A. L. (1973). Computer aided mathematics instruction for low-achieving students. *Dissertation Abstracts International, 33,* 553A. (University Microfilms No. 73-17, 131)

Broderick, W. R., & others. (1973). *Off-line computer aided learning project: The development of educational material. The second report.* London: Social Science Research Council. (ERIC Document Reproduction Service No. ED 129 279)

Burns, P. K., & Bozeman, W. C. (1981). Computer-assisted instruction and mathematics achievement: Is there a relationship? *Educational Technology, 21,* 32–39.

Chamberlain, E., Beck, D., & Johnson, J. (1983). *Language development component, compensatory language experiences and reading program* (Final Evaluation Report). Columbus, OH: Columbus Public Schools, Department of Evaluation Services. (ERIC Document Reproduction Service No. ED 249 247)

Chiang, A., Stauffer, C., & Cannara, A. (1978). *Demonstration of the use of computer-assisted instruction with handicapped children. Final report.* (Report No. 446-AH-60076A). Arlington, VA: RMC Research Corporation. (ERIC Document Reproduction Service No. ED 166 913)

Clements, D. H. (1986). Effects of Logo and CAI environments on cognition and creativity. *Journal of Educational Psychology, 78,* 309–318.

Coffman, W. E., & Olsen, S. A. (1980). *The first two years of PLAN: An evaluation of program impact.* Iowa City, IA: Iowa Testing Programs. (ERIC Document Reproduction Service No. ED 190 674)

Cohen, P. A., & Dacanay, L. S. (1991, April). *Computer-based instruction and health professions education: A meta-analysis of outcomes.* Paper presented at the annual meeting of the American Educational Research Association, Chicago.

Cohen, P. A., Kulik, J. A., & Kulik, C.-L. C. (1982). Educational outcomes of tutoring: A meta-analysis of findings. *American Educational Research Journal, 19,* 237–248.

Cole, W. L. (1971). The evaluation of a one-semester senior high school mathematics course designed for acquiring basic mathematical skills using computer-assisted instruction. *Dissertation Abstracts International, 32,* 2399A. (University Microfilms No. 71-29, 729)

Confer, R. W. (1971). The effect of one style of computer assisted instruction on the achievement of students who are repeating general mathematics. *Dissertation Abstracts International, 32,* 1741A. (University Microfilms No. 72-76, 160)

Coomes, P. A. (1986). The effects of computer assisted instruction on the development of reading and language skills. *Dissertation Abstracts International, 46,* 3302A. (University Microfilms No. 85-27, 359)

Cooperman, K. S. (1985). An experimental study to compare the effectiveness of a regular classroom reading program to a regular classroom reading program with a computer-assisted instruction program in reading comprehension skills in grades two through four. *Dissertation Abstracts International, 46,* 1234A. (University Microfilms No. 85-15, 764)

Cranford, H. R. (1976). A study of the effects of computer assisted instruction in mathematics on the achievement and attitude of pupils in grades five and six in a rural setting. *Dissertation Abstracts International, 37,* 5660A. (University Microfilms No. 77-5932)

Crawford, A. N. (1970). A pilot study of computer assisted drill and practice in seventh grade remedial mathematics. *California Journal of Educational Research, 21,* 170–174.

Davies, T. P. (1972). An evaluation of computer assisted instruction using a drill and practice program. *Dissertation Abstracts International, 32,* 6970B. (University Microfilms No. 72-18, 627)

Degelman, D., Free, J. U., Scarlato, M., Blackburn, J. M., & Golden, J. (1986). Concept learning in preschool children: Effects of a short-term Logo experience. *Journal of Educational Computing Research, 2,* 199–205.

Delon, F. G. (1970). A field test of computer assisted instruction in first grade mathematics. *Educational Leadership, 28,* 170–180.

Diamond, J. J. (1969). *A report on project GROW: Philadelphia's experimental program in computer assisted instruction.* Philadelphia: Philadelphia School District. (ERIC Document Reproduction Service No. ED 035 272)

Diamond, R. C. (1986). Traditional method versus computer-game instruction in teaching keyboarding skills to kindergarten children. *Dissertation Abstracts International, 46,* 2555A. (University Microfilms No. 85-26, 333)

Dunn, A. (Ed.). (1974). *Computer-assisted instruction program. A three-year report covering July 1, 1971, through June 30, 1974.* Rockville, MD: Montgomery County Public Schools. (ERIC Document Reproduction Service No. ED 100 361)

Durward, M. (1973). *Computer assisted instruction in arithmetic at South Hill Elementary School.* Vancouver, BC: Vancouver Board of School Trustees. (ERIC Document Reproduction Service No. ED 088 915)

Easterling, B. A. (1982). The effects of computer assisted instruction as a supplement to classroom instruction in reading comprehension and arithmetic. *Dissertation Abstracts International, 43,* 2231 A. (University Microfilms No. 82-23, 032)

Fejfar, F. L. (1969). ISU lab school fourth graders learn through CAI. *Contemporary Education, 40,* 296–297.

Feldhausen, M. W. (1986). The effects of computer review assistance modules (CRAM) on student achievement in United States history. *Dissertation Abstracts International, 47,* 68A. (University Microfilms No. 86-06, 961)

Ferrell, B. G. (1985, April). *Computer immersion project: Evaluating the impact of computers on learning.* Paper presented at the annual meeting of the American Educational Research Association, Chicago. (ERIC Document Reproduction Service No. ED 259 951)

Fisher, M. E. (1973). A comparative study of achievement in the concepts of fundamentals of geometry taught by computer managed individualized behavioral objective instructional units versus lecture-demonstration methods of instruction. *Dissertation Abstracts International, 34,* 2161A. (University Microfilms No. 73-25, 330)

Fletcher, J. D. (1990). *Effectiveness and cost of interactive videodisc instruction in defense training and education* (IDA Paper P-2372). Alexandria, VA: Institute for Defense Analyses.

Fletcher, J. D., & Atkinson, R. C. (1972). Evaluation of the Stanford CAI program in initial reading. *Journal of Educational Psychology, 63,* 597–602.

Foster, T. E. (1973). The effect of computer programming experiences on student problem solving behaviors in eighth grade mathematics. *Dissertation Abstracts International, 33*, 4239A. (University Microfilms No. 72-31, 527)

Gershman, J., & Sakamoto, E. (1981). Computer-assisted remediation and evaluation: A CAI project for Ontario secondary schools. *Educational Technology, 21*, 40–43.

Glass, G. V., McGaw, B., & Smith, M. L. (1981). *Meta-analysis in social research*. Beverly Hills, CA: Sage Publications.

Grocke, M. (1982). *Interactive Development of Reading Skills in an Educational Clinic*. Paper presented at the annual national conference of the Australian Group for the Scientific Study of Mental Deficiency. (ERIC Document Reproduction Service No. ED 223 993)

Haberman, E. L. (1977). Effectiveness of computer assisted instruction with socially/emotionally disturbed children. *Dissertation Abstracts International, 38*, 1998A. (University Microfilms No. 77-21, 221)

Hartley, S. S. (1978). Meta-analysis of the effects of individually paced instruction in mathematics. *Dissertation Abstracts International, 38(7-A)*, 4003. (University Microfilms No. 77-29, 926)

Hatfield, L. L. (1970). Computer-assisted mathematics: An investigation of the effectiveness of the computer used as a tool to learn mathematics. *Dissertation Abstracts International, 30*, 4329A. (University Microfilms No. 70-5569)

Hedges, L. V., & Olkin, I. (1985). *Statistical methods for meta-analysis*. Orlando, FL: Academic Press.

Henderson, R. W., Landesman, E. M., & Kachuk, I. (1983, April). *Effects of interactive video computer instruction on the performance of underachieving students in mathematics*. Paper presented at the annual meeting of the American Educational Research Association, Montreal, Canada. (ERIC Document Reproduction Service No. ED 233 690)

Horner, C. M., & Maddux, C. D. (1985). The effect of Logo on attributions toward success. *Computers in the Schools, 2*, 45–54.

Horton, J., & Ryba, K. (1986). Assessing learning with Logo: A pilot study. *Computing Teacher, 14*, 24–28.

Hughes, W. R. (1974). A study of the use of computer simulated experiments in the physics classroom. *Dissertation Abstracts International, 34*, 4910A. (University Microfilms No. 74-3205)

Hunter, J. E., Schmidt, F. L., & Jackson, G. B. (1982). *Meta-analysis: Cumulating research findings across studies*. Beverly Hills, CA: Sage Publications.

Jamison, D., Fletcher, J. D., Suppes, P., & Atkinson, R. C. (1976). Cost and performance of computer assisted instruction for education of disadvantaged children. In J. Froomkin & R. Wadner (Eds.), *Education as an Industry* (pp. 201–247). New York: Columbia University Press.

Jhin, K. R. (1971). A statistical comparison of the effectiveness of non-tutorial computer aided and conventional teaching of algebra. *Dissertation Abstracts International, 32*, 5734A. (University Microfilms No. 72-11278)

Johnson, R. E. (1971). The effect of activity oriented lessons on the achievement and attitudes of seventh grade students in mathematics. *Dissertation Abstracts International, 32*, 304A. (University Microfilms No. 71-18, 720)

Jones, J. E. (1974). Computer-simulated experiments in high school physics and chemistry. *Dissertation Abstracts International, 34*, 6903A. (University Microfilms No. 73-3897)

Katz, S. (1971). A comparison of the effects of two computer augmented methods of instruction with traditional methods upon achievement of Algebra Two students in a comprehensive high school. *Dissertation Abstracts International, 32*, 1188A. (University Microfilms No. 71-19, 986)

Kieren, T. E. (1969). The computer as a teaching aid for eleventh grade mathematics: A comparison study. *Dissertation Abstracts International, 29*, 3526A. (University Microfilms No. 68-17, 690)

Krull, S. M. (1980). An analysis of the effects of learning to program on student math performance and attitude toward school. *Dissertation Abstracts International, 40*, 5711A. (University Microfilm No. 80-10, 736)

Kulik, C.-L. C., & Kulik, J. A. (1986). Effectiveness of computer-based education in colleges. *AEDS Journal, 19,* 81–108.

Kulik, C.-L. C., & Kulik, J. A. (1991). Effectiveness of computer-based instruction: An updated analysis. *Computers in Human Behavior, 7,* 75–94.

Kulik, C.-L. C., Kulik, J. A., & Bangert-Drowns, R. L. (1990). Effectiveness of mastery learning programs: A meta-analysis. *Review of Educational Research, 60,* 265–299.

Kulik, C.-L. C., Kulik, J. A., & Shwalb, B. J. (1986). The effectiveness of computer-based adult education: A meta-analysis. *Journal of Educational Computing Research, 2,* 235–252.

Kulik, C.-L. C., Shwalb, B. J., & Kulik, J. A. (1982). Programmed instruction in secondary education: A meta-analysis of findings. *Journal of Educational Research, 75,* 133–138.

Kulik, J. A., & Kulik, C.-L. C. (1984). Effects of accelerated instruction on students. *Review of Educational Research, 54,* 409–426.

Kulik, J. A., & Kulik, C.-L. C. (1989). Meta-analysis in education. *International Journal of Educational Research, 13,* 221–340.

Kulik, J. A., & Kulik, C.-L. C. (1991). Ability grouping and gifted students. In N. Colangelo & G. Davis (Eds.), *Handbook of gifted education* (pp. 178–196). Boston: Allyn & Bacon.

Kulik, J. A., Kulik, C.-L. C., & Bangert-Drowns, R. L. (1985). Effectiveness of computer-based education in elementary schools. *Computers in Human Behavior, 1,* 59–74.

Lang, C. R. (1976). Computer graphic simulations in high school physics. *Dissertation Abstracts International, 37,* 903A. (University Microfilms No. 76-17, 116)

Larrea-Peterson, M. (1986). A comparison of reading and mathematics achievement and cost effectiveness: Traditional and computerized "Prescription Learning" methods; Grades 2–6, Salt Lake City School District, 1983–1984. *Dissertation Abstracts International, 47,* 39A. (University Microfilms No. 86-04, 742)

Levy, M. H. (1985). An evaluation of computer assisted instruction upon the achievement of fifth grade students as measured by standardized tests. *Dissertation Abstracts International, 46,* 860A. (University Microfilms No. 85-13, 059)

Litman, G. (1977). Relation between computer-assisted instruction and reading achievement among fourth, fifth, and sixth grade students. *Dissertation Abstracts International, 38,* 2003A. (University Microfilms No. 77-20, 883)

Lunetta, V. N. (1972). The design and evaluation of a series of computer simulated experiments for use in high school physics. *Dissertation Abstracts International, 33,* 2785A. (University Microfilms No. 72-32, 153)

MacLean, R. F. (1974). A comparison of three methods of presenting instruction in introductory multiplication to elementary school children (total computer, partial computer, and noncomputer). *Dissertation Abstracts International, 35,* 1430. (University Microfilms No. 74-19, 759)

Mandelbaum, J. (1974). A study of the effects, on achievement and attitude, of the use of the computer as a problem solving tool with low performing tenth grade students. *Dissertation Abstracts International, 34,* 3700A. (University Microfilms No. 74-1809)

McEwen, N., & Robinson, A. (1976). *Computer-assisted instruction in secondary school French. Final Report.* Edmonton: Alberta University. (ERIC Document Reproduction Service No. ED 150 846)

Melnik, L. (1986). An investigation of two methods for improving problem solving performance of fifth grade students. *Dissertation Abstracts International, 47,* 405. (University Microfilm No. 86-05, 549)

Mendelsohn, M. (1972). CAI in New York City: The slow learner in mathematics. *National Council of Teachers of Mathematics Yearbook,* 355–364.

Metric Associates. (1981). *Evaluation of the computer-assisted instruction Title I Project, 1980–81.* Chelmsford, MA: Metric Associates. (ERIC Document Reproduction Service No. ED 233 122)

Miller, S. W. (1984). A comparison of computer-assisted instruction with prescription learning and the traditional "pull-out" program used in supplementing of mathematics basic skills to Chapter I (Title I) students. *Dissertation Abstracts International, 44*, 2397A. (University Microfilms No. 83-26, 453)

Mitzel, H. (1971). *A commonwealth consortium to develop, implement, and evaluate a pilot program of computer assisted instruction for urban high schools. Final Report.* Pittsburgh: University of Pittsburgh. (ERIC Document Reproduction Service No. ED 059 604)

Morgan, C. E., Sangston, B. J., & Pokras, R. (1977). *Evaluation of Computer-Assisted Instruction, 1975–76*. Rockville, MD: Montgomery County Public Schools. (ERIC Document Reproduction Service No. ED 139 655)

Mravetz, P. J. (1980). The effects of computer-assisted instruction on student self concept, locus of control, level of aspiration, and reading achievement. *Dissertation Abstracts International, 41*, 994A.

Nabors, D. G. (1974). A comparative study of academic achievement and problem-solving abilities of black pupils at the intermediate level in computer-supported instruction and self-contained instructional programs. *Dissertation Abstracts International, 36*, 3241A. (University Microfilms No. 75-26, 294)

Niemiec, R. P., & Walberg, H. J. (1985). Computers and achievement in the elementary schools. *Journal of Educational Computing Research, 1*, 435–440.

O'Connell, W. B., Jr. (1973). An investigation of the value of exposing slow-learner ninth year mathematics pupils to a relatively short computer experience. *Dissertation Abstracts International, 34*, 124A. (University Microfilms No. 73-14, 846)

Odom, M.L.N. (1984). The effect of learning the computer programming language Logo on fifth and sixth grade student's skill of analysis, synthesis and evaluation. *Dissertation Abstracts International*, Vol. 45, p. 2390A (University Microfilms No. 84-26, 197)

Pachter, S. N. (1979). A computer assisted tutorial module for teaching the factoring of second degree polynomials to regents level ninth year mathematics students. *Dissertation Abstracts International, 40*, 1843A. (University Microfilms No. 79-23, 610)

Palmer, H. (1973). *Three evaluation reports of computer-assisted instruction in drill and practice mathematics*. Los Angeles, CA: Los Angeles County Superintendent of Schools. (ERIC Document Reproduction Service No. ED 087 422)

Porinchak, P. M. (1984). Computer-assisted instruction in secondary school reading: Interaction of cognitive and affective factors. *Dissertation Abstracts International, 45*, 478A. (University Microfilms No. 84-10, 506)

Prince, J. D. (1969). *A practitioner's report results of two years of computer-assisted instruction in drill and practice mathematics*. McComb, MS: McComb Schools. (ERIC Document Reproduction Service No. ED 032 769)

Ragosta, M. (1983). Computer-assisted instruction and compensatory education: A longitudinal analysis. *Machine-Mediated Learning, 1*, 97–127.

Reimer, G. (1985). The effects of Logo computer programming experience on readiness of first grade, creativity, and self concept. *AEDS Monitor, 23*, 8–12.

Rieber, L. P. (1987). Logo and its promise: A research report. *Educational Technology*, 12–16.

Roberts, A. S. (1982). The effects of split-day scheduling and computer-managed instruction on the reading achievement of intermediate students. *Dissertation Abstracts International, 43*, 1482A. (University Microfilms No. 82-23, 584)

Roblyer, M. D. (1988). The effectiveness of microcomputers in education: A review of the research from 1980–1987. *Technological Horizons in Education Journal, 16*(2), 85–89.

Rodefer, J. C. (1986). Teaching higher level thinking skills through Logo. *Dissertation Abstracts International*. (University Microfilms No. 86-803)

Ronan, F. D. (1971). A study of the effectiveness of a computer when used as a teaching and learning tool in high school mathematics. *Dissertation Abstracts International, 32*, 1264A. (University Microfilms No. 71-23, 861)

Rosenthal, R. (1984). *Meta-analytic procedures for social research.* Beverly Hills, CA: Sage Publications.

Schmidt, M., Weinstein, T., Niemiec, R., & Walberg, H. J. (1985, April). *Computer-assisted instruction with exceptional children: A meta-analysis of research findings.* Paper presented at the annual meeting of the American Educational Research Association, Chicago.

Shaw, D. G. (1986). Effects of learning to program a computer in basic Logo on problem-solving abilities. *AEDS Journal,* 176–189.

Slavin, R. E. (1990). On making a difference. *Educational Researcher, 19*(3), 30–34, 44.

Smith, E. S. (1980). The effect of computer-assisted instruction on academic achievement, school daily attendance, and school library usage at Margaret Murray Washington Career Center. *Dissertation Abstracts International, 41,* 2431A. (University Microfilms No. 80-26, 342)

Sperry, J. W. (1977). Computer simulations and critical thinking in high school biology. *Dissertation Abstracts International, 37,* 5370A. (University Microfilms No. 77-4669)

Staniskis, C. C. (1977). A comparison of student content achievement in biology between computer managed instructional and non-computer managed instructional biology courses. *Dissertation Abstracts International, 37,* 7665A. (University Microfilms No. 77-13, 528)

Summerlin, L., & Gardner, M. (1973). A study of tutorial-type computer assisted instruction in high school chemistry. *Journal of Research in Science Teaching, 10,* 75–82.

Suppes, P., & Morningstar, M. (1969). Computer-assisted instruction. *Science, 166,* 343–350.

Taylor, R. P. (Ed.). (1980). *The computer in the school: Tutor, tool, tutee.* New York: Teachers College Press.

Thompson, B. B. (1973). Effect of computer-assisted instruction on the language arts achievement of elementary school children. *Dissertation Abstracts International, 33,* 4077–4078A. (University Microfilms No. 73-3574)

Todd, W. E. (1986). Effects of computer-assisted instruction on attitudes and achievements of fourth grade students in reading and mathematics. *Dissertation Abstracts International, 46,* 3249. (University Microfilm No. 85-27, 393)

Turner, L. G. (1986). An evaluation of the effects of paired learning in a mathematics computer-assisted-instruction program. *Dissertation Abstracts International, 46,* 3641A. (University Microfilms No. 86-02, 860)

Vincent, A. T. (1977). The effects of supplementary computer-assisted instruction on the mathematics achievement and attitude toward mathematics of EMR high school students. *Dissertation Abstracts International, 39,* 736A.

Wainwright, C. L. (1985). The effectiveness of a computer-assisted instruction package in the supplementing teaching of selected concepts in high school chemistry: Writing formulas and balancing chemical equations. *Dissertation Abstracts International, 45,* 2473A. (University Microfilms No. 84-24, 757)

Warner, T. (1979). *The Jackson elementary school computer based education mathematics project.* Akron, OH: University of Akron, Computer Based Education Center.

Way, J. W. (1984). *Evaluation of computer assisted instruction.* Kansas City, MO: Kansas City School District. (ERIC Document Reproduction Service No. ED 247 840)

Willett, J. B., Yamashita, J. J., & Anderson, R. D. (1983). A meta-analysis of instructional systems applied in science teaching. *Journal of Research in Science Teaching, 20,* 405–417.

Wilson, H. A., & Fitzgibbon, N. H. (1970). Practice and perfection: A preliminary analysis of achievement data from the CAI elementary English program. *Elementary English, 47,* 576–579.

Wilson, P. M. (1982, July). *Computer-based education and proficiency testing: A model of cost-effectiveness.* Paper presented at the SALT Conference on Training Effectiveness and Evaluation.

Wolf, F. M. (1986). *Meta-analysis: Quantitative methods for research synthesis.* Beverly Hills, CA: Sage Publications.

2 An Ecological Approach for Information Technology Intervention, Evaluation, and Software Adoption Policies

Zimra Peled
Elad Peled
Gad Alexander
Ben-Gurion University of the Negev

This chapter reviews an approach that guided a 5-year (1985–1986 to 1988–1989) research-oriented information technology innovation (Project Comptown) that extensively computerized school systems in two localities in Israel (E. Peled, Z. Peled, & Alexander, 1989). The intervention, evaluation, and resulting software adoption policies all evolved from a single conceptual formulation that we call "ecological" (Gibbs, 1979; Z. Peled, E. Peled, & Alexander, 1991). This formulation treats the constituents of large-scale interventions and evaluations and combines their multisystemic and treatment-specific components into a model of educational change.

The chapter is divided into three parts. The first part presents the ecological formulation and briefly describes the Comptown project. The second part elaborates principles, considerations, and procedures that are central for the evaluation of large-scale information technology interventions. This part presents a model that within the same evaluation handles two types of processes that are modeled by two types of fundamentally different paradigms:

1. Cultural ecological processes that cannot be subjected to experimentation: The evaluation of these processes is based on paradigm modeling processes that evolve from complex cultural-ecological arrangements. The use of this paradigm prescribes longitudinal explorations, multiple ecological contrasts, identification of systemic interdependencies, and hypotheses generation.

2. Treatment specific processes that are subjected to experimental manipulations: The evaluation of these processes is based on a paradigm that modeling processes evolve from mindful (Salomon & Perkins, 1989) computer software manipulations (i.e., conscious manipulation of the elements of the software).

The use of this paradigm prescribes the use of experimental and quasi-experimental frameworks that make it possible to test causal hypotheses and treatment-specific effects.

The complementary use of the two paradigms leads to the third part of the chapter. This part elaborates a paradigm that models information technology software adoption policy implied by the ecological approach.

THE MULTISYSTEMIC ECOLOGICAL FORMULATION

The leading concept in this chapter is presented by a multisystemic ecological formulation based on Bronfenbrenner's theory of nested ecological frameworks (Bronfenbrenner, 1977, 1979) and on ecological notions of educational theories (e.g., Goodlad, 1979; Guba & Lincoln, 1988; Salomon, 1990a; Sarason, 1982). This formulation perceives the ecology of the classroom as a concentric arrangement of four nested systems that act and interact. Figure 2.1 schematically maps these ecological arrangements.

The innermost and core construct of this arrangement is the classroom, containing learners and teachers. This system consists of three open-ended functional settings (physical, activity, content) in which instruction and learning occur. Next is the school, containing the school administrative staff. This system is the primary operational unit in which resources and policies are transformed into the classroom settings. The third ring comprises the community's political, administrative, business, and social systems, containing the community's key personalities as well as the learners' parents. All three systems express needs and expectations, and exercise pressures that may directly affect (advance or disrupt) learning and instruction.

Finally the outer ring includes educational policy-making institutions containing elected and appointed officials at the regional and national levels. Through

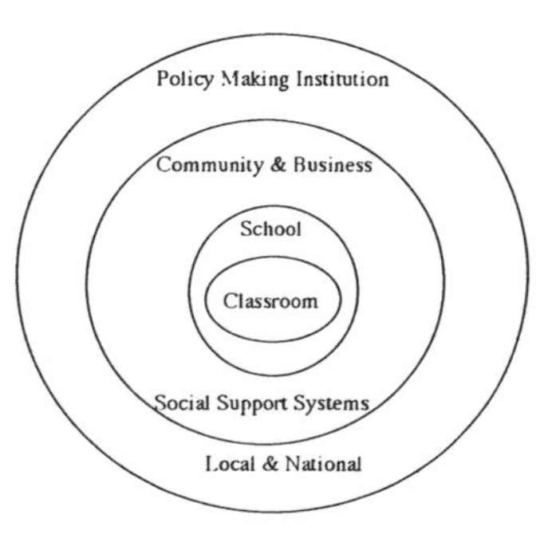

FIG. 2.1. Schematic of the innovation's ecology.

laws, administrative regulations, and resource allocation this outer ring, markedly separated from the school and the classroom, may generate new sources of stimulation that either enhance or discourage new developments in the immediate educational system.

The mapped arrangements are not merely structural. Their mapping is based on five assumptions:

1. Each system consists of implicit cultural, and explicit functional-instrumental components.
2. All the ecological systems are interrelated by a common "cultural blueprint" that sets the pattern for the structures and processes that occur within and across the systems.
3. Classrooms, schools, and social-political institutions are culturally dependent systems. To a large extent, their properties and activities are dominated by cultural traditions, and their cultural messages affect behaviors and have ripple effects in related systems.
4. Ordinarily cultural functioning is implicit. Its reproduced patterns and processes remain unnoticed. Their effect becomes explicit, and their critical evaluation becomes possible, only through interventions that introduce enduring innovations into the ongoing activities of the existing systems.
5. Enduring educational innovations are generated and carried on by two types of parallel and mutually stimulating change processes: cultural-ecological and treatment-specific. Cultural-ecological change processes result from combinations of acting and interacting factors, within and across the ecologically interconnected systems. Treatment-specific (mostly cognitive) change processes result from particular treatments that are applied within the ecologically specified educational settings. Information technology interventions and information technology policy decisions must therefore equally aim at the individual participants, the school and classroom, and their expanded ecological environment.

Project Comptown empirically implemented this formulation.

PROJECT COMPTOWN: AN ECOLOGICALLY ORIENTED INFORMATION TECHNOLOGY INTERVENTION

Comptown was designed to create an ecology in which the correspondence between cultural-ecological and individual changes could be identified; it was to be one in which the interplay between individual activities and environmental opportunities and constraints (Gallimore, 1990) could be better understood and exploited. The project was therefore carried out in two localities that differed

TABLE 2.1
Demographic, Administrative, and Political Characteristics of the Two Comptown Sites

Characteristics	*Locality "A"*	*Locality "B"*
Demographic		
Population	13,000	54,000
Composition	homogeneous mainly middle class	heterogeneous
Administrative and Political	centralized	decentralized
Educational administration		
Interest groups	insignificant	pronounced
Political pressure	insignificant	dominant
Main educational issues	improvement and innovations of schools	provision of quality education to large groups of advantaged and disadvantaged students

greatly in their demographic, administrative, and political characteristics; in their educational agendas; and in their approach to educational issues (see Table 2.1).

In Locality A the entire educational system participated in the project. In the second locality (Locality B) only a subset of the elementary schools participated. Table 2.2 provides a summary description of the educational system and the scope of the intervention in each site.

The demographic factors—the political and administrative systems, along with other "situational" factors (that emerged throughout the intervention)—created contrastable ecological environments in which the project's premises,

TABLE 2.2
A Summary Description of the Educational Systems and the Scope of the Intervention in the Two Comptown Sites

Characteristics	*Locality "A"*	*Locality "B"*
General		
Scope of the experiment	the entire city	three neighborhoods
School structure		
elementary school	grades 1-6	grades 1-8
secondary school	junior high 7-9 senior high 10-12	grades 9-12
Scope of the Intervention		
Elementary schools		
Schools	6 (all)	9 (of 23)
Students	2,000	3,400
Teachers	200	260
Secondary Schools		
Schools	1,	none
Students	1,430	none
Teachers	125	none

goals, and operational principles were implemented and its posited educational change expectations could be explored and evaluated.

COMPTOWN'S PREMISES, GOALS, OPERATIONAL PRINCIPLE, AND CHANGE PERSPECTIVES

The project built on three universally applicable and ecologically oriented premises: First, in the "information era" the computer is a "major cultural tool" (e.g., Calfee, 1985; Olson, 1985; Papert, 1987; Salomon, 1990a, 1990b; Shavelson & Salomon, 1985) that "defines and redefines man's role in relation to nature" (Bolter, 1984, p. 13). Realizing information technology potential in schools augments the educational environment and narrows the gap between the "school culture" (Sarason, 1982) and the "real-world culture."

Second, "sound" educational usages of information technology (Winkler, Shavelson, Stasz, Robyn, & Feibel, 1985) provide opportunities to generate educational innovations and activate unrealized learning and teaching potentials.

Third, collaborative politicians, community leaders, and parents create a "supportive ecology" in which "information technology culture" (directly or indirectly affecting schools) can germinate.

Following its premises the project's intervention goals were to:

1. Create a computer culture in schools: that is, create a learning environment in which information technology redefines teachers' and students' roles in relation to teaching and learning processes.
2. Utilize the computer's potential for innovative teaching and learning both in and outside school.
3. Create a supportive ecology in which a "computer culture" can expand.

The following are seven operational principles that complementarily implemented the three goals in each Comptown site:

1. "High density" allocation of computers enabling each student to have access to a computer for 2 to 3 hours a week in a computer laboratory as well as in the regular classroom.

2. Integration of varied computer applications into as many subject matters as possible focusing on "open tools" rather than on "closed" and "structured" software.

3. A system approach selecting ways and means aimed at the whole educational system (i.e., all the participants and all the activities), as well as its related environments.

4. A multimedia approach where participants interacting with diverse representations of the same task could change the course of learning and instruction and develop exploratory processes.

5. Use of computer tools in a mindful manner where students and teachers could be encouraged to reflect on their work and develop new understanding of the learned task.

6. Involvement of the classroom nesting systems (school, community, ministry) in the project's issues and implementing policies.

7. Cultivation of positive attitudes and beliefs toward the project within and across the systems that create the ecological environment in which the innovation is designed to take place.

Comptown introduced these goals and principles to dramatically change the nature of the traditional print-and-book-dominated classroom. It assumed that the long-term intervention would have three additional educational (cognitive) consequences. First, repeated choices mindfully carried on, such as weighing the benefits and costs of information technology and traditional alternatives, will enhance teachers' and learners' awareness of two sets of relations: those prevailing in the old setting and its underlying culture, and those prevailing in the innovative setting and its underlying culture. Second, these cultural insights will enable learners and teachers to (a) test their old and new learning environments by comparison, and (b) mindfully change their course of learning and teaching as they progressively augment their higher order thinking skills (Salomon, 1985, 1990a; Salomon & Perkins, 1989; Salomon, Perkins, & Globerson, 1991). Third, understanding the links between information technology and older strategies may cultivate two properties that are critical to educational change: (a) an intuitive understanding of the unique contributions of alternative learning environments to the ongoing cumulative learning process, and (b) the use of multiple perspectives in a learned task.

The implementation of the ecological model in a complex ecological environment followed a multilevel-multisystemic design (described in E. Peled, Z. Peled, & Alexander, 1989; Project Comptown, 1986, 1988, 1989) that (a) distinguished preparatory, implementation, and (b) the use of multiple perspectives in a learned task.

The implementation of the ecological model in a complex ecological environment followed a multilevel-multisystemic design (described in E. Peled, Z. Peled, & Alexander, 1989; Project Comptown, 1986, 1988, 1989) that (a) distinguished preparatory, implementation, and adoption phases of the innovation conditions and functions; and (b) used specified intervention strategies in the classroom and in the nesting systems.

The evaluation of the project showed that, unlike the claim often made in "experimental" (e.g., Becker, 1987, 1988; Clark, 1983a, 1983b, 1985a, 1985b;

Pea, 1987; Walker, 1987) or "cultural" (e.g., Papert, 1987; Salomon, 1990a, 1990b; Scarr, 1985) research literature, processes and outcomes that were demonstrated in information technology classrooms were neither specific nor holistic. Rather, they resulted from two types of interrelated developments: (a) continuous (often long-term) and complex ecological developments that were contingent on the specific nesting arrangements of the intervention and (b) treatment (often short-term) generated processes that were realized through interactions between learners and particular information technology devices (applied within an ecologically specified framework). The assumptions and concerns that guided this evaluation were not specific to Comptown. They were conceptually rooted in the general ecological formulation.

MAJOR CONCERNS OF AN ECOLOGICALLY ORIENTED EVALUATION

In the systematically nested ecological formulation the basic structure components are dynamic classroom settings. The basic process components are intersystemic and intrasystemic interactions that create and carry on the cultural-ecological and treatment-specific innovations. An evaluation that is guided by these conditioning assumptions is consequently concerned with three issues that are ordinarily bypassed by conventional input–output evaluations and are central to the ecological evaluation.

The first issue involves the identification and study of parallel and mutually stimulating cultural-ecological processes that are contingent on the intervention. These processes often act in complex and cyclical ways. Accordingly, the evaluation is concerned with (a) combinations of dynamic factors that contribute to particular results, although the relations among these factors and the unique effect of each single factor may remain unknown; and (b) developments that need to be studied in cyclical ways, so that new knowledge gained leads to new hypotheses that refer to new and previously unanticipated combinations of factors that both affect and are affected by the intervention.

The second issue is the design of multiple ecological contrasts in which different combinations of structure and process constituents that are not given to experimentation can be studied and evaluated. This design implies the construction of basic data structures that (a) formally define the building blocks (facets) of contrasted ecologies, and (b) translate these specifications into reproducible observations.

The third concern of an ecological evaluation is the understanding of the effects of specific treatments that are compatible with the ecological model and are part of the intervention. These understandings, which are essential for further intervention manipulations, imply the design of an ecologically sensitive experimentation that is theory driven and that rules out counterinterpretations within the well-specified ecology.

The following examples from Comptown elaborate these concerns.

ECOLOGICAL CHANGE PROCESSES: THE COMPTOWN EXAMPLE

In Comptown, ecological processes that were repeatedly activated by interactions in each and all ecological systems were realized through interconnected classroom accommodations, school modifications, centralized policies, and beliefs and attitude-based behaviors. Tables 2.3, 2.4, 2.5, and 2.6 examine some of

TABLE 2.3
Indicative Physical, Activity, and Content Accommodations in Classroom 6, School Y, Locality A (1985, 1988)

Addommodation	*1985*	*1988*
Physical		
Instructional aids	Whole class* oriented	Group work**oriented
Table and chair organization	Facing classroom's front (facilitating frontal teaching)	Optionally organized in activity centers for group work
Activity		
Essential student learning activities	Attentive listening and imitating	Group and machine interactions; exploring and modeling
Classroom behavior	Essentially controlled and quiet; occasional misbehavior	Noisy and constantly moving; minimal misbehavior
Dominant teacher delivery modes	Lecturing and demonstrating	Tutoring and guiding group and student machine interactions; using computer-based activity as a main delivery channel
Content		
Curricular goals	Knowledge and basic skills acquisition	Development of new and enriched content areas such as handling of information and use of multiple technologies and multiple knowledge sources

*The concept of "whole class" work has three components: (a) The classroom is organized as a single whole with the teacher as a sole vehicle of instruction; (b) The same instruction, conditions, and resources are available to all classroom students; (c) The acquisition of basic skills and knowledge are the end goals to be achieved.

Accommodations promoting whole class work are demonstrated by physical, activity, and content indicators characterizing Classroom 6 in 1985.

**The concept of "group work" has three components: (a) The classroom is divided into simultaneously operating groups; (b) alternative systems for group work are maintained by alternative instructional provisions, conditions, and resources that are available to the different groups; (c) acquisitions of basic skills and knowledge is accompanied by the acquisition of higher order skills, use of multiple technologies, and multiple information resources.

Accommodations promoting group work are demonstrated by physical, activity, and content indicators characterizing Classroom 6 in 1988.

the indicative developments in the first 3 years of the intervention (1985–1988). Each of the four tables focuses on preproject and project-triggered characteristics that realize one of the four ecological change processes involved in the innovation.

Table 2.3 focuses on accommodations (physical, activity, and subject matter content) observed in Classroom 6 (School Y, Locality A). The developments in this classroom (managed by the same teacher, in the same school, and in same locality) accurately represent the changing trends in classrooms that actively and continuously tried to implement the project's goals.

Furthermore, the analysis of the accommodations showed that (a) the contrasted characteristics realized inseparable aspects of interrelated classroom events, (b) the emerging patterns could neither be understood nor valued in terms of isolated classroom settings, and (c) the observed accommodations were nested; that is, additional ecological processes that converged in the classroom were differently realized in the 1985 and the 1988 situations.

Table 2.4 demonstrates some of the school's modifications that framed the classroom's "move" from one educational orientation (frontal teaching) to the other (interactive group work).

The listed administrative, social, and curricular modifications reveal a dynamic school policy that was fruitful both inside and outside the school. Inside the school it reshaped some of the prevailing principles, reinforced existing trends, and nurtured interactive relations between the school and its classrooms.

TABLE 2.4
Administrative, Social, and Curricular Modifications in School Y, Locality A (1985, 1988)

Policy Modification	*1985*	*1988*
Administrative Allocation policy of instructional aids	Supply of identical aids to different classrooms	Supply of aids chosen by teachers to meet their needs
Special Role assignment	Complete separation between teaching and learning activitities and responsibilities	Assignment of technical and teaching roles to students (e.g., older students teach the young)
Curricular Curricular emphases	Basic skills acquisition and accumulation of information	Development of interdisciplinary inquiries; information handling and use of multiple learning and teaching strategies
Special programs	Special extra classes for low achievers	Promotion of IT-based school activities: e.g., computer game library; school desk top publishing; IT training for teachers in and outside school; parents IT training

Outside the school it produced new ideas that activated local support systems and influenced centralized policy-making institutions. The policy modifications of School Y and its generated internal and external interactions were typical processes in Locality A. In this locality involvement, support, and intervention actions progressively increased, moving in the same direction. These interdependencies did not develop in Locality B. Table 2.5 presents examples that demonstrate the different intersystemic interactions in the two Comptown sites (Project Comptown, 1986, 1988).

These examples show that the distinctive ecological arrangements of Lo-

TABLE 2.5
Community Support and Centralized Educational Policies in the two Two Comptown Sites (1985, 1988)

Centralized Policy	*Locality A*	*Locality B*
Physical Support: Infrastructure and equipment	1985: Firm municipal commitment to build an IT infrastructure; firm commitment of the Ministry of Education to support introduction of IT infrastructure and supply computers to schools	1985: Vague municipal commitment to build an IT infrastructure; vague commitment of the Ministry of Education to support introduction of IT infrastructure and supply computers to schools
	1988: Private contributions of computers to schools; municipal maintenance of IT infrastructure and of computers installed and used in classrooms	1988: The commitment of the municipality and the ministry do not exceed regular support to nonexperimental school systems
Professional Support Planning	1985: Municipal appointment of experts to advise purchase of computers and develop networking	1985: Municipal appointment of experts to advise purchase of computers and develop networking
	1988: Experts follow up development of networking	1988: Experts follow up the purchase of hardware
Special Programs	Promotion of special training programs (e.g., parents and senior citizens training)	
Social Support Involvement	1985: Voluntary parents activity in classrooms	1985: Parents attempt to affect intervention program
	1988: Parents' participation in the project's inside and outside school activity	1988: Parents do not demonstrate special interest in the project

calities A and B generated different ecological processes. Furthermore, the examples that follow show that these processes interacted differently with the fourth type of ecological change processes: "belief-and attitude-based behaviors" (Jagodzinski & Clarke, 1986).

In Comptown, belief- and attitude-based behaviors operated across the ecological levels in two ways. First, at the introduction of the innovation, they provided a bridge between the intervention and its unknown results (Schank & Abelson, 1977). Second, as the intervention evolved, they tested the initial promises of the intervention against its particular outcomes. Table 2.6 describes belief- and attitude-based behaviors in the two Comptown sites.

Although contradictory in their consequences, belief- and attitude-based behaviors played identical roles in the two localities. They aimed at the project's promises and cultivated theoretical expectations that were not based on already existing experience. In Locality A, realized expectations augmented positive attitudes toward the project. In Locality B, the real events contradicted expectations, nurtured critical attitude-based behaviors, and augmented the negative approach toward the project.

Taken together, the previous examples reveal (a) systematic relations between an implicit "community culture" and explicit school and classroom characteristics, and (b) cyclical progressions of dynamic multisystemic ecologies that cannot be modeled by conventional hypotheses-testing paradigms.

The evaluation of Comptown showed that classroom accommodations and school modifications demonstrated in Locality A did not develop in Locality B. However, the evaluation could not determine, or experimentally show, whether the radically different project histories reviewed in this chapter resulted from different political and social constellations, different physical settings, different school cultures, different attitude-based behaviors, or a combination of these factors. This experience implies that the evaluation of complex ecological arrangements should build on a paradigm that models multisystemic linear and nonlinear functioning and that emphasizes (a) an explorative, hypotheses-generating approach that contrasts ecologies (rather than an hypothesis-testing approach that builds on randomized experiments), and (b) a data structure that formally and empirically characterizes variations within the contrasted ecologies.

FORMALIZATION OF BASIC ECOLOGICAL DATA STRUCTURES

The nested systems formulation assumes that classroom occurrences reflect and permit the tracing of developments across the ecological levels. In ecological evaluations the formal specification of basic data structures is based on this assumption.

Furthermore, the proposed ecological paradigm treats within Guttman's facet

TABLE 2.6
Beliefs and Attitude-Based Behaviors in the Two Comptown Sites

System	*Belief and Attitude-Based Behavior*	
	Locality A	*Locality B*
Ministry 1985	Positive attitude toward the research project generates support in the project	Lack of confidence in the local authorities generates limited support in the project
1988	Positive field outcomes and current demands result in longtime commitments	Attitudes and support remain unchanged
Local, Political Authorities 1985	Convinced that computer culture in schools serve local interests; participate in progress and difficulties	Approach Comptown as one of the competing projects; make no effort to support
1988	Demonstrate consistent attitudes; increase involvement and commitment to the project's success	Approach and support remain unchanged
School Principals 1985	Led to believe that the promised innovations can improve learning and teaching; set priorities that match the project's operational principles	Led to believe that the innovation can improve learning and teaching; express support in the project
1988	As the project moved toward promised targets augment involvement and express specific interests	Doubt and dispute the project's policies and disappointed by results
Teachers 1985	Convinced that additional work caused by the project is worthwhile; voluntarily praticipate in training	Internalize the project's objectives; voluntarily participate in training
1988	Gained success in work leads to interest and involvement in the achievement in specific goals	Difficulties in implementing Comptown's working principles result in no commitment while continuing to use the training offers of the project
Parents 1985	Believe the computers carry a promise for better education; they support and are involved in the project	
1988	Responding to enthusiastic reactions of children, parents' involvement is increased	

theory (Canter, 1985; Guttman, 1957; Shye, 1978) structure and process components that (a) represent the classroom and delimit its ecology, and (b) translate ecological variations into reproducible observations that can be used in a contrast-based evaluation.

A two-stage design is required to achieve this type of data representation. The first stage involves the specification of three structure and four process components that are essential and necessary for the design of the ecological evaluation. The second stage elaborates specific properties and processes that characterize each specific phase of the intervention.

The structure components that are essential in a first-stage design are the physical, activity, and content settings, often discussed in ecological and educational literature. The physical setting accounts for technology, materials, and learning aids available in the classroom (e.g., Bronfenbrenner, 1977, 1979; Calfee & Brown, 1979; Project Comptown, 1988, 1989, 1990). The activity setting accounts for all management, delivery, learning, and misbehavior activities enacted in the classroom (e.g., Doyle, 1986; Lamm, 1976; Leontiev, 1964; Project Comptown, 1988, 1989, 1990; Vygotsky, 1978). The content setting accounts for instructional, social, and technical goals, and for curricular emphases and students' motivation generated emphases (e.g., Doyle, 1988; Lamm, 1976; Project Comptown, 1988, 1989, 1990; Shavelson, Winkler, Stasz, Robyn, & Shaha, 1984).

The process components that are essential in a first-stage design are four facets that enable characterization and contrast of the newly introduced cultural-educational frameworks, and the preproject old frameworks. These process facets are (a) the inventory of the items that distinguish the setting, (b) the organization of the items within the setting, (c) the intrasystemic accommodations that involve the setting, and (d) the intersystemic relations that affect the settings.

Because any situation or event in the classroom can be characterized as a particular combination of these settings and facets, all three settings and four facets are considered essential and necessary for the design of the evaluation. Table 2.7 presents preliminary, first-stage specifications for the construction of reproducible ecological observations.

Tables 2.3, 2.4, 2.5, and 2.6 can be taken as typical observations that built on these specifications. The presented examples were derived from Comptown's longitudinal exploration of multiple ecologies that contrasted: same classroom within the same school, different classrooms within the same school, classrooms in different schools within the same locality, different schools within the same locality, different schools in different localities.

Local and regional policy-making institutions were represented by district and regional superintendents, who in turn represented the national policy formulated by the Ministry of Education and Culture. Figure 2.2 schematically lays out the ecological units of analysis used in this study.

The Comptown intervention was carried out in three phases: (a) preparation, (b) implementation, and (c) adoption of the innovation. Each phase had different foci and different characteristics that first-stage design could not capture. The second-stage design introduced detailed refinements that clarified specific objectives and referent systems and thereby operationalized first-stage specifications.

The ecological paradigm developed in this section has four distinguished characteristics:

TABLE 2.7
Preliminary First-Stage Specifications for the Construction of Reproducible Ecological Observations

Facet Setting	*Inventory*	*Organization*	*Intrasystemic Accommodations*	*Intersystemic Changes*
Physical	Available: Technology Materials Learning aids	Supporting: Whole class Group Individual learning and instruction	Accommodations in physical inventory and/or organization appear in combination with accommodations in additional settings	Demonstrated changes in: Social Political Other Involvement Support Commitment
Activity	Enacted: Management style Delivery mode Learning mode Misbehaviors Minimal Occasional Severe	Supporting: Whole class learning Group interactions Individual learning Student x machine interaction Session: Shortened Regular Shortened	Changes in activity inventory and/or organization appear in combination with accommodation in additional settings	Demonstrated changes in: Social Political Other Involvement Support Commitment Other
Content	Enacted: Goals: social; instruction; technical Curricular emphases: Basic skills High order skills Technical skills Other Enhanced motivation: High Average Low	According to: Hierarchical principle Nonhierarchical principles Mixed principles	Stimulated by: New needs Student feedback Ideological consideration Professional consideration	Demonstrated changes in: Social Political Other involvement in content issues

1. Properties and processes that have no effect on classroom occurrences and that cannot be traced through properties and processes in classroom settings are omitted from the evaluation design.

2. The units of analysis are the natural systems. Behaviors included in the design are not separated from their natural settings and can be studied as culturally and ecologically dependent behaviors.

3. The settings and facets that guide the construction of the observations remain intact across different ecological arrangements.

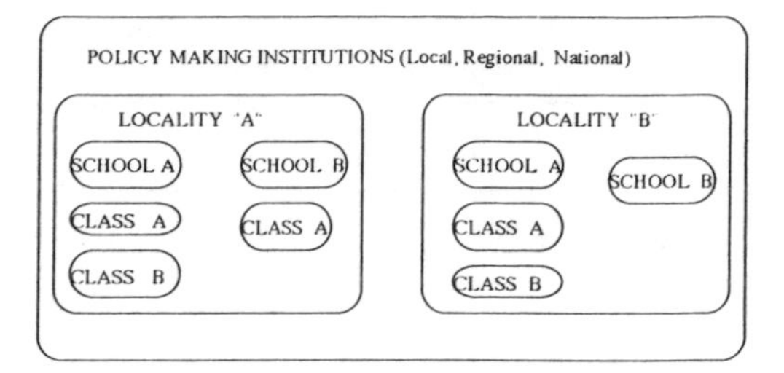

FIG. 2.2. Ecological units of analysis used in Comptown.

4. The two-stage design allows for additions, corrections, deletions, and accommodations that conceptually elaborate and empirically validate the ecological model.

ECOLOGICALLY SENSITIVE EXPERIMENTATION

The ecological assumption implies that information technology treatments cannot be separated from their ecological contexts, or from the cultural comparisons and educational activities they enhance. Accordingly information technology treatments should be defined in terms of (a) interactions between learners in an ecologically characterized classroom, and a particular type of educational software, and (b) the alternating representations (conventional and computer-based) introduced.

The ecologically sensitive experimentation that we propose elaborates this formulation in four facets. These facets are (a) the type of information exchanged and processed in the interaction (i.e., subject-matter-bound and applicable to specific topics or procedural and applicable to a variety of subject matters; Give'on, 1988); (b) the cognitive demands set on the learner (i.e., low-reactive or high-level-interactive processing demands; Give'on, 1988; Salomon, 1985; Salomon & Globerson, 1987; Salomon & Perkins, 1989); (c) the proximity between processes generated throughout the interaction and processes that are encouraged by the already functioning educational frameworks (i.e., processes producing "more of the same" and leaving the learner's "zone of proximal development" [Vygotsky, 1978; Wertsch, 1985a, 1985b] intact,[1] or processes that trigger an innovative experience that augments the learner's zone of proximal development; Project Comptown, 1990); and (d) the control of alternating

[1]Vygotsky defined the zone of proximal development as the distance between a child's "actual developmental level as determined by independent problem solving" and the higher level of "potential development as determined through problem solving under adult guidance or in collaboration with more capable peers" (in Wertsch, 1985, pp. 67–68).

TABLE 2.8
A Faceted Design for the Characterization of IT Software Ecologically Sensitive Experimentations

Facet	*Facet Element*
Type of information	1. Subject matter bound 2. Procedural
Cognitive demands	1. Low level (reactive) 2. Low level supplemented by a limited number of higher level demands 3. High level and interactive (reflecting on and constructing own learning preocesses)
Proximity to existing learning processes	1. "More of the same" (not augmenting "zone for proximal development") 2. "Different and complementary" (augmenting "zone for proximal development")
Control of alternating representations	1. Use of software in a nonselective manner 2. Use of software in a selective manner

representations (i.e., alternating use of conventional and nonconventional software representations in a nonselective or a critical selective manner; (Bamberger & Schon, 1983; Gal, 1990, 1991). Table 2.8 presents the faceted design for the characterization of information technology software used in ecologically sensitive experimentations.

Because information technology treatments are nested within natural ecological settings, the generality and validity of the treatment cannot be routinely handled. They must be demonstrated in two ways. First, the treatment and the stimulated cognitive processes must be relevant to a variety of learning and teaching contexts. Second, the implementation of the treatment and control conditions must be equivalent and representative in relation to similar learning and instruction activities in regular classroom settings. A design that satisfies these conditions, and tests the implications of a mindful use (Salomon & Perkins, 1989)[2] of a particular type of software in natural classroom settings, is presented in Table 2.9.

This design was repeatedly used in Comptown for the evaluation of the cognitive benefits of a mindful use of types of software that encourage the development of higher order cognitive skills and meet the ecological criteria of generality and validity. The "algebraic linear functions" and the "database" stud-

[2]Salomon and Perkins (1989, pp. 125–126) define *mindfulness* as "the volitional, metacognitively guided employment of nonautomatic (controlled) processes (Salomon & Globerson, 1987) typical of deeper processing (Kintsch, 1977), of greater cognitive capacity usage (Kerr, 1973), of greater mental effort expenditure (e.g., Salomon, 1983), and of the conscious manipulation of the elements of one's environment (Langer & Imber, 1979)."

TABLE 2.9
A Stepwise Facet Design of an Ecologically Sensitive Experiment

Step	*Treatment*	*Control*	*Posttest*
Precondition	Equivalent: IQ and score distribution Equivalent teacher evaluations		
Step 1	Teacher trained in subject matter concepts and in a mindful use of the specific software	Teacher trained in subject matter concepts	Skilled and selective use of software in a classroom session (treatment only)
Step 2	Students trained to mindfully use the specific software with familiar subject matter	Students learn identical and familiar subject matter in a different way	Students' skilled use of software (treatment only)
Step 3	Software used by teacher and student with curricular subject matter	Students learn identical subject matter without the software	Achievement test (treatment and control)
Step 4	Software used with personal assignment	Personal assignment prepared without software	Tests:* Abstraction and application of basic principles of the learned subject matter; learning modes; perception of learner and teacher role

*Abstraction and application were tested with paper-and-pencil problem-solving tasks. Learning modes were observed and analyzed. Questionnaires and interviews were used to document and evaluate perception of student's and teacher's roles.

ies are two examples. The design of the experiments combined (a) a careful selection of an information technology treatment that involved formal thinking operations (Piaget & Inhelder, 1969); (b) the definition and the prediction of measurable outcomes; and (c) the use of control and treatment groups with equivalent student distributions, equivalent classroom settings, and equivalent ecological environments.

The algebraic linear functions study evaluated the relation between a mindful use of computer-generated simulations and the users' ability to abstract the basic principles of these functions and apply these principles to new types of algebraic functions. This study was carried out over 6 months (teacher training included) with eighth- and ninth-grade students and concluded with three tests: a regular achievement test that evaluated learners' ability to apply familiar algebraic principles to familiar problems, a one-step inference test that evaluated learners' ability to apply familiar principles to new and unfamiliar problems, and a multiple inference test that evaluated learners' ability to use general abstractions for the generation of new principles and to apply the newly generated principles to new and unfamiliar problems. Interestingly, classrooms that selectively and critically used computer simulations coped best with multiple inference problems but did not score higher than their control groups on the regular achievement and the one-step inference tests.

The database study evaluated the relation between the mindful use of database software and the learners' ability to organize data, identify meaningful variables, and formulate and test hypotheses. This study was carried out over 6 months (teacher training included) with sixth-grade students and was concluded with a paper-and-pencil test that evaluated learners' ability to apply database inquiry procedures to new information that is not studied in schools. The results indicated that a mindful use of computer database software might help to realize IQ potentials. The correlations between IQ and database scores in the treatment classrooms were consistently and significantly higher (with low, medium, and high IQ students) as compared to the same correlations in the control classrooms.

Comptown's ecological sensitive experiments were carried out in natural classroom settings that were part of a complex multisystemic ecology. Using methods associated with quasi-experimental studies (Campbell & Stanley, 1963; Cook & Campbell, 1979) the Comptown experiments satisfied two needs: (a) They enabled the identification relations between specific types of software and specific cognitive gains and thereby test theory-driven, cause-and-effect hypotheses. (b) They created contexts in which systemic conditions in the treatment classrooms differed from their controls. They thereby delimited systemic aspects (of a complex classroom ecology) that affect the specific intervention and deserve more attention. One paramount characteristic was the congruence between the generic properties of the instruments of learning and teaching and the teacher's pattern of instruction. This finding motivated the construction of a "taxonomy for information technology adoption policy" (Z. Peled, E. Peled, & Alexander, 1992): an information technology software selection procedure guided by the ecological approach.

A TAXONOMY FOR INFORMATION TECHNOLOGY ADOPTION POLICY: AN INFORMATION TECHNOLOGY SOFTWARE SELECTION PROCEDURE IMPLIED BY THE ECOLOGICAL APPROACH

In the ecological model a pattern of instruction and the use of means and methods of instruction derive from a single conceptual framework that, to a large extent, is culturally and ecologically dominated. An intervention that introduces new instructional technologies may either disrupt an existing harmony and reveal the multifaceted nature of these implicit, ordinarily "hidden" connections, or lead to inadequate and fruitless use of the newly introduced technologies. Recognizing the vital importance of adequately matching teacher and technology, Comptown's ecologically sensitive experiments introduced information technology software while changing the teacher's pattern of instruction. The "taxonomy for information technology adoption policy" tries to generalize the Comptown experience and reveals the possible correspondences between the generic properties of patterns of instruction and six types of information technology software ordinarily used in education (drill & practice, tutorials, games, simulation, open tools, and educational programming).

More specifically, the taxonomy consists of three components: one that characterizes instructional processes that determine teachers' patterns of instruction, one that specifies properties of software, and one that defines the range of congruence between instructional processes and software.

Instructional processes are further elaborated by five decision-making processes (facets) that delimit the diversity of patterns of instruction. Software properties are further elaborated by five facets that specify these properties in terms of their managerial and instructional qualities (i.e., elements of these facets reinforce elements of practiced patterns of instruction). Table 2.10 presents the five instructional decision-making facets and their elements.

Table 2.11 presents the five software facets and classifies educational software accordingly.

The linear functions and database experiments are concrete examples that demonstrate the benefits of congruence. In these experiments congruent software properties augmented instructional methods. We use these studies as representative applications of the more general framework delimited by the taxonomy.

The instructional goals emphasized by the linear functions treatment teachers (who internalized the project's operational principles and were trained to use the simulation software mindfully) were (a) derivation of a set of abstract principles (Facet A, Element 3) that permit each student to rediscover abstract sets of relations and construct new functions (Facet D, Element 3), and (b) development of computer skills that allow each student to systematically and mindfully manipulate computerized simulations (Facet A, Elements 1, 2). The learning activities enhanced by these teachers were either group directed or individualized and autonomous (Facet C, Elements 2, 3). To this end, the treatment classroom teachers were constantly engaged in curricular decisions (Facet B, Element 2) that involved (a) mapping of elements of instructional patterns onto elements of the simulation software, and (b) selection and integration of computer-based activities into the ongoing instruction and learning procedures.

The software's managerial properties enabled teachers to deliver some control responsibilities (Facet F, Element 2) to software users and act as facilitators (Facet E, Element 2). The software's information-processing properties reinforced the teachers' tendency to enhance (a) use of semistructured learning

TABLE 2.10
Instructional Decision-Making Facets and Their Elements

Facet	*Element*
A. Goals of instruction*	1. Knowledge and comprehension 2. Application 3. Analysis and synthesis 4. At least two of the above
b. Responsibility for the design of the content to be learned (who decides?)	1. Curriculum expert 2. Teacher 3. Student 4. Two or all of the above
C. Type of learning activities that teacher decides to enhance**	1. Teacher-directed activities 2. Group-directed activities 3. Individualized and autonomous activities 4. At least two of the above activities
D. Enhanced learning styles***	1. Reaction to uniform structured learning materials 2. Interaction with peers and learning materials 3. Rediscovery and construction of new knowledge 4. Learning in more than one of the above modalities
E. Teachers" perception of their pedagogical role****	1. Dominating 2. Facilitating

*The elements of Facet A are specified in accord with Bloom's taxonomy (Bloom et al., 1956).
**Types of learning activities that teachers decide to enhance (Facet D) are discussed by Clements (1989).
***Facet D combines learning styles distinctions and concepts discussed by Henson and Borthjwick (1984); characteristics of interactive learning defined by Vygotsky (in Wertsch, 1985b, and applied by Tharp and Gallimore (1988); and discovery and constructivism notions elaborated by Bruner (1966), Giveon (1987), Clements (1989), Cohen (1988), Papert (1990).
****The distinctions presented in Facet E are based on Lamm (1976) and on Bennet, Jordan, Long, and Wade (1976).

materials (Facet I, Element 2), (b) joint computer and user generation of information (Facet H, Element 2), and (c) discovery of software's algorithm (Facet J, Element 2).

Similar developments took place in the database study. The treatment teachers emphasized the acquisition of computerized database strategies and higher order information handling skills (Facet A, Element 4). Responsibility for the design of the content, to a large extent, devolved on software users (Facet B, Elements 2, 3). Teachers facilitated (Facet E, Element 2) group-directed (Facet C, Element 2) learning activities that were essential to new knowledge construction operations (Facet D, Elements 2, 3).

The database software information-processing requirements induced learners to supply information and use software's algorithm for the construction of new knowledge (Facet H, Element 3; Facet J, Element 3). These requirements intensified an already existing pattern of instruction developed by teachers who had

TABLE 2.11
Faceted Specifications of Software Properties and Software Classification

Facet	*Elements*	*Software*
Managerial properties A. Software control devices	1. Control devices preprogrammed into software	Drill and practice Tutorial
	2. Software partially controls user's activity	Simulation Games
	3. Software is not equipped with a user's device	Open tools Ed. programming
B. Record keeping	1. Programmed record keeping provides automatic feedback to user	Drill and Practice Tutorial
	2. Software provides optional record keeping	Games Simulation
	3. Record keeping device is not available	Open tools Ed. programming
Information Processing** C. Provision of information being processed	1. Information is entirely provided by software	Drill and practice Tutorial
	2. Information is jointly provided by software and user	Games Simulation
	3. Information is provided by user	Open tools Ed. programming
D. Relation between software and content being processed	1. Structured: Curricular content and software cannot be separated	Drill and practice Tutorial
	2. Semistructured content provided by software	Games Simulation
	3. Software is content free	Open tools Ed. programming
E. Users involvement in informtion processing***	1. Software directed information acquisition	Drill and practice Tutorial
	2. User is required to discover and react to a software's algorithm	Games Simulation
	3. User is required to use software's algorithm and construct content	Open tools Ed. programming

*Feedback to learners and teachers concerning the student's progress is frequently discussed in the educational literature (e.g., Clements, 1989; Ediger, 1988; Give'on, 1988).
**The distinctions provided by Facets A, B, and C elaborate Give'on's Taxonomy of Educational Software (1988).
***The assumption that directed activities exclude generative information processing is based on Wittrock's theory of generative thinking (Wittrock, 1974).

internalized Comptown's operational principles. Hence, data construction procedures could be practiced in an enriched educational environment.

Both experiments spell out congruence in terms of fluid interdependencies between instructional patterns and instructional properties of software and demonstrate pedagogical, psychological, and administrative implications of software selection and use. Furthermore, the experiments suggest that congruence rests on a dual verification process: examination of the elements that characterize a pattern of instruction and examination of the correspondence between a pattern of instruction and generic software properties. Table 2.12 maps elements of patterns of instruction on elements of software properties and reveals optional software and instructional cross-classifications that support these processes.

Two arguments that are embedded in the proposed matrix further stress its educational implications. First, software instruction correspondences provide an

TABLE 2.12
Mapping Elements of Patterns of Instruction on Elements of Software Properties

	Software properties											
Pattern of Instruction Properties	*Software Control Devices*			*Provision of Info. Being Processed*			*Relation Between Software and Content*			*Users' Involved in Info. Processing*		
	1	*2*	*3*	*1*	*2*	*3*	*1*	*2*	*3*	*1*	*2*	*3*
Goals of Instruction												
1. Knowledge and comprehension	PT	MS										
2. Application		MS	LSR	PT	MS	L	PT	MS		PT	MS	
3. Analysis and synthesis			LSR		LS	LS		MS	LR		MS	LR
4. At least two of the above*						LSR			LR			LR
Curricular Decisions (Who decides?)												
1. Curriculum expert	PT	MS		PT	MS		PT	MS				
2. Teacher		MS			MS			MS	L			
3. Student		MS	LSR		MS	LR		MS	L			
4. At least two of the above												
Learning Activity												
1. Teacher directed	PT	MS		PT	MS		PT	MS	LR	PT	MS	LR
2. Group directed		MS	LR		MS	LR		MS			MS	LR
3. Individual and autonomous	PT	MS	LR	PT	MS	LR		MS	LR	PT	MS	LR
4. At least two of the above												
Enhanced Learning Style**												
1. Reaction to structured learning materials	PT			PT	MS		PT	MS		PT		
2. Interaction with peers and learning materials		MS			MS			MS			MS	
3. Rediscovery and construction of knowledge		MS	LR		MS	LR		MS	LR			LR
Perception of Teacher's Pedagogical Role												
1. Dominates	PT	MS		PT	MS		PT	MS		PT	MS	
2. Facilitates		MS	LR		MS	LR		MS	LR		MS	LR

Notes: Types of software: P - drill & practice; T - tutorial; M - games; S- simulation; L - open tools; R - programming.
*Cross-classifications of software properties and a combination of instructional elements depend on the specific combination selected.
**The numbers (1, 2, 3) refer to the elements of the facets.

immediate context in which instruction and knowledge construction reinforce each other. Second, a systematic and a reasoned choice among educational alternatives may enhance educational change.

However, it should be noted that the proposed theoretical classification leaves open practical constraints and opportunities that characterize each specific educational context and should be part of any change considerations.

CONCLUDING REMARKS

This chapter reviews an ecological formulation that applies equally to information technology intervention, evaluation, and software adoption policies. The formulation is based on the assumptions that (a) classrooms, schools, and social political institutions are culturally dependent systems; (b) their cultural functioning, ordinarily implicit, becomes explicit through interventions that introduce innovations into the ongoing activities of the existing systems; and (c) enduring educational innovations are generated and carried on by two types of parallel and mutually stimulating change processes: cultural-ecological and treatment-specific processes.

Furthermore, the elaboration of this overarching formulation leads to the complementarity of three paradigms: (a) a paradigm that models processes evolving from complex cultural arrangements that cannot be subjected to experimental manipulations, (b) a paradigm that models processes evolving from treatment manipulations in quasi-experimental settings, and (c) a paradigm that models decision-making considerations that are implied by the intervention and may yield congruence or dissonance in the immediate educational environment.

These paradigms prescribe the use of fundamentally different methods within the same intervention and same evaluation. The cultural-ecological framework leads to the design of multilevel systems intervention that requires longitudinal explorations of multilevel systems with ever-changing interdependencies (linear and nonlinear). The treatment-specific intervention leads to the introduction and manipulation of "external," independent variables. The evaluation of these treatments implies a quasi-experimental framework that focuses on causal relations with comparison of equivalent groups, and analyses of sequences of discrete events that offer predicted and measurable results, in response to narrow questions. The congruence framework combines cultural-ecological and quasi-experimental methods that facilitate analyses of educational innovations in progress.

The facet definitions of the evaluation framework directly evolve from a project's operational principles of the type under discussion in this chapter. These definitions (a) guide the design of reproducible observations for the cultural-ecological, treatment-specific and congruence studies; and (b) generate the entire map of multisystemic functioning that creates the educational innovation.

The ecological approach has four additional characteristics:

1. It uses the same conceptual formulation for both the design and the evaluation of the intervention, eliminating inconsistencies between intervention and evaluation.

2. It accords importance to ecological contexts and, if necessary, trades off internal for external validity.

3. It examines the assumption that multiple ecological contexts and multiple educational treatments encourage the development of higher order skills, whereas single-context educational environments are less likely to do so.

4. It tries to maintain a mutually stimulating and constructive relationship between parallel hypotheses-generating and hypotheses-testing operations.

Finally the ecological approach suggests five indicators that are useful for the identification of ecological change processes important for education.

1. Realization of parallel and mutually stimulating change processes: cultural-ecological and treatment-specific types.

2. Extensive and varied interactions with information technology devices that are mindfully integrated into the print-and-book-dominated classrooms.

3. Use of multiple perspectives in learning and teaching.

4. Awareness of the unique contributions of alternative and alternating learning environments.

5. Mindful developments of new and changing courses of learning and teaching that result from repeated comparisons of the print-and-book and the information-technology-based learning environments.

REFERENCES

Bamberger, J., & Schon, D. A. (1983). Learning as reflective conversation with materials: Notes from work in progress. *Art Education, 56*(2), 68–73.

Becker, H. J. (1987). *The impact of computer use on children's learning: What research has shown and what it has not.* (Report No. 18). Baltimore, MD: Johns Hopkins University, Center for Research on Elementary and Middle Schools.

Becker, H. J. (1988). *A field experiment at a distance: Studying on a national scale the effectiveness of instructional practices that use computers.* Paper presented at the annual meeting of the American Educational Research Association, New Orleans.

Bennett, N., with Jordan, J., Long, G., & Wade, B. (1976). *Teaching styles and pupil progress.* Cambridge, MA: Harvard University Press.

Bloom, B. S., Engelhart, M. D., Furst, E. J., Hill, W. H., & Krathwohl, D. R. (Eds.). (1956). *Taxonomy of educational objectives.* New York: David McKay.

Bolter, D. J. (1984). *Turing's man: Western culture in the computer age.* Chapel Hill, NC: Toward an experimental ecology of human development. *American Psychologist, 32,* 513–531.

Bronfenbrenner, U. (1979). *The ecology of human development: Experiments and design*. Cambridge, MA: Harvard University Press.

Bruner, J. S. (1966). *Toward a theory of instruction*. Cambridge, MA: Harvard University Press.

Calfee, R. (1985). Computer literacy and book literacy: Parallels and contrasts. *Educational Researcher, 14*(5), 8–13.

Calfee, R., & Brown, R. (1979). Grouping students for instruction. In D. L. Duke (Ed.), *Classroom management: The 78th Yearbook of the National Society for the Study of Education* (pp. 144–181). Chicago: NSSE.

Campbell, D. T., & Stanley, J. C. (1963). *Experimental and quasi-experimental designs for research*. Skokie, IL: Rand McNally.

Canter, D. (Ed.). (1985). *Facet theory: Approaches to social research*. New York: Springer-Verlag.

Clark, R. E. (1983a). Evidence for confounding in computer-based instruction studies: Analyzing the meta-analyses. *Educational Communication and Technology Journal, 33*(4), 249–262.

Clark, R. E. (1983b). Reconsidering research on learning from media. *Review of Educational Research, 53*, 445–459.

Clark, R. E. (1985a). Confounding in educational computing research. *Journal of Educational Computing Research, 1*(2), 137–148.

Clark, R. E. (1985b). The importance of treatment explication: A reply to J. Kulik, C-L. Kulik, and R. Bangert-Drowns. *Journal of Educational Computing Research, 1*(4).

Clements, D. H. (1989). *Computers in elementary mathematics education*. Englewood Cliffs, NJ: Prentice-Hall.

Cohen, D. K. (1988). Educational technology and school organization. In R. S. Nickerson & P. P. Zodhiates (Eds.), *Technology in education: Looking towards 2000*. Hillsdale, NJ: Lawrence Erlbaum Associates.

Cook, T. D., & Campbell, D. T. (1979). *Quasi-experimentation: Design and analysis issues for field settings*. Skokie, IL: Rand McNally.

Doyle, W. (1986). Classroom organization and management. In M. C. Wittrock (Ed.), *Handbook of research on teaching* (3rd ed., pp. 392–431). New York: Macmillan.

Doyle, W. (1988, April). *Curriculum in teacher education*. Vice Presidential address presented at the annual meeting of the American Research Association, New Orleans.

Ediger, M. (1988). Philosophy of microcomputer use in mathematics curriculum. *Journal of Computers in Mathematics and Science Teaching, 8*(1), 32–45.

Gal, S. (1990, March). *Knowledge-based systems, and more: A multimedia environment for learning structural engineering*. Paper presented at American Association for Artificial Intelligence, Spring Symposium, Stanford, CA.

Gal, S. (1991, April). *Building bridges: Design, learning, and the role of computers*. Unpublished manuscript, MIT, APSP, Research Program.

Gallimore, R. (1990, April). *Rousing school reforms to life*. Prepared for an invited address to the annual meeting of the Social Contexts of Education Division, American Educational Research Association, Boston.

Gibbs, J. C. (1979). The meaning of ecologically oriented inquiry in contemporary psychology. *American Psychologist, 34*(2), 127–140.

Give'on, Y. S. (1987). *Computer applications in education: Dimensions and conclusions*. Unpublished manuscript, Tel-Aviv. (Hebrew)

Give'on, Y. S. (1988). Taxonomy of educational software applications. *Proceedings of the Fifth International Conference on Technology and Education*, 480–483.

Goodlad, J. L. (1979). Perspectives on theory, research, and practice. In D. L. Duke (Ed.), *Classroom management: The 78th Yearbook of the National Society for the Study of Education* (pp. 391–412). Chicago: NSSE.

Guba, E., & Lincoln, Y. S. (1988). Do inquiry paradigms imply inquiry methodologies? In D. M.

Fetterman (Ed.), *Qualitative approaches to evaluation in education: The silent scientific revolution* (pp. 89–116). New York: Praeger.

Guttman, L. (1957). Introduction to facet design and analysis. In *Proceedings of the 15th International Congress of Psychology, Brussels*. Amsterdam: North-Holland Publishing, pp. 130–132.

Henson, K. T., & Borthjwick, P. (1984). Matching styles: A historical look. *Theory and Practice, 23*(1), 3–9.

Jagodzinski, A. P., & Clarke, D. D. (1986). A review of methods for measuring and describing users' attitudes as an essential constituent of systems analysis and design. *Computer Journal, 29*(2), 97–102.

Kerr, B. (1973). Processing demands during mental operations. *Memory & Cognition, 1*, 401–412.

Kintsch, W. (1977). *Memory and cognition*. New York: Wiley.

Lamm, Z. (1976). *Conflicting theories of instruction: Conceptual dimensions*. Berkeley, CA: McCutshan.

Langer, E. J., & Imber, L. E. (1979). When practice makes imperfect: Debilitating effects of overlearning. *Journal of Personality and Social Psychology, 37*, 2014–2024.

Leontiev, A. N. (1964). *Problems of mental development*. Washington, DC: U.S. Joint Publication Research Service.

Olson, D. R. (1985). Computers as tools of the intellect. *Educational Researcher, 14*(5), 5–8.

Papert, S. (1987). Computer criticism vs. technocentric thinking. *Educational Researcher, 16*(1), 22–30.

Papert, S. (1990). Introduction. In E. Harel (Ed.), *Constructionist learning* (pp. 1–8). Cambridge, MA: The Media Laboratory, MIT.

Pea, R. D. (1987). The aims of software criticism: Reply to Professor Papert. *Educational Researcher, 16*(1), 4–8.

Peled, E., Peled, Z., & Alexander, G. (1989). Project Comptown: Educational intervention and action research. *British Journal of Educational Technology, 20*(2).

Peled, Z., Peled, E., & Alexander, G. (1991). Ecology and experimentation in the evaluation of information technology interventions in natural classroom settings. *Studies in Educational Evaluation, 17*, 419–448.

Peled, Z., Peled, E., & Alexander, G. (1992). A taxonomy for computer software adoption policy. *Journal of Educational Computing Research, 8*(1), 81–100.

Piaget, J., & Inhelder, B. (1969). *The psychology of the child*. New York: Basic Books.

Project Comptown (1986). *Intermediate Report 1985–1986*. Beer Sheva, Israel: Ben Gurion University, Dept. of Education, Project Comptown. (Hebrew)

Project Comptown (1988). *Intermediate Report 1985–1987*. Beer Sheva, Israel: Ben Gurion University, Dept. of Education. Project Comptown. (Hebrew)

Project Comptown (1989). *An intermediate report: IT treatment studies 1987–1989*. Beer Sheva, Israel: Ben Gurion University, Dept. of Education, Project Comptown. (Hebrew)

Project Comptown (1990). *An observational report*. Beer Sheva, Israel: Ben Gurion University, Dept. of Education, Project Comptown. (Hebrew)

Salomon, G. (1983). The differential investment of mental effort in learning from different sources. *Educational Psychologist, 18*, 42–50.

Salomon, G. (1985). The new information technologies: What you see is not (always) what you get. *Educational Psychologist, 20*, 207–217.

Salomon, G. (1990a). Studying the flute and the orchestra: Controlled vs. classroom research on computers. *International Journal of Educational Research, 14*(6), 521–531.

Salomon, G. (1990b). *Transcending the qualitative/quantitative debate: The analytic and systemic approaches to educational research*. Unpublished manuscript.

Salomon, G., & Globerson, T. (1987). Skill may be not enough: The role of mindfulness in learning and transfer. *International Journal of Educational Research, 11*, 623–637.

Salomon, G., & Perkins, D. N. (1989). Rocky roads to transfer: Rethinking mechanisms of a neglected phenomenon. *Educational Psychologist, 24*(2), 113–142.

Salomon, G., Perkins, D. N., & Globerson, T. (1991). Partners in cognition: Extending human intelligence with intelligent technologies. *Educational Researcher, 20,* 10–16.

Sarason, S. B. (1982). *The culture of school and the problem of change.* (2nd ed.) Boston: Allyn & Bacon.

Scarr, S. (1985). Constructing psychology: Making facts and fables for our times. *American Psychologist, 40,* 499–512.

Schank, R., & Abelson, R. (1977). *Scripts, plans, goals and understanding.* New York: Wiley.

Shavelson, R. J., & Salomon, G. (1985). Information technology: Tool and teacher of the mind. *Educational Researcher, 14*(5), 4.

Shavelson, R. J., Winkler, J. D., Stasz, C., Feibel, W., Robyn, A. E., & Shaha, S. (1984). *Teaching mathematics and science: Patterns of microcomputer use.* Santa Monica, CA: Rand.

Shye, S. (1978). On the search for laws in the behavioral sciences. In S. Shye (Ed.), *Theory construction and data analysis in the behavioral sciences* (pp. 2–24). San Francisco: Jossey-Bass.

Tharp, R. G., & Gallimore, R. (1988). *Rousing minds to life.* Cambridge, UK: Cambridge University Press.

Vygotsky, L. S. (1978). *Mind in society.* Cambridge, MA: Harvard University Press.

Walker, D. F. (1987). Logo needs research: A response to Papert's paper. *Educational Researcher, 16*(1), 9–11.

Wertsch, J. V. (1985a). *Vygotsky and the social formation of mind.* Cambridge, MA: Harvard University Press.

Wertsch, J. V. (Ed.). (1985b). *Culture, communication, and cognition: Vygotskian perspectives.* Cambridge, UK: Cambridge University Press.

Winkler, J. D., Shavelson, R. J., Stasz, C., Robyn, A. E., & Feibel, W. (1985). Pedagogically sound use of microcomputers in classroom instruction. *Journal of Educational Computing Research, 13,* 285–293.

Wittrock, M. C. (1974). Learning as a generative process. *Educational Psychologist, 11,* 87–95.

3 Assessment of Distance Learning Technology

Richard E. Clark
University of Southern California

The history of positive claims for distance learning technology (Benjamin, 1988; Cuban, 1986; Saettler, 1968) and, on the other hand, a number of negative reports (Clark & Salomon, 1986; Clark & Sugrue, 1989; Gardner & Salomon, 1986) have led many to accept the need for a change in the way we evaluate new technologies for distance learning. The number of new and complex technological devices that could be applied to distance learning is increasing. Cuban (1986), in his history of technology use in schools, cautioned that "determining what levels of [technology] use now exist is like trying to snap a photograph of a speeding bicyclist" (p. 77).

With adequate evaluation in place, we may be able to "tune" existing technologies so that they meet our needs, anticipate new developments, and settle disputes, in time to plan and operate rational, cost-effective K–12 local, regional, and national distance learning systems. Underlying all evaluation plans are beliefs about how we employ technology so that we enhance the delivery of instruction and the quality of learning experiences. At the heart of every evaluation plan is a curiosity about how new technologies can increase students' access to quality instruction and thereby increase their academic achievement, motivation, and value for learning.

The purpose of this discussion is to (a) discourage evaluation questions that have not proved useful in the past; (b) suggest that future evaluations distinguish between the effects of delivery and instructional technologies; (c) offer some generic evaluation plans, questions, and examples associated with delivery and instruction; and (d) discuss issues related to the cost-effectiveness of distance learning.

FORMING AND ASKING EVALUATION QUESTIONS

Evaluation is the process by which we judge the worthwhileness of something in order to make decisions (Baker, 1991). Technology assessment encompasses a number of analytic and measurement strategies that produce information that helps make worthwhileness judgments about technologically based educational programs. Judgments made during the development of a program are termed *formative*. Evaluation that seeks to describe the results of an operating program is often referred to as *summative*. Because our values govern both formative and summative evaluation activities, we need to be clear about the kinds of distance learning evaluation questions that will meet the needs of our schools and communities. The questions we decide to ask about distance learning and the evaluation instruments we employ will necessarily keep us ignorant about some matters while informing us about others. Evaluation questions carry implicit assumptions and beliefs about the significance of different elements of distance learning and their impact on desired outcomes. For example, if we ask whether a new teaching medium produces more student achievement than traditional media, we have assumed that media are able to influence student achievement—an assumption that has been seriously questioned (Clark & Salomon, 1986; Clark & Sugrue, 1989; Gardner & Salomon, 1986).

One of the most important recommendations underlying this discussion is that all evaluations should explicitly investigate the relative benefit of two different but compatible types of distance learning technologies found in every distance learning program. One technology influences the delivery of schooling and another technology influences learning from instruction.

Delivery technology is characterized by the equipment, machines, and media that provide access to instruction. Familiar examples of delivery technology are books, computers, and teachers. Instructional technology seeks to influence the learning of students. Examples of instructional technology are ways to sequence and structure lessons, the use of examples, provisions for practice, and tests. Instructional technology is transported to the student by delivery technology. Any instructional technology can be provided to students by a variety of delivery technologies. For example, information, examples, practice, and tests can all be delivered to students by either books, computers, or teachers.

These two different technologies are typically confused in distance learning evaluations. Student achievement gains or losses influenced by instructional technology are most often attributed to delivery technologies. Reductions in the cost or time it takes to access special student populations (for example, rural or disadvantaged students) are incorrectly attributed to instructional technology. Confusion about technological benefits can lead to inappropriate and expensive policy mistakes. At the root of the confusion one finds many different definitions of technology (Clark & Salomon, 1986).

Which Technology for What Purpose?

In its most general sense, the term *technology* suggests the application of science and experience to solving problems (Heinich, 1984). The major obstacle in our past struggle to understand the contribution of new technology in distance learning is that we have confused the contributions of these two different technologies.

One distinct class of technologies results from the application of various scientific and engineering principles to the development and use of equipment, materials, and procedures that record and transmit instruction. These educational media technologies are associated with the physical sciences that have produced the new electronic media (for example, fiber optics, interactive video disc, and computers). Delivery technologies increase student and teacher access to learning resources, which is one of the most important goals of distance learning.

A second type of technology applies various social science principles and past experience to develop teaching methods and curriculum choices (Reigeluth, 1983, 1987). This instructional technology draws primarily on research in teaching, learning, and motivation to enhance student achievement. The "products" of an instructional technology are new instructional design theories (Gagne, Briggs, & Wager, 1992; Merrill, Jones, & Li, 1992; Reigeluth, 1983, 1987), teaching methods, and motivational strategies (Clark & Salomon, 1986; Weiner, 1992) that can be embedded in "courseware" (instructional materials) for distance learning. A primary goal of this chapter is to recommend that all evaluations of distance learning programs attempt to provide reliable and valid determinations of the separate influences of delivery and instructional technologies.

Separating Delivery and Instructional Evaluation Questions

Support for a separate consideration of delivery and instructional technologies in evaluation is well established in the research literature but rare in evaluations or program planning. Schramm (1977), historically the most established reviewer of media studies in education, concluded that "learning seems to be affected more by what is delivered than by the delivery medium" (p. 273). More recently, analyses of media and technology research that compared the learning benefits of different media (Allen, 1971; Clark, 1983, 1985; Clark & Salomon, 1986; Clark & Sugrue, 1989; Clark & Voogel, 1985; Gardner & Salomon, 1986; Jamison, Suppes, & Wells, 1974; Kearsley, Hunter, & Seidel, 1983; Levie & Dickie, 1973; Lumsdaine, 1963; Mielke, 1968; Salomon, 1981, 1984; Schramm, 1977; Winn, 1982) could be summarized with the analogy that media "do not influence learning any more than the truck that delivers groceries influences the nutrition of a community" (Clark, 1983, p. 3.). Distance learning media are vehicles that transport instruction to students. The choice of vehicle influences the important outcomes of student access, and the speed or cost of the delivery but *not* the learning impact of the instruction that is delivered to the "consumer." Delivery vehicles indiscriminately carry helpful, hurtful, and neutral instruction.

CHOOSING CRITICAL INDICATORS FOR EVALUATION

Among the specific issues that must be addressed in future evaluations of local applications of distance learning technology are: What aspects of evaluation planning enhance the usefulness of information for decision makers? How might we collect information that will aid in our judgment about the different influences of the delivery and instructional features of the program? (Baker, 1989; Clark, 1985; Congress of the United States, 1988). Whereas a number of evaluation concerns apply to some but not all programs, three generalizations seem useful to all: (a) adopt an early concern for evaluation, (b) use a multilevel evaluation plan, and (c) conduct formal cost-effectiveness analyses.

Adopt an Early Concern for Evaluation

Both evaluation specialists and administrative decision makers need to be involved early and actively in distance learning system design. Past experience suggests that waiting until a system is designed before thinking about evaluation has been a familiar but very wasteful pattern (Baker, 1989). It is critical to have early information about, for example, exactly what set of conditions are being replaced by new distance learning programs. One way to accomplish this would be to spend an ample amount of time during the program planning stages carefully describing the specific problems we wish the new approach to solve. We should describe how we will measure the current conditions (e.g., a baseline measure of the existing situation, including the views and impressions of the stakeholders) and thoroughly discuss what we believe to be the *alternative* solutions to the problem(s).

If an evaluation plan is developed as the program is planned and implemented, a number of advantages are realized. In the area of computer-assisted learning, Levin (1983, 1988; Levin & Meister, 1985) described eight exemplary cost-effectiveness evaluation programs. Each of these examples collected baseline measures of the problems they were trying to solve. Each of the eight programs began their concern with evaluation at the start of their planning.

Early evaluation makes it possible to determine which aspects of a distance learning program were positive and which were negative. Negative aspects can then be modified and the positive accentuated to achieve maximum benefit. For example, most distance learning programs attempt to bring a much richer set of curriculum choices and quality teaching to K–12 school programs. Program planners might begin with an analysis of options (the variety of media available to deliver new curricula) and their audience (for example, measure the number of students who would enroll in new courses). Early concern with evaluation results in the collection of information on both the need and the audience for distance learning as well as the existing alternatives. Another advantage of early evaluation involvement is that an ongoing evaluation plan can be developed. Too often programs are developed and implemented, then at some later stage the program planners remember that "we have to do some evaluation." As a result, very little is learned about the program being studied that is useful either for the immediate program or for other distance learning ventures. Early evaluation planning most often yields useful information, yet it is a rare phenomenon. Levin noted that his search for adequate cost-effectiveness evaluations was difficult. He found that only one in six published reports was adequately designed. Because most reports are not published, one suspects that early evaluation is not our typical procedure at the moment. The second general direction that is useful for all distance learning programs is to adopt a multilevel evaluation plan.

Use a Multilevel Evaluation Plan

The two levels of evaluation that most often seem to give useful development information are measures of (a) participant reactions, and (b) the achievement of program objectives.

Participant reactions to distance learning program effectiveness is the most common (and unfortunately, often the only) level of evaluation attempted by K–12 school districts. Typically, this level of evaluation employs printed forms containing a combination of questions designed to inquire about the "feelings" and "impressions" of different groups involved in the program. A common question is "How would you rate the quality of the teaching in this program?" (typically rated on a 5-point scale that ranges from exceptional through average to poor). Items such as "List what you think are the STRONG (or WEAK) points of the program" permit the respondent to write in personal views and comments. Questionnaire forms are most often used for reactions because they protect the anonymity of respondents and therefore, we presume, increase the candor of the responses. Forms are often sent to all of the program participants but are filled out and returned by only a small percentage of those who receive them. Participant reactions are useful provided they do not serve as the *only* level of evaluation data. They should be used primarily to uncover both informal participant impressions and *unanticipated* benefits and problems. Reaction items should be divided between those that deal with the medium (e.g., ease of access, reliability or technical quality of transmission or machines, space allocation issues) and those associated with the instruction (e.g., the quality of teaching, how things learned in the program were used outside of class).

Collecting participant reactions has the advantage that program managers get informal impressions of the programs and often uncover unanticipated results. For example, the Northeastern Utah Telelearning project, which uses microcomputer-based instruction transmitted between remote schools over telephone lines, found an unexpected problem because they used open-ended reaction forms (Congress of the United States, 1989). Students complained that in the early stages of the program it was very difficult to contact a teacher to get help when it was needed. On the other hand, the Interact Instructional Television Network in Houston, Texas (Congress of the United States, 1989), used a similar instrument and discovered an unexpected positive outcome of its project. It was observed that students in small television reception rooms tended to help each other a great deal during the instructional program. They could help while the program was continuing without disrupting the teacher or other students. This "peer tutoring" seemed to be having a positive impact on student learning and motivation. On closer inspection, the tutoring activity seemed to be due to the fact that the microphone the students used to communicate with the teacher at another location had to be turned on to function. When the microphone was turned off, the students could consult among themselves before they turned it on to answer a question or discuss a point with the teacher. When following up on the peer tutoring finding, the Houston project uncovered the fact that some of the tutors hired to supervise the student television reception rooms were demanding that the students "keep quiet," which discouraged the peer tutoring. The tutors had assumed that talking indicated a "discipline problem" that had to be corrected. Once discovered, the peer tutoring might be encouraged and its barriers eliminated (e.g., through adjusting the training of tutors as in the Houston example).

The problem with participant reaction data is that it is most often collected in such a way that it is not a reliable or a valid indicator of program effects. Yet, unreliable information might occasionally provide useful information as it did in the Houston project. Questionnaire data can be representative if evaluators select a random sample of participants large enough to engage a meaningful number of each group involved in the project. To increase participation evaluators have found it useful to send each randomly chosen participant a card telling them they have been selected, that their response is vital, and to expect the questionnaire soon. Follow-up notes to all those chosen can encourage laggards to send in their forms without violating anonymity. Depending on the numbers involved in the entire program, a small (5% to 10%) random sample of participants can give a very accurate impression of the reactions of the entire group (see Fowler, 1984, for a discussion of sample size in evaluation studies.

Questionnaires should be used at various stages in the program development, including very early on. Unanticipated problems and benefits uncovered by questionnaires usually require much more careful study. For example, when students in most distance learning programs are asked, a majority will typically state they would *not* continue to elect a distance learning option if they could choose a "traditional class" as they did in the Northeastern Utah Telelearning

Project (Congress of the United States, 1989). The fact that students would elect a traditional program if one was offered does not indicate that the Utah project failed. On closer inspection it is often found, as is suspected in the Utah case, that students sometimes feel isolated in distance learning settings and would therefore select more traditional options for social and "nonacademic" reasons. This is particularly true of middle school and high school students. They typically have strong social needs that are not always met in distance learning programs.

Other problems that can be spotted using the "early warning system" of reaction questionnaires are communication problems between participants, the extent and impact of technical difficulties, inappropriate implementation of plans, and opportunities to extend the program into new areas. Yet in even the best of circumstances, reaction forms will not give solid information about the achievement of most delivery and instructional goals. For this purpose, programs need to adopt a second level of evaluation.

Achievement of program objectives is the second and most substantive evaluation goal. Formal measurement of objectives is usually considered by evaluation specialists to be the most crucial information to be gathered. Objectives should be divided into at least two categories: those associated with delivery and those associated with instruction. One category of outcome that is common to both types of technology is cost-benefit and cost-effectiveness. In cost-benefit and cost-effectiveness evaluation, we attempt to measure "bang for the buck," that is, the cost of the impact obtained from various features of the program. The discussion turns next to outcomes specific to instructional technology, then to delivery technology outcomes and finally to cost-benefit and cost-effectiveness measurement.

Instructional technology objectives include changes in student learning, values, motivation, and the transfer of and application of knowledge outside of the classroom. These important goals are influenced by the "courseware" or instructional programs that are developed and/or chosen and transmitted to distant learners. In some cases, instruction is designed by teachers. In other cases, already developed courseware is purchased and transmitted to remote sites. The instructional decisions embedded in each lesson influence student learning and motivation. Different teaching method and curriculum options have very different effects on student learning, which might be explored in evaluation. So, distance learning evaluation might include at least the following four types of questions related to instructional technology.

1. Which of the curriculum and teaching method choices in a given distance learning program impacted student achievement and subsequent ability to use (transfer) the knowledge acquired outside of the instructional setting?

Achievement can be tested with teacher-made or standardized achievement tests. Increasingly, schools are interested in the extent to which students transfer what they learn outside of school. Transfer might be estimated by open-ended questions on reaction forms. If the school district has other schools receiving similar curricula from different delivery forms, an obvious opportunity exists to check on any achievement or motivation differences between the options. When possible, alternative teaching methods and curriculum choices should be explored in order to maximize the learning of different kinds of students. For example, highly structured and supportive instruction might be contrasted with a more "learner-directed" and discovery approach to curriculum (Clark, 1983, 1985). Many programs have found that students who are anxious or have learning problems profit a great deal from added structure and support, whereas students who are more independent are able tend to benefit more from a discovery approach (Clark, 1983).

2. What impacted student and teacher *motivation* to learn and invest effort in making this program a success?

Current theories of motivation (Weiner, 1992) have introduced a very counterintuitive element in distance learning programs and evaluation. Formerly, it was thought that media choices greatly influenced both student and teacher motivation. Now it is understood that motivation is influenced by beliefs and expectations and is therefore due to individual differences in beliefs about media and *not* to the media per se (Clark, 1983; Clark & Sugrue, 1989; Salomon, 1984). Yet a number of studies of media preferences agree with O'Neil, Anderson, and Freeman (1986) that "in general, students' attitudes are positive while instructors' attitudes are negative" (p. 977). There is recent but solid evidence that when students expect that a new medium will make learning easier and more "entertaining," they like it. However, there is good evidence that their liking does not lead them to work harder (Clark & Sugrue, 1989; Saettler, 1968). Quite to the contrary, the more they think a medium makes learning "easy," the less effort they will invest to learn (Kozma, 1991; Mielke, 1968; Salomon, 1984). This effect has been explained as a student misjudgment about the kind of effort required to learn based on our previous experience and expectations. For example, U.S. students typically assume that television is an "easier" medium than books or teachers, probably because of their use of the medium for entertainment. This reaction on the part of our students is quite different than that of Israeli students who, on the average, have been found to invest more effort in television because their early experiences with television have been less entertaining and more demanding intellectually (Salomon, 1984).

There is additional evidence that students will not invest effort if they believe a medium to be very difficult. With U.S. children, this is sometimes the reason for their lack of willingness to read (Kozma, 1991; Salomon, 1984). So the greatest motivation is invested in media and instructional programs that are perceived as being moderately difficult. This evidence would suggest that one way to influence student motivation would be to select "moderately difficult" media. However the evidence also suggests that student and teacher beliefs about media difficulty change over time, sometimes radically (Clark & Sugrue, 1989). The more stable predictor of motivation seems to be student beliefs about their own ability and the demands placed on them by different instructional tasks (Salomon, 1984). This would suggest that we should evaluate the students' perceptions and beliefs about the *learning tasks* contained within the media employed by distance learning programs and their own *self-efficacy* as learners. This form of evaluation could be embedded in reaction questionnaires.

3. Which of the curriculum and teaching method choices in a given distance learning program impacted: (a) student and teacher values for what was learned and, (b) subsequent motivation to teach and learn and to use what was learned outside of the instructional setting?

Reaction questionnaires that are carefully constructed and administered will give a good indication of student and teacher values related to the program, teaching, and the curriculum. Negative value statements do not always reflect negatively on the program (recall the students in the Utah project who liked traditional classrooms better than distance learning because of social opportunities). Generally, one hopes to foster a positive value for learning and new curriculum options with distance learning. Shifts in attitude that result from *changes* in the program can be monitored *if* reaction forms are sent periodically (every few months) throughout the development stages.

4. Which of the curriculum and teaching method choices in a given distance learning program impacted the cultivation of different kinds of knowledge, including procedural skills *and* higher order thinking, learning-to-learn, and metacognitive skills?

Although higher order skill learning is more difficult to assess than ordinary "achievement," few programs have been successful in this area. One current example of a technology-based thinking skills program is the Higher Order Thinking Skills (HOTS) program, which focuses on Chapter 1 (disadvantaged) students (Congress of the United States, 1988). The program originates at the University of Arizona and is distributed to member schools in many states. Teachers in the program use computer lessons, class exercises, and discussion to increase the thinking and study skills of students. HOTS evaluation involves the ongoing use of standardized tests, noting changes in the quality of questions students ask and analyses of their class assignments. Although a few formal measures of thinking and study skills exist (and more are being developed), program managers might consult with evaluation specialists about selecting and developing tests to measure problem-solving and study skill development (Congress of the United States, 1988; Levin & Meister, 1985).

Whereas learning, values, and study skills are important instructional outcomes for distance learning, the delivery technology will influence yet another type of outcome.

Delivery technology transmits various forms of instruction to students. The recent introduction of computers to schools has resulted in more attention to technology delivery benefits (Congress of the United States, 1988; Kearsley, Hunter, & Seidel, 1983). Evaluation questions associated with delivery technologies include attempts to assess the effect of medium on (a) student *access* to a greater variety of curriculum choices, (b) school or program *utilization of resources,* and (c) the *reliability* of delivery choices. Questions one typically finds in the evaluation of media include:

1. Did the distance learning media maximize student access to new, and/or high-quality courses and teaching when compared with other choices?

Access to new or beneficial courses and instructional techniques or teachers is one of the primary objectives of most distance learning programs. Collecting access data often involves comparisons between different ways to deliver courses or the size of enrollments in classes both before and during the implementation of the program. For example, the Share-Ed program in Beaver County, Oklahoma (Congress of the United States, 1989), used a new fiber optic network to provide new curriculum to rural schools. They collected participant reactions on the advantages of the increased curriculum choices offered to students who are allowed to take college credit courses in high school as a result of the new system. These reactions, when combined with baseline and process data on actual enrollments, provide good evidence of the extent of access provided by the innovation. Evaluators should carefully consider increased or enhanced access of minority, older, or widely dispersed student groups.

Although "access" usually suggests the availability of new curriculum options, it can also imply teacher access to students on a more personal level. Teachers in the Houston, Texas, Interact Instructional Television systems (Congress of the United States, 1989) report problems with their personal and immediate access to students during instruction in order to "check their reactions or mood" and adjust their teaching accordingly. On the other hand, teachers using computer-delivered courses often report increased "individualized" access to students and enjoy the opportunity to "watch them learn."

2. Did the media influence the utilization of school and community educational resources (e.g., space, equipment, skilled teachers, new courseware developed at one site but not readily available at others)?

It is often the case that because distance learning programs are recorded and distributed to many different sites, the best teachers are made available to many more students. Evaluators might track statistics about how the background and/or training of teachers in distance programs compare with district averages. An instance of a different kind of utilization is to be found in the Beaver County, Oklahoma, Share-Ed program (Congress of the United States, 1989). The local telephone company was installing fiber optic communication lines to improve local service. The system was capable of handling far greater transmission volume than the existing usage anticipated in the communities served. The school systems' use of fiber optic lines for television and voice transmission for distance learning utilized unused space on the system. Because distance learning courses are often provided to fewer students per school than the average course, they often make use of underutilized rooms (e.g., storage spaces) and equipment.

3. Are distance learning media more reliable than other alternatives?

One of the primary concerns expressed by the critics of distance media is their technical reliability. In the Beaver County, Oklahoma, television system, for example, the reaction forms used in evaluation only picked up technical problems when the students were asked to describe "weak points" of the system. None of the administrators noticed technical problems, 11% of the teachers mentioned reliability, but 36% of the students responded to the reaction form by going into detail about microphone feedback, distracting equipment, out-of-focus pictures, equipment noises, and color problems. This difference in reporting reliability problems probably stems from the amount of experience each group had with the actual television transmission. However, program evaluation should establish regular checks by technical staff on these problems in order to judge the severity of participant reactions and make repairs when necessary. When technical transmission problems are not solved, they can decrease achievement scores and reduce participant commitment to the system.

In successful distance learning programs, delivery (media) technology and instructional technology must work together. The delivery features of new media must be employed so that they will eventually save precious educational resources. Curriculum and instructional design must be utilized so that they support the effective learning and transfer of important concepts. Instruction must be developed to reflect the special delivery characteristics of different media. In addition, however, communities and funding agencies are increasingly concerned not only with the effectiveness but also the cost of distance learning programs. Cost is a "goal" or "outcome" of both delivery and instructional technologies.

COST-EFFECTIVENESS EVALUATION

During an evaluation of the separate delivery and instructional value of distance learning program effectiveness, *cost* data should also be collected. This parallel activity allows us to combine "effectiveness" (i.e., delivery and instructional outcomes) with "cost" data to provide cost-effectiveness information to decision makers. Cost-effectiveness evaluation requires that the cost of two or more different alternative technology options are compared for the same outcome measures (Levin, 1983).

In many ways, cost-effectiveness ratios are the most interesting information we can supply to school officials, taxpayers, and their elected representatives. Limited educational resources will eventually require a much greater emphasis on both the monetary and time cost of new programs.

Delivery Technology Cost

Evaluations that precede the introduction of new media should explore the costs of various alternatives. In many cases, older technologies (e.g., tutors, books, cassette television programs, the mail system) are cheaper in monetary cost. Evaluations of costs should always consider trade-offs with cheaper and more traditional delivery options. There is evaluation data indicating, for example, that tutors who are trained and paid minimum wage are much cheaper than computers for many instructional tasks (Levin, 1983). An excellent discussion of cost-effectiveness analysis is provided by Fletcher (1990), who reviewed previous studies and presented cost data for interactive video disc programs used in military training. He noted that some programs divide costs into categories such as (a) initial investment, (b) technology support (maintenance and replacement), and (c) operating costs; other programs lump all costs together. He advised that separation gives a better picture of the source of costs and helps cost containment. He noted that cost-effectiveness ratios vary widely in past reports. Some studies find huge cost benefits for technology-based distance learning. Other studies report large cost disadvantages. Clearly this question involves a number of factors, many of which have not yet been identified. Fletcher implied that cost-effectiveness analyses can be (and are) manipulated when he suggested that "basically, these cost ratios can be as low as we want, depending on the actual equipment being simulated" (p. 19).

Evaluations conducted during the introduction and maintenance of a distance learning program are advised to adopt the "ingredients" costing approach described later.

Instructional Technology Cost

There are a great variety of different school and community goals that influence evaluation criteria under the general heading of instructional effectiveness costs. The cost required to increase student motivation, learning, and transfer is being questioned with greater frequency (Congress of the United States, 1988; Jamison, Suppes, & Wells, 1974). School districts may wish to consider collecting cost data as a way to support the development of policy. The development of an instructional technology yields a variety of teaching, motivation, and transfer outcomes at very different monetary costs (Congress of the United States, 1988; Levin & Meister, 1985).

Besides monetary cost, schools are increasingly interested in the time costs associated with the mastery of different learning or performance goals. Some types of learning tasks consume much more "teaching time" and/or "learning time" (Clark & Sugrue, 1989). For example, it takes much longer to teach a student study skills than to teach memorization of facts. It also takes longer for a student to learn procedural knowledge to the point where it becomes automatic—about 100 hrs of practice for even simple procedures is the current estimate (Clark, 1989; Gagne, Briggs, & Wager, 1992). Fletcher (1990) reviewed a number of military applications of computer-based instruction and found time savings to average about 30% across many different sites. It is therefore likely that there will be more and more emphasis on the time costs of different instructional technology options.

In some applications, the cheapest and/or quickest options are not necessarily the best. Students who learn cheaper or faster do not necessarily learn better. The new "cognitive" learning theories provide the insight that it may be more important to know *how* students reach learning goals than to know that they get correct answers on examinations. It often takes longer for students to learn in such a way that their correct answer on a test reflects "deep cognitive processing" and the exercise of higher order cognitive learning skills, than to take a surface level shortcut (Clark & Voogel, 1985; Merrill, Jones, & Li, 1992). Educators need to be wary of focusing evaluations on time savings at the expense of the quality of learning.

Generally, once a distance learning team has worked out the list of goals associated with both monetary and time costs, an evaluation design can be chosen. One of the first issues to be confronted is the choice of how the data reflecting costs will be gathered. There are a number of methods, but Levin's (Levin, 1983, 1988; Levin & Meister, 1985) *ingredients* method seems particularly applicable to both delivery and instructional technologies.

The Ingredients Method of Determining Costs. Although there are a number of emerging ways to determine local costs and efficiencies, one of the soundest and most comprehensive is the "ingredients method" developed by Levin at Stanford University (Levin, 1983, 1988). It "requires identification of all of the ingredients required for the . . . [distance learning] intervention, a valuation or costing of these ingredients and a summation of the costs to determine the cost of the intervention" (Levin, 1988, p. 3). In the K–12 setting, cost is defined as the value of what is given up by using resources in one way rather than for its next best alternative use. For example, if teacher time is given up then it may not be used for other purposes. Therefore, the cost of teacher time is assessed by assigning a value to what is lost when teachers are assigned to distance learning technology programs.

The ingredients method is implemented in two stages. In the first stage, all necessary program ingredients are listed. The identification of ingredients requires that we list distance learning program necessities associated with five categories: (a) personnel, (b) facilities, (c) equipment, (d) materials and supplies, and (e) all other. In the second stage, each of the ingredients listed in each of the five categories is valued.

Space limitations preclude a complete description of the ingredients method but a review of Levin (1988; Levin & Meister, 1985) will provide most of the information needed to determine ingredient costs. Levin gave specific technology examples that are very relevant to the kinds of programs now evolving in many schools, and he urged complete listings of ingredients. For example, he required that all "donated" time of volunteers and outside organizations be included as a personnel ingredient if it is necessary for the conduct of the program. He reasoned that failure to cost donated time will give an unrealistic picture of the "replication" expense. He also claimed (Levin & Meister, 1985) that, in the rare instance where one finds a complete costing of technology-based programs, one often finds evidence that the organizational climate greatly influences cost-benefit ratios. He presents evidence that when the same distance learning program is presented in many different sites, the cost of implementation can vary by 400% (Levin & Meister, 1985). Some organizational designs seem much more efficient than others for technology-based, distance learning program delivery.

CONCLUSION

In the past, distance learning evaluations have typically been conducted as afterthoughts and have relied heavily on reaction questionnaires that may be unreliable and nonrepresentative of the participants involved. Even when evaluations attempted to collect information about changes in student achievement, questions were asked that confused the separate contributions of delivery media and instructional technology.

In order to identify the strong features of distance learning programs and eliminate weak features, more robust evaluation plans must be adopted in the future. These plans should be firmly based on the experience of those who have struggled with technology evaluations in the past (Levin, 1988). Three features are recommended: First, evaluation should begin at the start of distance learning program planning. An early commitment to evaluation will provide much more useful information about the strengths of a program as it develops. Changes can be made during the formative stage in time to strengthen the plan. The second recommendation is that all programs should adopt a multilevel evaluation plan. The different roles of qualitative (e.g., questionnaires, diaries, and open-ended participant reactions) and quantitative (e.g., student achievement scores, monetary costs) data should be decided. Delivery and instructional evaluation should be separated and a variety of goals assessed. Finally, new techniques are available for cost-effectiveness evaluation of distance learning programs. Levin's "ingredients" method is suggested.

ACKNOWLEDGMENTS

This chapter is based in part on the report *Evaluating Distance Learning Technology,* commissioned by the U.S. Office of Technology Assessment in 1988. This report was part of the support documentation for the OTA report *Linking for Learning: A New Course for Education,* Document OTA-SET-430, U.S. Government Printing Office, November 1989. The views presented here are the author's and do not necessarily reflect those of the Office of Technology Assessment.

REFERENCES

Allen, W. H. (1971). Instructional media research: Past, present and future. *A V Communication Review, 19,* 5–18.

Baker, E. L. (1989). Technology assessment: Policy and methodological issues. In Air Force Systems Command, *Proceedings of the Second Intelligent Tutoring Systems Research Forum* (pp. 151–158).

Baker, E. L. (1991). Technology assessment: Policy and methodological issues for training. In H. Burns, J. W., Parlett, & C. L. Redfield (Eds.), *Intelligent tutoring systems* (pp. 243–263). Hillsdale, NJ: Lawrence Erlbaum Associates.

Benjamin, L. T. (1988). A history of teaching machines. *American Psychologist, 43*(9), 703–712.

Clark, R. E. (1983). Reconsidering research on learning from media. *Review of Educational Research, 53*(4), 445–459.

Clark, R. E. (1985). Evidence for confounding in computer-based instruction studies: Analyzing the meta-analyses. *Educational Communication and Technology Journal, 33*(4), 249–262.

Clark, R. E. (1989). Current progress and future directions in research on instructional technology. *Educational Technology Research and Development, 37*(1), 57–66.

Clark, R. E., & Salomon, G. (1986). Media in teaching. In M. C. Wittrock (Ed.), *Handbook of research on teaching* (3rd ed., pp. 464–478). New York: Macmillan.

Clark, R. E., & Sugrue, B. M. (1989). Research on instructional media: 1978–1988. In D. Ely (Ed.), *Educational media and technology yearbook* (Vol. 14, pp. 19–36). Denver, CO: Libraries Unlimited.

Clark, R. E., & Voogel, A. (1985). Transfer of training for instructional design. *Educational Communications and Technology Journal, 33*(2), 113–1232.

Congress of the United States, Office of Technology Assessment. (1988, September). *Power on: New tools for teaching and learning.* Washington, DC: U.S. Government Printing Office.

Congress of the United States, Office of Technology Assessment. (1989, November). *Linking for learning: A new course for education* (Report No. OTA-SET-430). Washington, DC: U.S. Government Printing Office.

Cuban, L. (1986). *Teachers and machines: The classroom use of technology since 1920.* New York: Teachers College Press.

Fletcher, J. D. (1990). *Effectiveness and cost of interactive videodisc instruction in defense training and education* (Institute for Defense Analysis Paper P-2372). Alexandria, VA: Institute for Defense Analysis.

Fowler, F. J. (1984). *Survey research methods.* Beverly Hills, CA: Sage Publications.

Gagne, R. M., Briggs, L. J., & Wager, W. W. (1992). *Principles of instructional design.* New York: Harcourt Brace Jovanovich.

Gardner, H., & Salomon, G. (1986, January). The computer as educator: Lessons from television research. *Educational Researcher,* 13–19.

Heinich, R. (1984). The proper study of instructional technology. *Educational Communication and Technology Journal, 32*(2), 67–87.

Jamison, D., Suppes, P., & Wells, S. (1974). The effectiveness of alternative instructional media: A survey. *Review of Educational Research, 44,* 1–68.

Kearsley, G., Hunter, B., & Sidel, R. J. (1983). Two decades of computer based instruction: What have we learned? *T.H.E. Journal, 10,* 88–96.

Kozma, R. B. (1991). Learning with media. *Review of Educational Research, 61*(2), 179–211.

Levie, W. H., & Dickie, K. (1973). The analysis and application of media. In R. M. W. Travers (Ed.), *Second handbook of research on teaching* (pp. 858–881). Chicago: Rand McNally.

Levin, H. M. (1983). *Cost effectiveness: A primer.* Beverly Hills, CA: Sage Publications.

Levin, H. M. (1988, May). The economics of computer-assisted instruction. *Peabody Journal of Education.*

Levin, H. M., & Meister, G. R. (1985). *Educational technology and computers: Promises, promises, always promises* (Report No. 85-A13). Stanford, CA: Center for Educational Research at Stanford, School of Education, Stanford University.

Lumsdaine, A. (1963). Instruments and media of instruction. In N. L. Gage (Ed.), *Handbook of research on teaching* (pp. 583–682). Chicago: Rand McNally.

Merrill, D. M., Jones, M. K., & Li, Z. (1992). Instructional theory: Classes of transactions. *Educational Technology,* 46–52.

Mielke, K. (1968). Questioning the questions of ETV research. *Educational Broadcasting Review, 2,* 6–15.

O'Neil, H., Jr., Anderson, C. L., & Freeman, J. (1986). Research and teaching in the armed forces. In M. C. Wittrock (Ed.), *Handbook of research on teaching* (3rd ed., pp. 971–987). New York: Macmillan.

Reigeluth, C. (1983). *Instructional design: Theories and models.* Hillsdale, NJ: Lawrence Erlbaum Associates.

Reigeluth, C. M. (1987). *Instructional theories in action.* Hillsdale, NJ: Lawrence Erlbaum Associates.

Saettler, P. A. (1968). *A history of instructional technology.* New York: McGraw-Hill.

Salomon, G. (1981). *Communication and education.* Beverly Hills, CA: Sage Publications.

Salomon, G. (1984). Television is "easy" and print is "tough": The differential investment of mental effort in learning as a function of perceptions and attributions. *Journal of Educational Psychology, 76*(4), 647–658.

Schramm, W. (1977). *Big media, little media.* Beverly Hills, CA: Sage Publications.

Weiner, B. (1992). *Human motivation: Metaphors, theories and research.* Newbury Park, CA: Sage Publications.

Winn, W. (1982). Visualization in learning and instruction. *Educational Communication and Technology Journal, 30*(1), 3–25.

4 Evaluating Intelligent Tutoring Systems

J. Wesley Regian
Valerie J. Shute
Armstrong Laboratory, Human Resources Directorate, Brooks Air Force Base, Texas

It has long been claimed that automated instruction has the potential for mass delivery of effective and efficient instruction (e.g., Pressey, 1926, 1927; Skinner, 1957; Woolf, 1988). Over the years, a variety of theoretical approaches have been adopted to pursue that potential (e.g., Burton & Brown, 1982; Carroll, 1963; Cohen, J. Kulik, & C. C. Kulik, 1982; Lewis, McArthur, Stasz, & Zmuidzinas, 1990; Sleeman & Brown, 1982; Wenger, 1987). As early as 1926, Pressey described a device that sought to apply then-contemporary learning theory to the task of automated instruction. The mechanical device, loaded with multiple-choice questions and answers by the teacher, would drill the student on the questions and provide immediate feedback in order to support learning:

> The somewhat astounding way in which the functioning of the apparatus seems to fit in with the so-called "laws of learning" deserves mention in this connection. The "law of recency" operates to establish the correct answer in the mind of the subject, since it is always the *last* answer which is the right one. The "law of frequency" also cooperates; by chance the right response tends to be made most often, since it is the *only* response by which the subject can go on to the next question. Further, with the addition of a simple attachment the apparatus will present the subject with a piece of candy or other reward upon his making any given score for which the experiment may have set the device; that is the "law of effect" also can be made, automatically, to aid in the establishing of the right answer. (Pressey, 1926, p. 375)

Pressey's ideas were probably viewed by some as quite promising, given their relationship to then-current learning theory, but they were never applied or even evaluated in any rigorous sense. Today, intelligent tutoring systems (ITS) epitomize the notion of theory-based, individualized, automated instruction. Many of us are just as excited about the potential of ITS as Pressey was about his teaching machine. Unfortunately, although ITS have been in existence for well over a decade, the degree to which they have been successful remains equivocal due to the relative dearth of controlled evaluations (Baker, 1990; Littman & Soloway, 1988; Shute & Regian, 1993).

Some of the more familiar ITS evaluations reported in the literature include the LISP tutor (e.g., Anderson, Farrell, & Sauers, 1984), instructing LISP programming skills; Smithtown (Shute & Glaser, 1990, 1991), a discovery world that teaches scientific inquiry skills in the context of microeconomics; Sherlock (Lesgold, Lajoie, Bunzo, & Eggan, 1992), a tutor for avionics troubleshooting; and Bridge (Shute, 1991; Shute & Kyllonen, 1990) teaching Pascal programming skills. Results from these evaluations show that the tutors can accelerate learning with, at the very least, no degradation in outcome performance compared to appropriate control groups.

How much can we make of these findings? As always, there is a selection bias for publication of unambiguous evidence for successful instructional interventions. Thus, we do not know how many studies found disappointing results. We are personally familiar with other (unpublished) tutor-evaluation studies that were conducted but were "failures." We are also aware of a great many ITS that have been built but never evaluated. We believe that a consistently applied, systematic, and rigorous approach to evaluation would speed the emergence of ITS into applied settings. The primary goals of this chapter are to outline a systematic approach to research and development of intelligent tutoring systems, and to present a set of steps to organize the design of evaluations for these systems.

RESEARCH AND DEVELOPMENT OF ITS: A GENERAL APPROACH

Our general approach has two main thrusts. First, in order to manage the tradeoff between internal and external validity, we believe ITS research and development should progress from laboratory studies of pedagogy in artificial tasks toward field studies of fully implemented ITS for real-world tasks. In other words, begin by identifying powerful instructional manipulations in controlled settings, and then work up to evaluating those manipulations in applied settings. Second, to maximize the efficiency of the research as well as the generality of the results, we believe ITS research and development should be driven by learning theory and constrained by evaluation data. In other words, if it should work, try it; if it doesn't work, change it.

Managing Experimental Validity

Experimental design involves arranging conditions to promote the validity of an experiment. If the causal link between independent manipulations and dependent measures is equivocal, the experiment is said to lack internal validity. If the ability to generalize from the experimental sample to the population of interest is equivocal, the experiment is said to lack external validity. In pedagogical research, increases in external validity are generally accompanied by decreases in internal validity. As you increase your ability to generalize pedagogical findings to applied settings, you lose the level of experimental control afforded within the laboratory. We believe the solution to this problem is to initially develop and test pedagogical principles in a laboratory setting with careful attention to experimental control. Promising approaches should then be tested in increasing fieldlike settings, and ultimately in applied settings with careful attention to external validity.

Figure 4.1 depicts the posited tradeoff between internal and external validity; as internal validity decreases, external validity increases. This relationship is particularly true with regard to research on pedagogy. Research in laboratory settings is desirable because of the experiment control that is possible in the laboratory. One can control for prior knowledge, assign subjects to groups, counterbalance for teacher (experimenter) effects, and so on. On the other hand, research in field settings (e.g., high school classrooms) is desirable because all aspects of the target setting are present in the experiment. Many of these aspects, however, are potential confounds to the experiment, making it difficult to relate outcome performance measures to the experimental manipulation. Field research on pedagogy, if done well, can have high external validity, but often at the expense of internal validity.

Our approach to managing the tradeoff between internal and external validity is to begin with laboratory research (high experimental control and internal validity) using carefully designed laboratory tasks. As we find instructional manipulations that are powerful, we attempt to replicate the effect with more realistic tasks, again within the laboratory. Eventually, we study the intervention

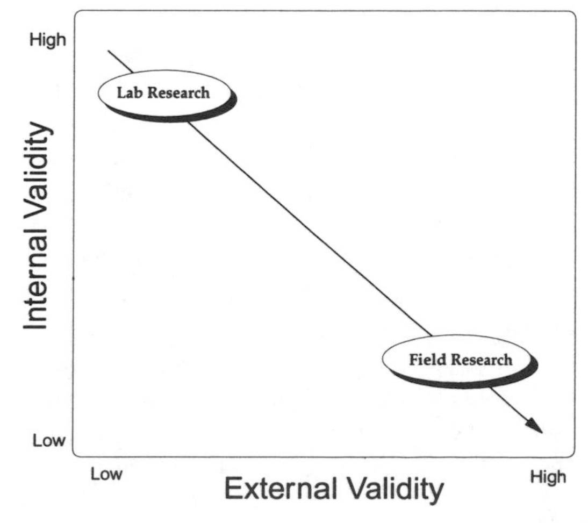

FIG. 4.1. Simple inverse relationship between internal and external validity.

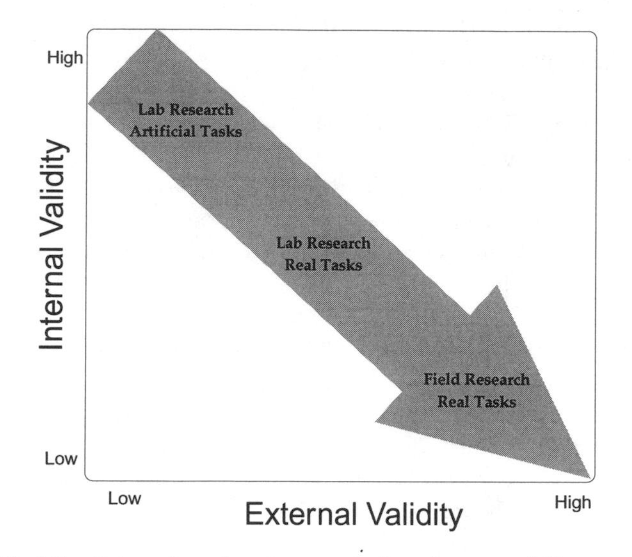

FIG. 4.2. Categories of pedagogy studies along a validity vector.

in an applied instructional context (field setting) with real-world tasks. Figure 4.2 depicts this flow, and places these stages of research on the validity vector from Fig. 4.1. We believe that neither laboratory nor field research alone will give a complete and accurate picture of the instructional effectiveness of a particular intervention. Further, we believe the choice of target tasks used to study instructional interventions at the various stages deserves careful consideration.

Managing Experimenter Bias

We believe that ITS research and development can advance more rapidly if the process is both driven by learning theory and constrained by empirical data. By *learning theory,* we mean a coherent, plausible body of ideas about how people acquire, store, retrieve, and apply knowledge and skill. We find that instructional prescriptions (or "theories" of instruction) that fail to address mechanisms of human knowledge acquisition and representation, are inadequate for our purposes. However, even if the design of an ITS is carefully linked to well-established theory, its value can only be ascertained from empirical testing. Theory is important in generating hypotheses about teaching and learning, and in driving generalizations about pedagogical effectiveness across instructional domains, but empirical testing is critical in order to judge how these ideas fare in reality. Only empirical data, with appropriate control conditions, can provide convincing documentation of the effectiveness of an intervention. Figure 4.3 shows this proposed cyclical relationship between theory and data, where

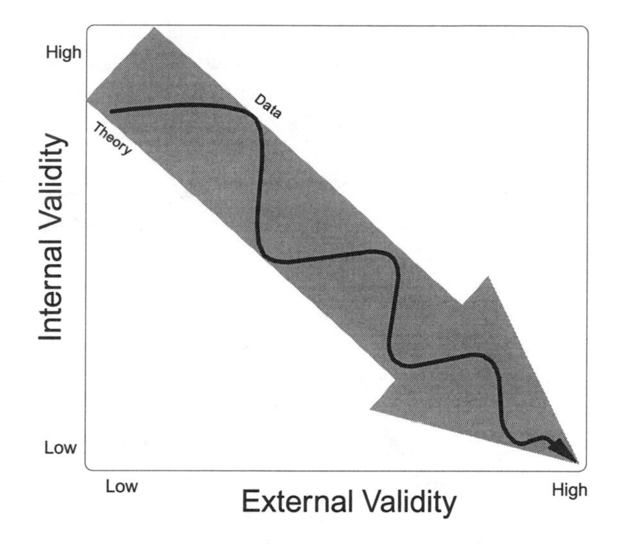

FIG. 4.3. Iterative process of experimentation—driven by learning theory and constrained by evaluation data.

research begins with theory that is progressively modified by empirical results.

In summary, empirical data about the effectiveness of theory-based instruction provides feedback about how well our implementation works, and may also lead to a revision of the original theory. We believe it is extremely important to evaluate systems rigorously and often in order to make progress in ITS effectiveness.

In the next section, we present examples of research that reside at each of three anchor points along the validity vector in Fig. 4.2. Our intention is to give a sense of the kinds of studies that are possible, and to indicate how the results of such studies can influence subsequent ITS work. It is important to keep in mind, however, that we view these three stages of research as relatively arbitrary points along a continuum, rather than truly distinct categories. We present examples of (a) laboratory research employing artificial tasks, (b) laboratory research employing real-world tasks, and (c) field research using real-world tasks.

Laboratory Research With Artificial Tasks

Artificial, or laboratory, tasks do not exist (in their exact form) in the real world. Examples of artificial tasks that have been used over the years in psychological research include memorization of nonsense syllables, cryptarithmatic, forced-choice reaction time tasks, and cursor-tracking tasks. Such tasks are devised to allow uncontaminated study of various phenomena of interest to the experimenter. Artificial tasks are useful in pedagogical research because they allow us to eliminate or reduce the effects of prior knowledge on learning, isolate very specific components of real tasks of interest, and study knowledge/skill acquisition in shorter time frames than would be required for real tasks.

Space Fortress *Research on Small-Group Pedagogy. Space Fortress* is an example of an artificial task that has a rich record as a research tool for studying issues of training and skill acquisition (see *Acta Psychologica,* Vol. 71, 1989). This gamelike dynamic control task was originally developed at the University of Illinois under funding from the Defense Advanced Research Project Agency (DARPA) as part of the Learning Strategies project (Donchin, 1989). We have developed an updated version of the program to run in our laboratory, with more flexibility than the original for our research purposes. Shebilske and Regian (1992), and Shebilske, Regian, Arthur, and Jordan (1992) report some of the research conducted in our laboratory using *Space Fortress*. For instance, we have found that it is possible to train up to four subjects on a single computer while achieving individual performance levels equivalent to those attained by subjects trained in the same amount of time on four separate computers. This is achieved by using a training protocol that involves a combination of whole-task practice, shared part-task practice, and observational learning among trainees. These findings are leading us to design prototype instructional systems that operate from the perspective of small-group pedagogy rather than individual pedagogy. In general, automated instruction is more cost-effective and sometimes more instructionally effective when designed for small groups rather than for individuals. When teaching multiple students simultaneously at a single computer, the hardware investment is reduced, as are demands on human instructor time. Also, students in small groups tend to teach one another, benefiting both the provider and the recipient of the instruction. Because students diagnose and remediate each other's performance, the difficult problems of automated diagnosis and natural language processing are avoided.

Space Fortress *Research on Gender-Related Performance Differences.* Another research area that we have been examining with *Space Fortress* involves the significant spatial component of the task. Typically, spatially loaded laboratory tasks yield robust gender effects with males outperforming females. This effect occurs on static spatial tasks (e.g., mental rotation, mental paper folding, form boards) as well as dynamic ones (e.g., collision estimation, dynamic control of moving figures). There has been a long-running argument over whether this gender difference in spatial performance is due to sex-related biological differences or differential developmental experiences. There is clear evidence that at least some of the difference is related to differences in testosterone levels (e.g., Kimura, 1992; Shute, Pellegrino, Hubert, & Reynolds, 1983). Recently, we have been examining instructional interventions that may overcome the hypothesized experiential deficits. We were surprised to find a very simple intervention that seems to go a long way in this direction; namely, placing women in discussion groups with men. We had female subjects participate in brief but regularly occurring (and specifically structured) discussion groups with male subjects, to talk about *Space Fortress* strategy and tactics. This simple intervention dramatically increased women's *Space Fortress* performance. Short discussion groups following practice sessions produced a small positive effect on men's skill acquisition, but a significant positive effect on women's. The women under this treatment performed nearly as well as the men. This very inexpensive intervention may help reduce gender differences in skill acquisition for other kinds of tasks as well.

Loader *Research on Mental Models During Training*. A second example of an artificial task from our laboratory is *Loader*—a complex procedural task (Farquhar, 1992). It requires subjects to execute long sequences of console-operation actions (e.g., button presses, switch actuations, dial rotations) to accomplish specific goals. The task is based on a computer-simulated console that controls railroad cars, tracks, and cranes in a fictitious railroad yard. The task is designed to be a laboratory analog of procedural console operations and process control tasks, which are common in industrial and defense settings.

We hypothesized that acquisition of *Loader* performance skill would be supported by the development of a dynamic mental model linking console actions to events in the "railroad yard." That is, in the process of learning to carry out a specific sequence of actions to accomplish a goal, the operator would come to imagine the corresponding events in the railroad yard, even if she could not actually see the yard while operating the console. We therefore conducted the following experiment (Farquhar, Shebilske, & Regian, 1992). Forty subjects were shown a simple static diagram representing a bird's-eye view of the railroad yard. The diagram depicted the layout of tracks, the initial location of cars, and the locations of bins and the crane. Subjects were told they would learn to operate a console that would enable them to move the cars around on the tracks, and to use the crane to move canisters between bins and cars. Subjects were randomly divided into two groups (i.e., dynamic model vs. no model). During training, both groups received identical text-based instruction in an instructional-window above the *Loader* interface. One group, however, additionally saw a *dynamic* version of the bird's-eye view of the railroad yard. After training, both groups were tested under identical conditions. They were asked to perform the complete procedure without guidance and without access to either type of railroad yard representation. The results were striking. Rather than becoming dependent on the animated rail yard model, subjects in the dynamic model condition apparently internalized the model, as evidenced by their performance after the model was removed. Posttraining performance was 33% faster and 50% more accurate for subjects trained with a dynamic graphical model compared to the no-model condition, even though the graphical model was not present during testing. This is an example of a very simple graphical aid that can be added to simulation-based ITS to produce significant and enduring performance enhancement.

Laboratory Research With Real Tasks

By real tasks, we mean tasks that constitute all or part of actual tasks that are performed in the world outside of the laboratory. In addition to having counterparts in the real world, they typically are more complex in structure than artificial tasks. Because real tasks tend to be more complex, they may take longer to acquire and performance may be more error-prone than artificial tasks.

Bridge Tutor. "Bridge" is the name of an ITS that teaches a subset of the Pascal programming language, which fits our criteria for being a *real* task (Bonar, Cunningham, Beatty, & Weil, 1988). We conducted a study using this tutor prior to conducting a full field evaluation of Bridge (Shute, 1991; Shute & Kyllonen, 1990). Approximately 200 subjects participated in the initial laboratory study. Many of them, however, had significant problems learning the programming curriculum because they lacked or had forgotten prerequisite knowledge presumed by the system (e.g., not knowing what an integer or variable was). Findings from this study highlighted about 10 weak concepts in programming and math: integer, real number, string, data, sum, product, constant, variable, expression, and value assignment. As a result of this laboratory investigation, we built a "pretutor,"an approximately 2-hr computer-assisted instruction (CAI) module that instructed those 10 concepts. Subjects received on-line definitions of concepts, followed by a series of questions pertaining to the concept (e.g., Is 5.24 an example of an integer?). After each response, feedback was provided on both the accuracy of the response and the item in question (e.g., "No, 5.24 is not an example of an integer because integers are positive or negative whole numbers without decimal points, and 5.24 contains a decimal"). This pretutor presented items in a learning-by-doing format with a strict mastery learning criterion. In the subsequent field study, once subjects encountered the Bridge tutor, they no longer had to ask, "What's a variable?" or "What's an integer?" The problem was solved, and learning Pascal programming skills was not confounded by inadequate knowledge of necessary concepts.

Electricity Tutor. MHO is a tutor that teaches basic principles of electricity (Lesgold, Bonar, Ivill, & Bowen, 1989). In one laboratory study (Shute, in press-a), we tested about 400 subjects using two instructional environments created as slightly different versions of MHO. These two environments differed only in the computer-generated feedback. All other aspects of the tutor were identical. In the rule-application environment, the ITS told the learners what the relevant principles were, and in the rule-induction environment, learners had to induce principles on their own, only given information about what variables were relevant. One learner characteristic that was examined was "exploratory behavior," a quantified measure of on-line tool usage (e.g., taking a meter reading from a circuit). Results from this laboratory study showed that learners with more exploratory behaviors learned significantly faster and scored significantly higher on outcome tests if they had been assigned to the inductive environment than the applied environment. On the other hand, less exploratory learners performed significantly better from the more structured, application environment compared to the inductive environment. It is interesting to note that there was no significant main effect due to learning environment on any of the many outcome or efficiency measures used in that study. Thus, neither of the instructional approaches was a clear "winner," overall. Instead, the study gave us critical information about how subsequent versions of the tutor should adapt to student behavior.

Field Research With Real Tasks

This section discusses studies that have employed real tasks tested in the field as opposed to in the laboratory. As noted earlier, the controls that are possible within laboratory environments may be more difficult, or impossible, to achieve during the conduct of field studies. For example, it may not be possible to randomly assign subjects to treatment conditions in a field study. However, with field research, the ability to generalize to the actual instructional context of interest is enhanced, increasing the study's external validity.

Smithtown. Shute and Glaser (1991) developed an ITS designed to improve an individual's scientific inquiry skills as well as provide a microworld environment for learning principles of basic microeconomics. Both of these foci constitute real knowledge and skills as they are applied outside of the laboratory in the real world. Shute, Glaser, and Raghavan (1989) reported that results from a field study comparing three groups of subjects: a group interacting with Smithtown, an introductory economics classroom, and a control group. The curriculum was identical in both treatment groups (i.e., laws of supply and demand). Results showed that whereas all three groups performed equivalently on the pretest battery (around 50% correct), the classroom and the Smithtown groups showed the same gains from pretest to posttest (26.4% and 25.2%, respectively), significantly outperforming the control group. Although the classroom group received more than twice as much exposure to the subject matter as did the Smithtown group (11 vs. 5 hrs, respectively), the groups did not differ on their posttest scores. These findings are particularly interesting because the instructional focus of Smithtown was not on economic knowledge, but rather on general scientific inquiry skills, such as hypothesis testing.

LISP Tutor. Another example of an ITS field was conducted by Anderson and his colleagues at Carnegie-Mellon University (Anderson et al., 1984). They developed a LISP tutor that provides students with a series of LISP programming exercises and tutorial assistance as needed during the solution process. In one study, Anderson, Boyle, and Reiser (1985) reported data from three groups of subjects: human-tutored, computer-tutored (LISP tutor), and traditional college instruction (subjects solving problems on their own). The time to complete identical exercises were 11.4, 15.0, and 26.5 hrs, respectively. Furthermore, all groups performed equally well on the outcome tests of LISP knowledge. A second evaluation study (Anderson et al., 1985) compared two groups of subjects: Students using the LISP tutor and students completing the exercises on their own. Both received the same lectures and reading materials. Findings showed that it took the group in the traditional instruction condition 30% longer to finish the exercises than the computer-tutored group. Furthermore, the computer-tutored group scored 43% higher on the final exam than the control group. So, in two different studies, the LISP tutor was successful in promoting faster learning with no degradation in outcome performance compared to traditional instruction.

In this section, we have provided examples of the types of studies we believe are useful at various stages in the development of ITS. We hoped to give a sense of the kinds of studies that are possible, and to indicate how the results of such studies can influence subsequent ITS work. In the following section, we turn to the goal of designing evaluation studies. We describe a set of steps that may be used to organize the design of ITS evaluation studies.

STEPS IN ITS EVALUATION

Outcomes of evaluation studies occasionally reflect the quality of an experimental design rather than the efficacy of the ITS. In our experience, we have seen evaluation studies fail due to poor experimental design, inadequately operationalized constructs and measures, and even deficient logistical planning and implementation. In the following sections, we present some general steps that may be followed to implement an effective ITS evaluation (see Shute & Regian, 1993, for a fuller discussion on this topic): (a) Clearly delineate the goals and methods of the tutor; (b) clearly define the goals of the evaluation study; (c) select the appropriate design to meet the defined goals; and (d) instantiate the design with appropriate measures, subjects, and controls.

Step 1: Clearly Delineate the Goals and Methods of the ITS

A careful review of the ITS goals and methods should be undertaken prior to designing an evaluation study. Occasionally, the instructional goals or methods may have shifted over the developmental life cycle of the ITS. In any event, if the designer of the evaluation study is unfamiliar with the tutor's goals and methods, then designing a good evaluation study is almost impossible. We believe the evaluation designer should be very clear about the following critical issues.

What Instructional Approach Underlies the Tutor? How, generally and specifically, does the system accomplish instruction? Is instruction guided or unguided, student directed or tutor directed? Is knowledge explicitly presented by the system or induced by the student? To what degree will all students have seen the same information or experienced the same interactions? Do students "complete" the tutor after a fixed time period or after reaching some performance criterion?

What Learning Theory Does It Assume? What knowledge or skill-acquisition theory motivates the instructional approach of the tutor? Which aspects of the tutor are directly theory-driven and which are arbitrary? How closely linked are the instructional approach and the learning theory? It is important to distinguish among a learning theory, a general instructional approach, and a specific instantiation of that instructional approach. Failure to do so can lead to over generalizations about evaluation results (e.g., Sleeman et al., 1989).

What Exactly Does It Teach? It is important to be very clear about what students are expected to learn as a result of interacting with the tutor. First, in a concrete sense, what exactly will they know or be able to do after tutoring that they did not know or could not do before? Specific and measurable knowledge or skills should be clearly delineated as the expected learning outcomes. For example, one might hope that students will be able to solve differential equations, list the bones in the human hand, or diagnose faults in a specific electromechanical system. It is also useful to characterize the goals of instruction in a more abstract manner. For example, one might hope to teach procedural skills, declarative knowledge retrieval, or logical problem solving. The ability to generalize findings across or within instructional domains is dependent on some type of theoretical characterization of domain dimensions.

What Other Impacts Is It Expected to Have? Are there other ways in which interacting with the tutor is expected to impact the student? For example, *Smithtown* explicitly instructed scientific inquiry behaviors, but it provided an environment that promoted learning about microeconomics. Less intentional side-effects of tutoring might include near or far transfer of skill, changes in perceived self-efficacy, or modification of attitudes about computers. If you believe such effects are probable and important, then appropriate and objective measures should be obtained to demonstrate the effect. So-called anecdotal evidence is usually the clearest indication of a missed opportunity during an evaluation.

In What Context Is It Supposed to Operate? Is the system intended to supplement existing instruction or provide stand-alone instruction? Is the system targeted to individuals or small groups? What prior knowledge, training, or demographic characteristics are assumed of students? Is the tutor supposed to be used in an academic setting to support declarative knowledge acquisition, or in an industrial training environment to support acquisition of procedural skills? It is important to clearly specify the environment in which the tutor is intended to operate in order to give it a fair chance of succeeding in evaluation, and in deciding on appropriate control conditions.

Step 2: Clearly Define the Goals of the Evaluation Study

Evaluation studies should not be fishing expeditions. A thoughtful consideration of what you want to know enables you to develop an experimental design that will unequivocally give you that information. You should also be realistic about the difficulties involved in implementing various designs, and adjust your goals at the outset to those that are realizable. Consider the following questions:

What Would You Like to Know After the Study is Completed? What is the primary question you want answered, or alternatively, what is the most important claim you want to be able to make? You may want to know if the tutor is more effective, more efficient, or both, than some instructional alternative at producing criterion performance on some task. You may want to see how much students learn beyond their incoming knowledge and skills, or as a function of their incoming knowledge and skills. You may want to see how tutor effectiveness is influenced by students' individual learning style. You should clearly specify your research questions and hypotheses before you design the study.

How Will You Measure Success, and By What Standard Will You Judge It? Think carefully about how to measure what is being taught, and how you will judge success. Suppose your instructional goal is to teach nine test-taking strategies, and you found that 1 week after students received 2 hrs of tutoring, they were able to state five of these strategies, on average. Was your tutor a success? What if you also learned that 1 week after students received 5 min of instruction using a simple mnemonic approach, they were able to state eight of the nine strategies. By comparison, your tutor would seem ineffective. But what if you found that students learning from your tutor could reliably apply five of the nine strategies, whereas students trained with the mnemonic approach can state, but not apply, eight strategies? Because any human performance is extremely sensitive to the methods used to measure it, your measures of learning should closely reflect the goals of instruction.

You may want to capture quantitative indices, protocols, and/or observational data. Because your subjects will be working at computers, it will be possible to plan for the online capture of quantitative measures of performance, such as latencies, accuracies, and behavioral counts. With considerably more effort and expense, protocol analyses can yield important information about learning that cannot be captured directly by the computer. Alternatively, trained observers may be employed to record aspects of learning and performance that are impossible to obtain otherwise (Schofield & Evans-Rhodes, 1989).

Step 3: Select an Appropriate Design to Meet Defined Goals

Only after reviewing the goals and methods of the tutor and clarifying the goals of the evaluation study is it appropriate to select an evaluation design. Researchers involved in the evaluation of automated instruction have sometimes chosen to distinguish between formative and summative evaluations (e.g., Kearsley, 1983) of courseware. Generally speaking, formative evaluations have an *internal* control condition, and ask the question: How can the system be improved? Summative evaluations have an *external* control condition, and ask the question: How does the system compare to other systems or approaches?

Originally, the formative/summative distinction was used to distinguish between diagnostic (formative) evaluation during student learning versus outcome (summative) evaluation after student learning (Bloom, Hastings, & Madaus, 1971). This distinction was only later adapted to the purpose of categorizing evaluations of courseware during development versus after completion. However, we have found that distinction too restrictive for our purposes. Concerning types of evaluation studies, we prefer to think in terms of the continuum described earlier (see Fig. 4.2) and a set of general evaluation categories. In particular, we present five broad design categories that may be used for evaluation studies. These include (a) *within-system designs* asking how two or more alternative versions of a single tutor compare to one another; (b) *between-system designs* addressing the effectiveness of one tutor in relation to another in terms of teaching the same subject matter; (c) *benchmark designs* asking how a tutor fares in relation to some standard instructional approach; (d) *hybrid designs* constituting combinations of the above options; and (e) *quasi-experimental designs* representing any of the previous categories, but without random assignment of subjects to conditions. Such an approach is often necessary for true field studies, but should be undertaken with some care (see Campbell & Stanley, 1968). Although these five categories do not represent an exhaustive set, they are common and useful design types for evaluation studies.

Step 4: Instantiate Design With Proper Measures, Subjects, and Controls

The next step is to carefully plan the details of the design. Carefully consider the selection of dependent and independent measures, the number and type of subjects, and the appropriate control conditions.

Dependent Measures. We have found that a common problem in failed evaluation is poor selection, design, or implementation of dependent measures to assess knowledge and skill acquisition. The dependent measures should directly reflect both the goals of the ITS and the goals of the evaluation study.

We prefer to obtain a variety of dependent measures. Because ITS instruction is done on computers, it is cheap and easy to capture data on virtually everything that happens during instruction. Given the expense and trouble involved in building an ITS and implementing a large-scale evaluation, we choose to err on the side of gathering too much data. Besides, it is the nature of learning and instructional research that the apparent effectiveness of an intervention will depend, in large part, on how you measure performance. If you measure performance in a variety of ways, you are more likely to pick up treatment effects if they exist. Possible dependent measures include performance latency, performance accuracy, declarative knowledge, procedural knowledge, procedural skill, automatic skill, secondary task performance, higher order knowledge, as well as measures of near transfer, far transfer, and skill retention or decay.

Independent Measures. It is likely that the effectiveness of an instructional intervention will vary with individual characteristics of students. Individuals come to any new learning situation with varying knowledge, skills, and abilities. Common individual difference measures include general intelligence, grade point average, standardized aptitude test scores, cognitive process measures (e.g., working memory capacity, information processing speed), personality measures (e.g., impulsivity, aggression, introversion), and demographic information (gender, age, years of school, experience with computers). Consider collecting these kinds of measures in order to control for potential confounds in your experimental design (e.g., two schools with different mean IQs for enrolled students).

Control Conditions. One of the most common arguments in interpreting the results of evaluation studies is over the suitability of the control conditions. The choice of treatment condition(s), as well as the proper control condition(s), must be principled, based on a reasonable consideration of the claims you hope to make. For example, if you choose only to include a no-treatment control, you may only be able to claim "My intervention is better than nothing." This assumes, of course, that data support the claim. Certain rules of thumb may be applied to help eliminate control-condition problems in ITS evaluation research (see Shute & Regian, 1993, for more on this topic). One problem that may arise in ITS research is the creation of Hawthorne effects (i.e., treatment differences due only to the fact that one group, usually the tutor-instructed group, receives special attention). Hawthorne effects, like placebo effects, are easily obtained, and thus must be carefully avoided. In the ideal case, the only difference between the control and treatment condition should be the treatment itself. Confounding difference you may want to avoid including differences in motivation, time-on-task, exposure to certain information, background characteristics, and so on.

Subjects. In addition to specifying rigorous control and experimental conditions, you will need to identify the right type and number of subjects that are needed in the study. In this regard, the most important considerations are the target population to which you would like to generalize, and the effect size that you expect to obtain.

For whom is the tutor intended? If the purpose of your ITS is to teach university graduate students a certain curriculum, and your test subjects come from an undergraduate population, you won't be able to accurately assess the effectiveness of your tutor on the target population.

As a rule of thumb, we believe evaluation studies looking for main effects of instructional treatments should use at least 30 subjects per condition. For aptitude-treatment variables (ATI) studies, using individual difference measures as independent variables, studies should use at least 100 subjects per treatment (Cronbach & Snow, 1977). This estimate can be relaxed somewhat for sufficiently powerful designs involving extreme groups or matched cases. Most investigators in the ATI tradition before 1980 used 40 or fewer subjects per treatment, and may have lacked the power to pick up even moderate effects. Keep in mind the relationship between sample size and power. The ability to pick up a given treatment effect goes up as sample size increases. Most basic experimental design textbooks describe how to estimate the required sample size for picking up a treatment effect of some hypothesized magnitude. When performing these calculations, keep in mind the difference between statistical significance and real-world importance. With enough power, you can pick up very small treatment effects, even though the effect size may be too small to be of practical importance.

CONCLUDING REMARKS

In this chapter, we have described our general approach to research and development of intelligent tutoring systems. The approach was based on the fundamental belief that ITS research should be driven by learning theory and constrained by evaluation data. We further described and illustrated a principled progression from laboratory studies using artificial tasks (with high internal validity), to field studies of fully implemented ITS teaching real tasks (with high external validity). We believe that early in this progression it is appropriate to identify effective instructional interventions in controlled laboratory settings using carefully designed laboratory tasks. Interventions that appear promising in this context should be applied to real-world tasks in controlled laboratory studies and eventually in field studies. Finally, we presented four steps we believe are useful in organizing the design of an evaluation study: (a) Delineate the goals and methods of the tutor, (b) define the goals of the evaluation study, (c) select the appropriate design to meet the defined goals, and (d) instantiate the design with appropriate measures, subjects, and controls.

It is important to note that even the most carefully designed evaluation study can fail during implementation due to incomplete logistical planning and preparation. Any evaluation effort has a multitude of details to attend to, and it is important to try to anticipate all of these in advance. Problems can be avoided with careful planning, training of personnel, and general preparation. For example, you can avoid a lot of problems by providing testing personnel with clear "scripts" and procedural checklists. You should also consider, in advance, the possible "worst-case" scenarios, such as what you would do if your hardware or software fails. These kinds of questions are best considered before the study begins (i.e., an ounce of prevention is worth a pound of cure).

If you succeed in carrying out a large evaluation study, you may be surprised at the difficulties involved in dealing with very large and diverse data sets. We recommend that you automate the storage, moving, recoding, and formatting of data as much as possible, and carefully check your automated procedures with dummy data sets having known distributions. Try to keep human recoding to a minimum to reduce errors. It is possible to be very efficient managing data that is initially collected on the computer.

We have found the evaluation of instructional interventions to be every bit as exciting as the development of these interventions. We are sometimes supported, sometimes humbled by data about how our instruction influences learning. Always, however, we benefit from the process.

ACKNOWLEDGMENTS

This chapter represents a synthesis and extension of some of our other work, especially Shute and Regian (1993) and Regian and Shute (1994). The research reported in this chapter was conducted by personnel of the Armstrong Laboratory, Human Resources Directorate, Brooks Air Force Base, Texas. The opinions expressed in this chapter are those of the authors and do not necessarily reflect those of the Air Force.

REFERENCES

Anderson, J. R., Boyle, C., & Reiser, B. (1985). Intelligent tutoring systems. *Science, 228,* 456–462.

Anderson, J. R., Farrell, R., & Sauers, R. (1984). Learning to program in LISP. *Cognitive Science, 8,* 87–129.

Baker, E. L. (1990). Technology assessment: Policy and methodological issues. In H. L. Burns,

J. Parlett, & C. Luckhardt (Eds.), *Intelligent tutoring systems: Evolutions in design* (pp. 151–161). Hillsdale, NJ: Lawrence Erlbaum Associates.

Bloom, B. S., Hastings, J. T., & Madaus, G. F. (1971). *Handbook on formative and summative evaluation of student learning*. New York: McGraw-Hill.

Bonar, J., Cunningham, R., Beatty, P., & Weil, W. (1988). *Bridge: Intelligent tutoring system with intermediate representations* (Tech. Rep. No. 88-7). Pittsburgh, PA: Learning Research & Development Center, University of Pittsburgh.

Burton, R. R., & Brown, J. S. (1982). An investigation of computer coaching for informal learning activities. In D. Sleeman & J. S. Brown (Eds.), *Intelligent tutoring systems* (pp. 77–123). London: Academic Press.

Campbell, D. T., & Stanley, J. C. (1968). *Experimental and quasi-experimental designs for research*. Chicago: Rand McNally.

Carroll, J. (1963). A model of school learning. *Teachers College Record, 64*, 723–733.

Cohen, P. A., Kulik, J., & Kulik, C. C. (1982). Educational outcomes of tutoring: A meta-analysis of findings. *American Educational Research Journal, 19*(2), 237–248.

Cronbach, L. J., & Snow, R. E. (1977). *Aptitudes and instructional methods: A handbook for research on interactions*. New York: Irvington.

Donchin, E. (1989). The learning strategies project. *Acta Psychologia, 71*, 1–15.

Farquhar, J. (1992). *Loader*. Unpublished computer program, Brooks Air Force Base, Texas.

Farquhar, J., Shebilske, W. L., & Regian, J. W. (1992). *Dynamic graphical models during training*. Unpublished manuscript.

Kearsley, G. (1983). Computer-based training: A guide to selection and implementation. Reading, MA: Addison-Wesley.

Kimura, D. (1992, September). Sex differences in the Brain. *Scientific American*, 119–125.

Lesgold, A. M., Bonar, J., Ivill, J., & Bowen, A. (1989). An intelligent tutoring system for electronics trouble-shooting: DC-circuit understanding. In L. Resnick (Ed.), *Knowing and learning: Issues for the cognitive psychology of instruction* (pp. 66–93). Hillsdale, NJ: Lawrence Erlbaum Associates.

Lesgold, A., Lajoie, S. P., Bunzo, M., & Eggan, G. (1992). A coached practice environment for an electronics troubleshooting job. In J. Larkin, R. Chabay, & C. Sheftic (Eds.), *Computer-assisted instruction and intelligent tutoring systems: Establishing communication and collaboration* (pp. 49–80). Hillsdale, NJ: Lawrence Erlbaum Associates.

Lewis, M. W., McArthur, D., Stasz, C., & Zmuidzinas, M. (1990). Discovery-based tutoring in mathematics. *AAAI Spring Symposium Series*. Stanford University, Stanford, CA.

Littman, D., & Soloway, E. (1988). Evaluating ITSs: The cognitive science perspective. In M. C. Polson & J. J. Richardson (Eds.), *Foundations of intelligent tutoring systems* (p. 209–242). Hillsdale, NJ: Lawrence Erlbaum Associates.

Pressey, S. L. (1926). A simple apparatus which gives tests and scores-and-teaches. *School and Society, 23*, 373–376.

Pressey, S. L. (1927). A machine for automatic teaching of drill material. *School and Society, 25*, 549–552.

Regian, J. W., & Shute, V. J. (1994). Basic research on the pedagogy of automated instruction. In T. de Jong, H. Spada, & D. M. Towne (Eds.), *The use of computer models for explication, analysis, and experiential learning* (pp. 121–132). New York: Springer-Verlag.

Schofield, F. W., & Evans-Rhodes, D. (1989). Artificial intelligence in the classroom: The impact of a computer-based tutor on teachers and students. In D. Bierman, J. Brueker, & J. Sandberg (Eds.), *Artificial intelligence and education: Synthesis and reflection* (pp. 238–243). Amsterdam, the Netherlands: IOS.

Shebilske, W. L., & Regian, J. W. (1992, October). *Video games, training, and investigating complex skills*. Paper presented at the annual meeting of the Human Factors Society, Atlanta, GA.

Shebilske, W. L., Regian, J. W., Arthur, W., & Jordan, J. (1992). A dyadic protocol for training complex skills. *Human Factors, 34*, 369–374.

Shute, V. J. (1991). Who is likely to acquire programming skills? *Journal of Educational Computing Research, 7*(1), 1–24.

Shute, V. J. (1992). Aptitude-treatment interactions and cognitive skill diagnosis. In J. W. Regian & V. J. Shute (Eds.), *Cognitive approaches to automated instruction* (pp. 15–47). Hillsdale, NJ: Lawrence Erlbaum Associates.

Shute, V. J. (1993a). A comparison of learning environments: All that glitters . . . In S. P. Lajoie & S. J. Derry (Eds.), *Computers as cognitive tools* (pp. 47–74). Hillsdale, NJ: Lawrence Erlbaum Associates.

Shute, V. J. (1993b). A macroadaptive approach to tutoring. *Journal of Artificial Intelligence and Education.*

Shute, V. J., & Gawlick-Grendell, L. A. (1993, August). *An alternative approach to learning probability: Stat Lady.* Proceedings of AI & ED 93, Edinburgh, Scotland.

Shute, V. J., & Glaser, R. (1990). A large-scale evaluation of an intelligent discovery world: Smithtown. *Interactive Learning Environments, 1*, 51–77.

Shute, V. J., & Glaser, R. (1991). An intelligent tutoring system for exploring principles of economics. In R. E. Snow & D. Wiley (Eds.), *Improving inquiry in social science: A volume in honor of Lee J. Cronbach* (pp. 333–366). Hillsdale, NJ: Lawrence Erlbaum Associates.

Shute, V. J., Glaser, R., & Raghavan, K. (1989). Inference and discovery in an exploratory laboratory. In P. L. Ackerman, R. J. Sternberg, & R. Glaser (Eds.), *Learning and individual differences* (pp. 275–326). San Francisco: Freeman.

Shute, V. J., & Kyllonen, P. C. (1990). *Modeling programming skill acquisition* (Report No. AFHRL-TP-90-76). Brooks Air Force Base, TX: Air Force Systems Command.

Shute, V. J., & Regian, J. W. (1993). Principles for evaluating intelligent tutoring systems. *Journal of Artificial Intelligence & Education*, 245–271.

Shute, V. J., Pellegrino, J. W., Hubert, L., & Reynolds, R. W. (1983). The relationship between androgen levels and human spatial abilities. *Bulletin of the Psychonomic Society, 26*(6), 465–468.

Skinner, B. F. (1957). *Verbal behavior.* Englewood Cliffs, NJ: Prentice-Hall.

Sleeman, D., & Brown, J. S. (1982). *Intelligent tutoring systems.* London: Academic Press.

Sleeman, D., Kelly, A. E., Martinak, R., Ward, R. D., & Moore, J. L. (1989). Studies of diagnosis and remediation with high school algebra students. *Cognitive Science, 13*(4), 551–568.

Wenger, E. (1987). *Artificial intelligence and tutoring systems.* Los Altos, CA: Morgan Kaufmann.

Woolf, B. P. (1988). Intelligent tutoring systems: A survey. In H. Schrobe (Ed.). Exploring artificial intelligence (pp. 1–44). Palo Alto, CA: Morgan Kaufman.

5 Assessment of Intelligent Training Technology

Alan Lesgold
University of Pittsburgh

Over the past decade, there has been considerable research and development in applications of artificial intelligence to education and training (e.g., studies in Larkin & Chabay, 1992; Polson & Richardson, 1988; Psotka, Massey, & Mutter, 1988). In several cases, training systems have been produced that are receiving practical use (e.g., Anderson, 1990; Corbett & Anderson, 1992; Govindaraj, 1988). More commonly, so far, managers are starting to face decisions about whether a prototype research system has potential utility. In this chapter, I view the assessment of intelligent training systems from a long-term perspective, discussing the different kinds of decisions that require assessment of intelligent training technology and a number of specific assessment issues, considered in light of current theory and experience. In particular, I draw on experiences with the Sherlock coached practice environment for electronics troubleshooting (Lajoie & Lesgold, 1990; Lesgold, Lajoie, Bunzo, & Eggan, 1992; Lesgold, Lajoie, Logan, & Eggan, 1990).

IMMEDIATE EFFECTIVENESS VERSUS POTENTIAL

Technology assessment in the world of intelligent training systems must consider not only the effectiveness of a training system but also the likelihood that it can be assimilated by the organizations that could use it. This can be seen either superficially as a marketing problem or more deeply as a problem in changing schooling or training. In either case, though, it is not enough for a product to be effective; it also must either fit the existing organizational structure and available technology or be so attractive as to bring about adaptive changes that make it usable.

When a product is assessed for its immediate utility, evaluation is extremely straightforward. We try it and see how it works. Sometimes we can develop quantitative assessment approaches that allow us to rank alternate products. For example, consumer testing laboratories have mechanical devices that simulate sitting in a chair and getting up. With such devices, we can count how many sitting/rising cycles it takes before a chair's springs fail. With a mixture of such tests, we can develop composite scores that assess the durability of chairs. In other cases, where more subjective judgments of adequacy are involved, we can ask potential consumers to rate properties of a product. So, we see ratings of orange juice, microwave popcorn, wine, and other food products by panels of tasters, either professional or from the lay public. For some products, the effect of using the product can be directly measured. For example, when testing razors, we can count the number of cuts received by a sample of razor users and perhaps even measure the lengths of hair roots left after shaving.

Instructional products are often evaluated the same way. We use the product and measure its positive and negative outcomes. Usually, this is done by testing students after their use of a product and seeing whether they do better on goal-relevant test items after using the product than after some alternative treatment. Costs, corresponding to the razor cuts of the preceding example, are also assessed. Often, there is an explicit comparison between requirements for the instructional treatment being tested and the resources available in some pool of representative schools. Other costs, such as teacher preparation time, student class time, and so on, are also considered.

User acceptance is also an important consideration when instructional products are evaluated. For example, certain textbook series are considered to have great instructional potential but to be market risks because teachers won't adopt them. Often, this occurs when a textbook series fails to match current curricular sequencing, requires significant teacher preparation time investment, or fails to provide certain aids to teaching that competitors make available. One of the costs likely to be associated with a technological aid to education is the investment of time teachers must make to learn how to use it. A particular problem for computer-based systems is whether the computer equipment it requires is broadly available.

In the case of computer-based consumer commodity products, assessment must consider user acceptance and installed platform base. Many a product has failed in the market, even though it was demonstrably better than its competitors, because it required a different operating system or more memory. More trivial sources of product failure include complex copy protection schemes, complexity in providing the right size of diskettes, and lack of compatibility of files with extant products in the marketplace. Clearly, from the standpoint of an educational product meant for use today, an assessment of the product must consider not only whether it is effective when used but also whether people are prepared and willing to use it.

When evaluating an educational product's potential for the future, these factors are harder to deal with. The computers that schools have today are primitive and characteristically inadequate for many of the most exciting educational technology possibilities.[1] For example, one big advance in the computer world is simpler, smarter interfaces that are more forgiving. Even the better-equipped schools, however, tend to have underpowered machines that cannot run the larger programs that are needed to provide easy-to-use information-processing tools. To restrict positive assessments to software that runs on underpowered machines is foolish, especially when schools show a continuing ability to upgrade their resources, albeit slowly and spasmodically, in response to technological change.[2] However, it is difficult to predict when enabling conditions will arise in any market, including the school market. Fortunes have been made and lost in guessing whether DOS, Unix, Windows, or OS/2 will prevail, for example. Accordingly, it seems very important at least to understand what conditions will be required for a promising prototype system to be used and valued, and it would be extremely helpful to have means of assessing the likelihood of those conditions arising.

In the case of intelligent training systems, some information is available concerning the hardware platforms that will be prevalent in the future, and there are also development platforms that can be used to produce software that will run under several different operating systems. For example, it is clear that Microsoft Windows is a major force in the computer world. Combined with other forces previously evidenced, Windows assures that there will be a relatively large population of computers with 80386, 80486, or 80586 processors; four or more megabytes of memory; and decent (VGA or better) graphics in the business and industry world. Recent market trends suggest that the Macintosh operating systems will have a long presence in the school world, the desktop publishing world, and perhaps other niches. Unix windowing systems such as X will also be supported by the next generation of multiple-platform operating systems.

On the software side, much of the research base in artificial intelligence depends on Common LISP running on large Unix™ work stations. Currently,

---

[1]The situation for the training world is often similar, though the exact current technology differs. Training directors would love to have highly adaptive intelligent software that will run on 386 MS Windows machines with 80 MB disks. However, because there are more direct economic forces in the business world than in the education world, training directors will generally buy new equipment if it is proven to be cost-effective.

[2]It is often alleged that schools cannot afford any incremental investments over teacher salaries. This is demonstrably untrue. What is true is that capital investments by schools are somewhat unpredictable and generally driven by broad social forces. However, the initial investment of schools in primitive computers, the massive broadening of school-provided transportation, the introduction and technological modifications of school lunch facilities, and the massive investments in asbestos removal (often uncorrelated with risk) show that schools can make major investments. What needs to be understood is what it takes to trigger such an investment.

delivered systems are often rewritten in C so they will run faster on standard work stations (major LISP vendors are working to complete adequate delivery systems for LISP that run efficiently on multiple platforms). Rather recently, Smalltalk has emerged as a programming language of choice for training system development, and it is what my team uses for its biggest and most applied project. Recent actions in the commercial software world suggest a move toward use of object-oriented languages such as Smalltalk (or C++ for teams with high programming skill levels) because they produce software that is more maintainable. I discuss these issues in more detail later in this chapter.

In the easy case, then, a decision maker can predict, with a high degree of confidence, that the hardware and the software architecture required to support a desirable prototype system will be in place. Often, however, given the requirements of development, there will be a gap between the hardware platform for a prototype system and the hardware broadly available in the short term. A conservative view of the problem of assessing both software quality and the likelihood of a hardware plant to run the software would be that only software that makes a striking contribution will succeed in navigating the hardware gap. From this viewpoint, assessment means a search for evidence that a product not only is effective but further that it is so effective that it cannot easily be avoided. A global finding of massive effect, though not particularly informative for product refinement, provides a basis for predicting that a product will be used, even if it requires improved hardware. More broadly, the bigger the infrastructural investment that would be needed to use a piece of software, the bigger the demonstration of general efficacy needs to be.[3]

These observations are informed by our own experience with the "Sherlock Project," a long-term effort to shape a technology of coached practice environments for training complex problem-solving jobs in the Air Force (Lajoie & Lesgold, 1990; Lesgold, Lajoie, Bunzo et al., 1992; Lesgold, Lajoie, Logan et al., 1990). Our first "product," Sherlock I, needed many refinements but it did produce the massive effect needed to assure likely adoption, and it led to support for ambitious efforts to refine and generalize the system and move it to different platforms. Consequently, the way in which we evaluated it may be worthy of examination. Later, I discuss this project, especially our approach to assessing it. I conclude by reflecting on some issues critical to assessment of training technology that became apparent in the course of the development of Sherlock.

---

[3]It is important to note that the "cost" of software is best seen in terms of the organizational barriers to its use. For example, one product might cost $10,000 whereas another might cost $1,000 but require a $1,000 modification to available hardware platforms. If it is easier for a decision maker to get $8,000 more than to work around organizational restrictions on hardware purchases or modifications, then to that decision maker, the $10,000 product is more feasible. In absolute terms, software will be seen as feasible if the effects it can produce outweigh the organizational costs, financial and otherwise, of putting it into use.

ASSESSMENT EXPERIENCES FROM THE SHERLOCK PROJECT

What Is Sherlock Like?

Since 1983, my associates and I have been developing a technology for training complex problem-solving expertise for the U.S. Air Force. The Sherlock Project has been an extended effort to develop improved approaches to the training of complex job skills, especially training that supports transfer to new but related jobs. After empirical studies of experts and trainees (Glaser, Lesgold, & Gott, 1991; Glaser, Lesgold, & Lajoie, 1987) the work has revolved around a family of prototype training systems called coached intelligent apprenticeship systems. The basic training approach of these systems is to present trainees with simulations of work problems that are among the most challenging that arise in real life. To help them through these problems, coaching is provided, that is, help of varying forms is available to the trainee on request. Artificial intelligence techniques are used to provide the work simulations and to provide coaching tailored to the trainee's capabilities. Two generations of coached intelligent apprenticeship environments have now been built. The first of these, Sherlock I, was evaluated extensively in the field. Its successor, Sherlock II, is largely a response to lessons we learned from the evaluations. Sherlock II includes a simulation of a very complex electronic device, a "test station"[4] with thousands of parts, simulated measurement devices for "testing" the simulated station, a problem selection scheme that presents fault diagnosis problems within the device simulation, a coach that provides assistance when help is requested in the course of diagnosis, and a reflective follow-up facility that permits a trainee to review his or her performance on a problem and compare it to that of an expert.

In developing the Sherlock systems, we had a number of psychological concerns. We wanted to afford opportunities for learning by doing, and this required simulation of complex job situations, not just of small devices. Also, we wanted

---

[4]The Air Force uses *test stations* to diagnose and repair components from aircraft. For example, when a navigation component malfunctions, it is replaced with a unit known to be working and then is sent back to a repair shop for diagnosis and repair. In that shop, a test station is used to facilitate the diagnosis. The test station is like a giant telephone switchboard, connecting the aircraft module being tested to both power sources and measurement devices. Automated test stations use computer programs to carry out a sequence of tests to localize aircraft module faults, whereas manual test stations rely on a technician setting switches in response to a printed protocol in the technical orders for the station. Sherlock is targeted at a manual test station job. The really hard part of the job, which is what Sherlock coaches, arises when the test station itself is not working right. Then, diagnosis must proceed without a protocol that has been totally prespecified, and meters must be attached by hand to various test points on the station. Test station failures often take 8 to 12 hrs of diagnosis before they are found and remediated. Much of this time is spent physically reaching various test points and waiting for spare parts to arrive from a central depot. Sherlock compresses test station diagnosis to about a half hour of concentrated cognitive activity per fault isolation problem.

to tailor the coaching provided by the system to the knowledge needs of the trainee. Ideally, trainees should be kept in the position of almost knowing what to do but having to stretch their knowledge just a little in order to keep going. Consequently, hints should be provided with some inertia. They should provide enough help to avoid total impasse but this help should come slowly enough so that it is easier to think a bit on one's own than to wait for the correct next step to be stated completely. This requires considerable modeling of student capability and may also require modeling of the course of trainee–machine interaction. Of course, it also requires expert modeling in order to know what advice to give.

During the course of difficult work, it is not likely that much extended learning can take place. Both psychological experimentation (cf. Owen & Sweller, 1985; Sweller, 1988; Sweller & Cooper, 1985) and theoretical models of case-based learning (e.g., Mitchell, Keller, & Kedar-Cabelli, 1986) indicate that learning from task situations requires a lot of cognitive effort. For this reason, we have put much of the power of our training systems in postproblem reflective follow-up. After solving a problem, which requires about a half hour of effort, trainees can review their actions step by step, asking what an expert would do at any point along the way. Or, they can simply ask for a trace of an overall expert solution. At each step in either trace, they can receive background information on why the step is being taken. Also, color diagrams at each step in the trace show what is known about different parts of the system being diagnosed (parts proven good in green; paths with incorrect information in them in red, etc.). Much of this capability rests on the same knowledge structures that support coaching during problem solution.

Sherlock I ran on a special artificial intelligence work station and was written in Interlisp and Loops, a proprietary object-based language for Interlisp.[5] Trainees interacted with the system by pointing to screen-graphic renderings of the front panels of devices and to schematic diagrams of their innards. Sherlock II runs on a standard 80386 machine, requires around 8MB (depending on the version used and research requirements for data collection), about 20MB of hard disk, a processor speed of 20 MHz or higher, a videodisc player and interface, and a GENLOCK card[6] to mix the video and computer graphics images. Trainees interact with Sherlock II by making selections from menus and by pointing to video views of test station components. For example, to make a resistance measurement, trainees would click on a screen icon of the hand-held digital multimeter to access the front panel display of the meter in video, indicate knob settings on the video image with the mouse, select the component he or

---

[5]Both Interlisp and Loops were developed at the Xerox Palo Alto Research Laboratory (Interlisp had a brief prior existence in precommercial form in the MIT Artificial Intelligence Laboratory), and later sold as commercial products by Xerox and then by Envos, a Xerox spin-off company.

[6]A GENLOCK card permits mixing of a video image and a computer screen image. The card is programmed to watch for a particular color in the computer screen image and to substitute the corresponding point in the video image for any pixel of that color. The net effect that can be created is of computer graphics "written on" a video recording.

she[7] wanted to test from a menu, and then indicate meter probe locations by pointing to a video image of the component. Coaching advice also is available via the menu system. Sherlock I, in spite of its more specialized artificial intelligence environment, was much less intelligent and more brittle in its knowledge than Sherlock II. In addition, it lacked the reflective follow-up capability that we now believe to be of great importance.

Basic Assessment Results for Sherlock I: The Massive Effect

Sherlock II has undergone multiple revisions, and major field tests were scheduled for Spring 1993. We do have field assessment data for Sherlock I. Overall, Sherlock I was excessively rigid but remarkably successful. Because the goal structures for each problem were hand coded and many hints were specific statements written in advance, the system was not very extensible, and the interaction between trainee and machine somewhat rigid. However, the bottom line is that 20–25 hrs of Sherlock I practice time for trainees in their first 4 years of duty produced improvements almost to the level of their more senior colleagues who had many more years on the job. In more practical terms, trainees could not generally troubleshoot test station failures before the Sherlock training, but they could afterward. Here is how this conclusion was established.

The goal of Sherlock I was to train the ability to diagnose test station faults, the hardest part of the F-15 manual test station job. So, we[8] used simulated test station diagnosis problems in the field evaluation (see Gott, 1989, or Nichols, Pokorny, Jones, Gott, & Alley, in press, for details). Virtually all of the job incumbents at two Air Force bases participated in the evaluation, a total of 32 airmen in their first 4-year term and 13 at more advanced levels. The 32 first-termers were split into an experimental and a control group of 16 each. The experimental group had a mean experience of 28 months in the Air Force, whereas the control group had a mean of 37 months (the difference was not statistically significant and worked against the comparison of interest). The advanced group had about 6 more years of experience, a mean of 114 months. The simulated test station diagnosis problems were presented verbally. An example problem is the following:

---

[7]In our own work, about 20%–25% of trainees are female. We occasionally use the term "airman" or "airmen," an official rank in the Air Force. Airmen are both female and male.

[8]The pronoun *we* is convenient but inaccurate. The Air Force Human Resources Laboratory carried out the evaluation study with our support. Official reporting of their results will appear in Nichols et al. (in press). The summary we provide is not endorsed by the Air Force. Although we have attempted to accurately convey our best understanding of the results, the official Air Force position on the methods employed and results obtained may deviate from our interpretation. We did conduct additional evaluations on our own, which are reported in Lajoie and Lesgold (1990). Those results are consistent with the present discussion as well.

> While running a Video Control Panel unit, Test Step 3.e fails. The panel lamps do not illuminate. All previous test steps have passed.

In such a situation, the unit being tested is usually defective, but in this particular case, it turns out that a relay card in the test station is bad. This type of problem is one that is extremely difficult for novice technicians. In the evaluation study, technicians would hear the problem statement and then be asked two questions: (a) *What would you do next?* (b) *Why would you do that?* They would then be told the result of their action and the cycle of questioning would repeat until the problem was solved or an impasse was reached. Verbal protocols of these problem-solving interviews were then given to Air Force experts who scored them blind to the condition assignments of the subjects. Scoring scales were derived from expert rankings of the problem-solving performances using "policy capturing" techniques (discussed later).

Figure 5.1 shows the results. Given group standard deviations ranging from 12 to 29, the results show that the experimental and control group pretest means and the control group posttest mean are at one level and the experimental posttest mean and the advanced group mean are at a second, much higher and significantly different, level. The data were also considered from a second viewpoint, the amount of on-the-job experience needed to produce gains equivalent to those produced by the Sherlock experience of 20–25 hrs of coached practice. The totality of the pretest data was used to generate a regression coefficient for predicting months of Air Force job experience from these test scores. Using the scale created by this regression, the gain shown by the experimental group from

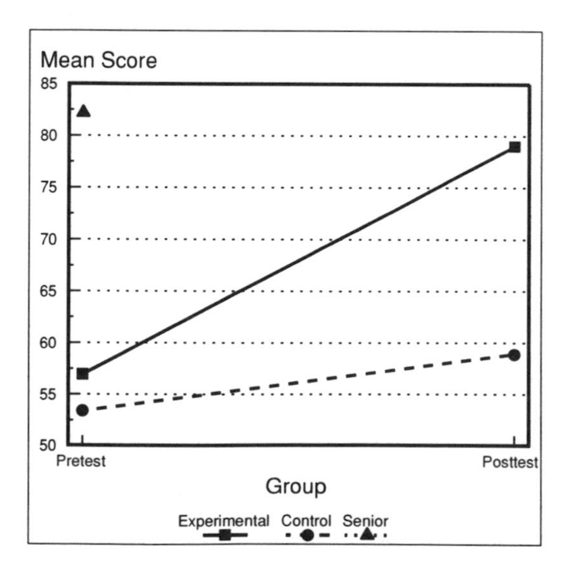

Fig. 5.1. Results of Sherlock I evaluation by the Air Force.

pretest to posttest is equivalent to about 4 years of job experience, using conservative estimates, although the confidence interval for this estimate is necessarily huge, given the small numbers of subjects. A follow-up testing 6 months after training (Pokorny, unpublished data) showed retention of over 90% of the gains made from pre- to posttesting. Overall, then, Sherlock was very successful, in terms of producing the ability to do the specific job of manual F-15 test station diagnosis, which is not readily acquired from simple on-the-job experience or from the training now available prior to reporting for work.

Interpreting the Massive Effect

The massive effect of Sherlock is real, but it requires interpretation. Basically, Sherlock is effective because it has no competition. That is, it affords opportunities for learning that were not available before, either on the job or in the classroom. A variety of logistic and other limitations make it very difficult for on-the-job training to be effective in teaching the hardest parts of the job. When those hard tasks appear, it is often an urgent situation, in which getting equipment back on-line takes precedence over providing training opportunities. Further, the specific events that would present good training opportunities with respect to our high threshold criterion (the hardest tasks in real-life work) are relatively rare. In the schoolhouse, it is even more difficult to create realistic situations in which the hardest diagnostic tasks can be practiced, and such practice seems to be critical to attaining high levels of skill.

When looking at high-end job performance, even in purely cognitive tasks like fault diagnosis, there often is no substitute for realistic practice. Abstract principles can be taught in the classroom, but it is rare for those principles to be applied automatically in the real world without some practice, especially in situations of great complexity and stress. Consequently, one interpretation of the massive effect of Sherlock I is that it provides practice, under simulated task conditions, that is sufficient for learning, whereas prior learning opportunities within on-the-job practice did not. Seen from this viewpoint, the assessment issues that are raised are somewhat different in character. We consider each of these, in the context of the Sherlock experience, in the next section.

ISSUES IN INTELLIGENT TRAINING TECHNOLOGY ASSESSMENT

Reality and Nature of the Main Effect

The first issue is the reality of the main effect. If one is going to assert that a system accomplishes a major chore that is otherwise not readily accomplished, this needs to be backed up. It is necessary to show that the system produces levels of competence that are worth more than the levels of competence achieved without using the system. At one level, this was easy. We could document the costs of not having technicians who could troubleshoot test station failures, and we were able to show that after Sherlock training, technicians could handle problems that they could not handle before. Because the Air Force was hiring civilian experts to stand by to assist uniformed personnel when test station faults occurred, the costs could be documented. However, we feel it is important to have a quantitative documentation of the training outcome as well as of the monetary value of the training. That is, we wanted to have quantitative scores of performance in the test station troubleshooting tasks whose value we had established.

To get this, we had two basic options. On the one hand, we could list a number of properties of good test station troubleshooting activity and then score troubleshooting episodes for the presence or absence of those properties. For example, one important property is making measurements instead of swapping components. We could decide arbitrarily to subject some number of points from a person's score for each action required to solve a problem, charging more for swapping than for testing. Further, we could almost certainly reduce the costs to dollars. Each action takes time, which has measurable cost, and swapping a good part generates a variety of measurable costs. Depleting an inventory has at least indirect costs, because the inventory must be kept higher if such depletions must be anticipated.

It is also important to note that Sherlock I was based on many design principles, some of which were enumerated earlier. Which design principles have what effect on the various possible outcome measures is difficult to establish. One implication of this difficulty in isolating the mapping of treatment parameters to effects is that once a main effect is established, detailed parametric research may be justified. In the case of Sherlock, the initial results have motivated support for such a program of research, which continues in the context of Sherlock II.

Transfer

On the other hand, we could have experts evaluate the performances of those who did or did not use the system, and then compare their ratings. At first blush, this seems considerably less satisfactory than the quantitative approach just described, and it would be if we were concerned only with immediate costs and performances. However, if we want to predict transfer to systems that may not yet exist or that may not be available for testing, especially when predictive studies of transfer may not have been carried out for the knowledge domain, then it may be necessary to rely on expert appraisals of competence. Expert judgments have known shortcomings. In the military context, it is not unusual for staff who are cooperative to be valued over those who are not, independent of their expertise, for example. With respect to assessing changes that we expect a tutoring system to introduce, such social factors represent error variance in an evaluation design.

The Air Force worked with us to find ways to use expert judgments to derive scorable properties. Nichols et al. (in press; see also Pokorny & Gott, 1989) applied techniques of policy capturing[9] to develop scoring schemes for the troubleshooting task we used in evaluating Sherlock I. The basic scheme is very straightforward. Difficult troubleshooting problems are posed verbally to the testee. Testees call for various actions to be performed in solving the problem. Results of each action are provided to the testee. A trace is kept of all the activity of each trainee in solving each criterion troubleshooting problem. Experts are asked to examine the traces and to rank order them. Then, they are questioned about the bases for their rankings. From this questioning, one derives a list of features that contribute to judgments of expertise. The next step is to assign point values to each of these features, so that they can be used to set a score for the trainee. Finally, the scoring scheme thus developed can be used to score additional performances by the same or other test subjects.

Setting the point values for each scoring feature can be done in several different ways. One approach is to set the point values to best predict the rank orderings assigned by experts to the whole performances. This is a common strategy and generally involves regression analyses. The strategy makes sense if we assume that the experts are making their holistic judgments solely with respect to issues of expertise we care about. Sometimes this is not the case. A second approach is to analyze the features cited by experts and to evaluate them. This can be done both empirically and theoretically. Empirically, it is possible to do clustering analyses of the scoring features. Once clusters are identified, some amount of theorizing is required to decide why certain features cluster. This may result in a decision that some features are good indicators of important job knowledge whereas others are mainly generic indicators of being "good airmen." For example, following recommended troubleshooting sequences religiously may be highly valued but may not correlate with indicators of deep domain knowledge.

When the policy capturing approach is used there is potential loss of explainability for scores. Saying that a trainee got a high score for doing things that experts value highly is not quite as satisfactory as saying that the high score was awarded for performance approximating that of an expert in identifiable ways.

---

[9]The policy capturing approach consisted of first having experts rank order protocols of trainees' solutions to troubleshooting problems. Then, they were asked to justify their rank orderings by pointing to features of the problem solutions that justified valuing one solution more than another. The next step was to ask the experts to assign relative value to these distinguishing features. Finally, a check was made to assure that protocols that were scored using the point scheme based on the valued features would receive expert rankings similar to their rankings based on the feature scores. With that validation, Nichols et al. (in press) then had a scoring rubric that could be used for evaluating additional protocols—even protocols from new but relatively similar problems.

For this reason, we are moving toward a modification of the pure policy capturing approach. We are now experimenting with an online evaluation scheme in which our expert model directly tallies various indications of expertlike and nonexpertlike actions (Katz & Lesgold, 1991; Katz, Lesgold, Eggan, & Gordin, 1992). These tallies can then be used in two ways. First, they can be summarized in ways that match the abstractions that are implicit in the expert model's goal hierarchies for performance. Second, regression analyses[10] can be done to predict human expert judgments of overall performance from the more microscopic objective tallies.

Nichols et al. (in press) probed for data beyond problem-solving steps. Test subjects were asked to explain each step they were taking, to indicate expected outcomes of tests, and to comment on what was learned from each new piece of information (such as a measurement made on the circuit). This approach was useful in providing information about performances that had high face validity. People who offer principled explanations for their problem-solving actions and who solve the problems efficiently are certainly candidates for good transfer performance. On the other hand, the very requirement of explaining steps that are being taken may produce performances that are more systematic, and even more generally expert, then otherwise would occur. The requirement to explain one's performances is a significant intrusion into task performances. So far, there is no indication that it distorts results, but further study seems advisable.

Overall, it seems well advised to ground the evaluation of a training system in performances of difficult tasks from the target task domain.

Mode of Presentation

In the first field tests of Sherlock I, some people in our client organization objected to using computer-administered problems for assessment, because the training program provided practice in using our computer system as well as job-specific practice. For the most part, this objection is attenuated as the evaluation becomes more heavily grounded in details of expertlike performance. Still, it is surely possible that a testee unfamiliar with the interface might appear to be performing less optimally than would otherwise be the case. For example, it is possible to "miss" in making choices from a pop-up menu, and such a "miss" might result in a tally of a nonoptimal choice during problem solution. Of course, the verbal problem simulation approach we have used so far in field evaluations is also problematic, because it requires trainees not only to be able to solve problems but also to be able to articulate their decision processes. However, the biases due to verbal aptitude requirements when verbal simulations of problem

---

[10]Because we use fuzzy variables rather than scalars in our current implementations, the summarizing is not done by standard regression. Conceptually, however, regression analysis is a good way to think about this aspect of our approach.

solving are used apply to both experimental and control conditions, whereas the biases due to computer-administered simulated problems apply only to the experimental group. Accordingly, we recommend that posttesting not be done via computer unless both experimental and control subjects are well trained in the interface.

It can still be useful to use the computer for administering and scoring the problems, however. The experimenter can sit at the computer and enact each action of the trainee. Further, the system could be modified to accept annotations along with actions, so as to log the trainee's explanations along with the trace of actions. A major advantage of using the computer in this way is that testing need not be done by a domain expert. The system simulation in a training system like Sherlock contains a verified device model. It therefore can provide the result of every action the testee proposes. In earlier field work, testees occasionally called for an action whose results the tester could not determine. Because some of our testing was done on third shift (between 11:00 PM and 7:00 AM), an expert had to be phoned in the middle of the night to determine what result to report back to the testee in response to the action proposed.

Ideally, systems will be developed for multiple jobs in a "job family." Again, once testees are familiar with the basic interface conventions used for a family of training systems, the systems themselves make good testing and data logging systems. Transfer can be assessed by noting the trajectory of performance over training sessions for both original training on one system and transfer training on a second. Given proper counterbalancing of order of training, it is possible to quantify transfer in terms of time (and its monetary value) saved in learning the second system given training on the first. Again, there are objections to using the training system as an assessment vehicle if prior experience with the interface is not controlled, and again the systems may make good examiner stations even when testing is done via verbal interactions.

Assessment Advantages of Object-Based Approaches

Object-based design has power that is making it the standard in the software development world (cf. Booch, 1991). For the very same reasons, object-based design may be key both in training for transfer and in assessment of transfer potential. More generally, intelligent training systems offer a peculiarly good opportunity for achieving synthesis of learning and assessment, which has been widely advocated as a goal for education and training generally.

The expertise in systems like Sherlock II is represented in computational "objects." An object is an independent piece of computer program that stores its own local data and can thus respond to various requests that other parts of the system might make of it. Components of the system being diagnosed are represented by objects. Knowledge about how to deal with a specific component is embedded in the object that represents that component. For example, component objects will have routines relevant for the objects they represent. The object for a given component, such as a particular type of printed circuit card, might "know" how to draw the component it represents on the screen. It also will likely know how to model its component as part of an electronic circuit, how to test that component, and how to coach trainees in their interactions with that component. Because most training systems will do some sort of student modeling, the object for a component also needs to know how to record the student's interactions with that object, how to score those interactions, and how to make the recorded information available to other parts of the system that might be generating more abstracted evaluations of the student.

Further, objects are generally arranged in an inheritance hierarchy[11] to facilitate system development. General objects are defined that have basic capabilities. When more specialized capabilities are needed, new objects are created that inherit general capability from their "parents" but add to that some specific functionality. For example, all component objects may need to tally the time of each action taken by a trainee that involves the component within their "scope." The time tallying routine would, in a good object-oriented programming system, be defined only once, for a general component object, and the routine would be inherited by more specialized objects that also require it.

At a higher level of expert function, a level that abstracts over specific components and even types of components, expertise is represented as a goal structure for problem solving. In our approach, a task analysis will lead directly to specifications for the computational objects to be used in training systems. The goals of training are represented by objects, and those objects, too, must be able to perform, coach, and illustrate their specific bits of expertise. Furthermore, they, too, can be readily modified to keep track of how well trainees approximate expertise in their performances.

A goal hierarchy represents one kind of abstraction of expertise, but there is also another kind. The concept of an inheritance hierarchy of knowledge, which is central to object-oriented programming (though lacking in some partial object-oriented programming languages!), also has potential for the prediction, training, and assessment of transfer, both potential and actual. This is especially the case when specialized objects do their work through a combination of a few specific actions combined with a "call" to a more generic routine. I currently believe that analyses of multiple jobs for transfer should result in products that specify inheritance hierarchies of knowledge components. Further, I believe that transfer

---

[11]An inheritance hierarchy is an arrangement of objects according to their generality. At each level of generality, computational methods for an object are defined. It is necessary to write specific computational methods for a specialized object in such an arrangement only if it cannot "inherit" a more general method. For example, in most systems, the most general class is called *object,* and it has some methods defined for it that are needed for every object, for example, the ability to report its name. These methods are "inherited" by more specialized objects.

can then be predicted by noting the relative amounts of knowledge that are shared, that require only minor specializations of what is already known, or that require major new learning. I am currently trying to refine such an approach to task analysis (a first effort is discussed in Lesgold, 1991).

Given the decision that task analyses will lead directly to specifications for the computational objects to be used in training systems, and given the scheme of having those objects able not only to simulate expertise and train, but also to assess trainee performance, it is a small step to systems that can assess transfer potential as well as job-specific learning as they train. The step entails objects' contributing to decisions about transfer.[12] For example, if there are cases where performance from the viewpoint of a specific object is expertlike, whereas performance from a more general viewpoint is not, this may indicate that the trainee has learned a successful algorithm that does not adequately generalize. Such an indication would count against any claims that the system teaches for transfer. For example, when technicians test a component by verifying its inputs and then verifying its outputs, or vice versa, they are exercising a general capability that should transfer to many components of many systems. If instead they trace those input-to-output paths that are relevant to a particular situation, they will still be able to decide whether the component is good, but their performance does not have the same guarantee of transferability.

Architectural aspects, and use of object-based approaches in particular, are considerations that should enter into assessments of software for integrated training and testing.

Durability of Effects

For the effects of intelligent training systems to be worthwhile, competence must not only develop and transfer, it must also persist. Training that is durable is much more valuable than training that requires regular "maintenance." Although complex, time-sensitive performances inevitably require maintenance, basic competences generally should not, provided they have been adequately taught and learned. Still, the training world is replete with courses taught, exams passed, predictable and overrehearsed performances carried out, with minimal long-term effect. Consequently, we felt it important to do retention testing of the Sherlock I system. In fact, retention was extremely high, in excess of 90%. Further, it was relatively uniform—few trainees showed precipitous drops in performance. We think such demonstrations are important, given the cost of intelligent system research and development.

Just as with transfer, it would be helpful to have predictors of retention.

---

[12]Objects should also know how to coach to maximize transfer, by emphasizing the generality of general procedures and giving situational specifics for more specific bits of knowledge, but that is not the direct focus of this chapter.

However, the development cycle for intelligent training systems is long even without adding extra months to separate initial from retention testing. I propose that instead, once a particular technology for training system development is well established, it would be possible to predict retention from the many micro-measures of competence that are used for assessing competence and transfer potential. In the Sherlock work, for example, if retention rests on conceptual understanding, then those specific performance indicators that depend on understanding the device being diagnosed and the methods of diagnosis should be good predictors of retention. If understanding plus efficiency of certain basic cognitive processes is needed, then indicators of both should be good predictors of retention. We did not conduct the needed analyses to support this approach when we field tested Sherlock I, but we expect to be able to with Sherlock II.

Predicting retention is not the same as measuring actual retention, especially when prediction formulas from one training system's history are used to estimate likely retention for a different system, but it is a start. To the extent possible, predicted retention measures should be supplemented by actual retention measures, at least on an occasional audit basis. However, predicted retention is an important aspect of assessment, especially because of the increased emphasis on rapid prototyping and more efficient development of computer-based training. Just as with conventional training approaches, it is always possible to audit performance with the system already in place and in use. Predicted retention would allow first tryouts of the system to be more informative, so that sound deployment decisions could be made earlier in the development cycle.

Boundary Conditions

Like any treatment, intelligent training systems will work only within certain boundary conditions. However, assessments of training seldom attend to boundary conditions. It is common to provide background data on the sample that was used to assess system capability. However, users are generally left to make their own inferences about how and when results from that sample might generalize. Some improvement over that state of affairs is possible and important. Consider the field testing of Sherlock I, for example. It was tested at operational Air Force bases, not at the training school. As a result, it could be assumed that a variety of basic electronics principles and procedures had been mastered by the test sample. Otherwise, they would not have been allowed job site roles. On the other hand, because they were on the job, they had daily concrete experience with the artifacts being simulated. It is conceivable that Sherlock I might not work well in the tech school environment. On the other hand, the scheme in which coaching is always available, so that true performance impasses are unlikely, seems rather robust and might be sufficient to permit a much wider range of trainees to use the system effectively.

From a research-and-development point of view, it seems appropriate to conduct, for each new design approach to intelligent training system design, specific studies of the boundary conditions under which the system works. This is not too unreasonable. It simply means keeping records and analyzing for data patterns as the first implementations of the approach are carried into broad use. Then, if boundary limitations emerge, they can be considered by future users.

Related to boundary conditions are interactions between components of the instructional treatment and trainees' prior knowledge. Consider, for example, the range of treatment possibilities present in Sherlock II or being considered for future versions. These include practice in solving problems presented according to a fixed progression, a student-model-determined progression, or a student-request-determined progression; opportunities to replay one's own or an expert solution to the problem just solved; opportunities or requirement to critique one's own, or a peer's, performance on a problem; and opportunities for any of the aforementioned activities as a member of a cooperating peer group. It is quite possible that some of these learning opportunities might work better for one type of student and others might work better for another. For example, there may be some threshold of domain knowledge that is required before one can frame effective questions about an expert performance. If so, then students yet to reach that threshold may not find opportunities to replay problem solutions and ask questions about them to be very helpful. A second possibility is that some students may have more successful practice with one or another of the approaches and therefore value it more.

Although much about the effectiveness of training approaches for trainees with differing prior knowledge remains to be elucidated, it seems appropriate for an assessment of a training system to consider what is known, and to take such information into account in interpreting the adequacy of the test samples used for evaluating the system. A further step is possible when a system records a detailed trace of system usage by the student. Then, it is possible, by examining the course of learning for specific members of the test sample, to use extant knowledge to make predictions about interactions of prior knowledge with treatment, and to proceed to partial verification of those predictions.

Maintainability and Extensibility

In addition to its utility in promoting learning, an intelligent training system must also be evaluated as a technological artifact. Too often, the process whereby training software is procured results in systems that cannot be maintained or extended. Initially, it will seem to the system purchaser that if the system works, there is nothing else to worry about. However, virtually all training systems require modifications over their lifetimes. Weaknesses in the training are discovered. Devices that are part of the task domain are modified or replaced. New duties are added to the job. New trainees, with different entering capabilities, become part of the training population. All of these things happen routinely in the training world.

The requirements for maintainable software are well known (cf. Booch, 1991). The software must be modular, with each module carefully documented. Detailed explanations and specifications of how the system works, and why, should be available. Standard computer languages should be used and only standard hardware should be required. We have found that a deeply object-oriented approach helps greatly in maintaining and extending software; indeed, we have had to rewrite virtually all code that did not reflect deep understanding of object-oriented practices.

Good object-oriented designs make use of inheritance, so that each knowledge component of the system is defined only once. This facilitates repairs and changes. In the object-oriented paradigm, actions are taken by passing a message to the object that is to act. When, in contrast, actions are taken directly, whenever a change is required, each instance of such actions must be detected and modified. This is very costly. Good object-based design, therefore, enhances productivity immeasurably. For example, having developed software that could display electronic circuit diagrams, with color coding of component states and explanation of components when their diagram representations are selected, our main software designer, Edward Hughes, was able to build a new system for inputting, displaying, and allowing interactions with troubleshooting flowcharts. He simply made a "flowchart editor object" that inherited most of its capabilities from the same "graphic editor object" that supports the "circuit editor object" he had programmed earlier. At a more mundane level, when I wanted to build a database of hints generated by Sherlock, all I had to do was modify the "hint display object" to dump all text to a file in addition to sending it to the relevant text window pane object.

Just as with any system, the learning time it takes a user to use a software development approach must be considered. Experience to date has been that object-oriented programming skill takes a long time to train—3 to 6 months for a topnotch programmer with good formal computer science background (roughly master's degree level in computer science). However, even at that high cost, the approach pays. From a software evaluation viewpoint, use of good object-oriented techniques, including the representation of core design principles and approaches in separable objects, makes a training system much more valuable, and makes changes in the system much more efficient. Moreover, user acceptability is very high. Our experience with several different object-based languages suggests that it would be difficult to wean software developers away from an object-based approach once they have practiced it.

CONCLUSIONS

The approach I have taken in this chapter is to view training system assessment from a long-term perspective. Therefore, I have assumed that transfer and retention, not just immediate rote performance of algorithms, is the key to a system's value. Similarly, I have assumed that modifiability and principled design are also to be valued highly. Surely, there are training systems for which these requirements may be excessive. However, for significant training of personnel for enduring organizations that perform work involving high levels of knowledge and cognitive skill, this "high road" will surely pay. Regrettably, it has not been followed sufficiently often. Training software is sometimes seen as extremely expensive. This is because it often is rigid and narrow, both in its realization as software and in its effects in promoting learning. It is unlikely that this "low road" approach will ever be more efficient at what it does than the human-centered alternative of quickly cobbling together stand-up lectures and mastery quizzes. I believe that a much more effective long-term strategy would be for workers to acquire some of the knowledge they need to work intelligently and adaptively through apprenticeship experiences simulated by intelligent and adaptive software.

ACKNOWLEDGMENTS

The research reported in this chapter was supported in part by a contract from the Defense Advanced Research Projects Agency (DARPA), administered by the Office of Naval Research (ONR), to the UCLA Center for the Study of Evaluation/Center for Technology Assessment. However, the opinions expressed do not necessarily reflect the positions of DARPA or ONR, and no official endorsement by either organization should be inferred.

The Sherlock project, from which my ideas come, is the joint work of Marilyn Bunzo, Gary Eggan, Robert Glaser, Maria Gordin, Linda Greenberg, Edward Hughes, Sandra Katz, Susanne Lajoie, Alan Lesgold, Tom McGinnis, Rudianto Prabowo, Rose Rosenfeld, Arlene Weiner, and a number of other colleagues, past and present, at the Learning Research and Development Center, along with Sherrie Gott, Robert Pokorny, Ellen Hall, Dennis Collins and others at the Air Force Human Resources Laboratory. AFHRL supported the work but does not necessarily endorse the statements made in this chapter.

REFERENCES

Anderson, J. R. (1990). Analysis of student performance with the Lisp Tutor. In N. Frederiksen, R. Glaser, A. M. Lesgold, & M. Shafto (Eds.), *Diagnostic monitoring of skill and knowledge acquisition* (pp. 27–50). Hillsdale, NJ: Lawrence Erlbaum Associates.

Booch, G. (1991). *Object oriented design: With applications.* Redwood City, CA: Benjamin/Cummings.

Corbett, A. T., & Anderson, J. R. (1992). LISP intelligent tutoring system: Research in skill acquisition. In J. Larkin & R. Chabay (Eds.), *Computer assisted instruction and intelligent tutoring systems: Shared issues and complementary approaches* (pp. 73–109). Hillsdale, NJ: Lawrence Erlbaum Associates.

Glaser, R., Lesgold, A. M., & Gott, S. (1991). Implications of cognitive psychology for measuring job performance. In A. K. Wigdor & B. F. Green, Jr. (Eds.), *Performance assessment for the workplace: Technical issues* (pp. 1–26). Washington, DC: National Academy Press.

Glaser, R., Lesgold, A., & Lajoie, S. (1987). Toward a cognitive theory for the measurement of achievement. In R. R. Ronning, J. Glover, J. C. Conoley, & J. C. Witt (Eds.), *The influence of cognitive psychology on testing and measurement* (pp. 41–85). Hillsdale, NJ: Lawrence Erlbaum Associates.

Gott, S. P. (1989). Apprenticeship instruction for real world cognitive tasks. In E. Z. Rothkopf (Ed.), *Review of research in education.* (Vol. 15, pp. 97–169). Washington, DC: American Education Research Association.

Govindaraj, T. (1988). Intelligent computer aids for fault diagnosis training of expert operators of large systems. In J. Psotka, L. D. Massey, & S. A. Mutter (Eds.), *Intelligent tutoring systems: Lessons learned* (pp. 303–322). Hillsdale, NJ: Lawrence Erlbaum Associates.

Katz, S., & Lesgold, A. (1991). Modeling the student in Sherlock II. In J. Kay & A. Quilici (Eds.), *Proceedings of the IJCAI-91 Workshop W.4: Agent modelling for intelligent interaction* (pp. 93–127). Sydney, Australia.

Katz, S., Lesgold, A., Eggan, G., & Gordin, M. (1992). Approaches to student modeling in the Sherlock tutors. In E. Andre, R. Cohen, W. Graf, B. Kass, C. Paris, & W. Wahlster (Eds.), *Proceedings of the Third International Workshop on User Modeling* (pp. 205–230). Dagstuhl Castle, Germany.

Lajoie, S., & Lesgold, A. (1990). Apprenticeship training in the workplace: Computer coached practice environment as a new form of apprenticeship. *Machine-Mediated Learning, 3,* 7–28.

Larkin, J., & Chabay, R. (Eds). (1992). *Computer assisted instruction and intelligent tutoring systems: Shared issues and complementary approaches.* Hillsdale, NJ: Lawrence Erlbaum Associates.

Lesgold, A. (1991, June). *An object-based situational approach to task analysis.* Paper presented at a NATO Advanced Study Workshop on Learning Electricity and Electronics with Advanced Technology, Marne-la-Vallee, France.

Lesgold, A. M., Lajoie, S. P., Bunzo, M., & Eggan, G. (1992). SHERLOCK: A coached practice environment for an electronics troubleshooting job. In J. Larkin & R. Chabay (Eds.), *Computer assisted instruction and intelligent tutoring systems: Shared issues and complementary approaches* (pp. 201–238). Hillsdale, NJ: Lawrence Erlbaum Associates.

Lesgold, A., Lajoie, S., Logan, D., & Eggan, G. (1990). Applying cognitive task analysis and research methods to assessment. In N. Frederiksen, R. Glaser, A. M. Lesgold, & M. Shafto (Eds.), *Diagnostic monitoring of skill and knowledge acquisition* (pp. 325–350). Hillsdale, NJ: Lawrence Erlbaum Associates.

Mitchell, T. M., Keller, R. M., & Kedar-Cabelli, S. T. (1986). Explanation-based generalization: A unifying view. *Machine Learning, 1,* 47–80.

Nichols, P., Pokorny, R., Jones, G., Gott, S. P., & Alley, W. E. (in press). *Evaluation of an avionics troubleshooting tutoring system* (Special Report). Brooks AFB, TX: Air Force Human Resources Laboratory.

Owen, E., & Sweller, J. (1985). What do students learn while solving mathematics problems? *Journal of Educational Psychology, 77,* 272–284.

Pokorny, R., & Gott, S. (1989). *The evaluation of a real-world instructional system: Using technical experts as raters.* Unpublished manuscript.

Polson, M. C., & Richardson, J. J. (1988). *Foundations of intelligent tutoring systems.* Hillsdale, NJ: Lawrence Erlbaum Associates.

Psotka, J., Massey, L. D., & Mutter, S. A. (1988). *Intelligent tutoring systems: Lessons learned.* Hillsdale, NJ: Lawrence Erlbaum Associates.

Sweller, J. (1988). Cognitive load during problem solving: Effects on learning. *Cognitive Science, 12,* 257–285.

Sweller, J., & Cooper, G. (1985). The use of worked examples as a substitute for problem solving in learning algebra. *Cognition and Instruction, 2,* 59–89.

6 Improving Intelligent Computer-Aided Instruction Via Explicit Instructional Strategies

Kazi G. Nizamuddin
Mt. San Jacinto Community College

Harold F. O'Neil, Jr.
University of Southern California/CRESST

This chapter discusses the design, development, and evaluation of a set of domain-independent instructional strategies for teaching problem-solving outcomes in elementary algebra through Intelligent Computer-Aided Instruction (ICAI).

The elementary algebra course is one of the most important for all entry-level freshman students of any major at most universities and 2-year colleges in the United States. Many students have a difficult time understanding the facts, concepts, and principles of algebra. As a result, the procedural portion in subsequent problem solving becomes a difficult task. Many students eventually fail the course.

Our long-term goal was to develop a computer-based tutor that will be as effective in algebra instruction as a human tutor. The purpose of this chapter is an attempt to combine artificial intelligence technology with instructional theories of problem solving to achieve an effective teaching environment in algebra. The design implemented various instructional strategies from various design theories, and developed a set of transformations in the context of linear algebra to improve an existing ICAI system.

INTELLIGENT COMPUTER-ASSISTED INSTRUCTION

In recent years there has been increased emphasis on individualized instruction and computer technology specially applying intelligent learning systems that facilitate learning at all levels of education and training (O'Neil, 1981).

The intelligent learning systems are known as intelligent tutoring systems

(ITS) or intelligent computer-assisted instruction (ICAI). The integral components of any ICAI system may consist of (a) the knowledge base: what the learner is to learn, that is, the expert model representing the relevant knowledge in the domain that solves problems like an expert (based on the domain); (b) a student model, which may be constructed by comparing the student's performance to the computer-based expert's behavior on the task; and (c) a tutor, that is, a model that should be composed of the desirable properties of a human tutor. The research analytic evidence for ICAI has been reviewed by Littman and Soloway (1988) and Wenger (1987).

An example of such an ICAI program is MicroSEARCH. MicroSEARCH, based on the work of Sleeman (1987), solves deductive-type problems using a heuristic search strategy. The program allows selection of transformations and examination of the solution tree as the transformations are applied (Park Row Software, 1987).

Any problem solving requires a certain amount of search. An integral part of AI today is the theory of heuristic search: search that departs from blind trial and error, which makes use of information drawn from the problem domain to guide itself selectively until it finds solutions or goals (Simon, 1984).

Algorithms in which arbitrary choice is required are known as nondeterministic algorithms. In general, beginning mathematics students react poorly to any use of nondeterministic algorithms. They expect all tasks to be solvable by well-defined algorithms. In addition, the teaching system seldom discusses search as a necessary strategy for solving a whole range of tasks (Anderson, 1981). Many tasks in high school and entry-level college mathematics involve nondeterministic searches such as in algebra. Nondeterministic algorithms are currently taught poorly. Students are not taught that search is a legitimate strategy. Sleeman (1987) suggested that students should be explicitly asked (a) to state all the transformations they consider to be appropriate to the task, and (b) to systematically explore the complete solution space. The major disadvantage of this approach is the potential size of the search space.

TSEARCH (Sleeman, 1987) was built to solve tasks that involved nondeterministic searches. It provided a variety of support facilities for its users. TSEARCH had been implemented using Rutgers LISP on the DEC-10. TSEARCH is a shell for building a class of intelligent tutoring systems. It does not allow the student to type in the transformed expression but merely the *number* of the transformation to be applied. TSEARCH works only in a domain in which the set of operators are specified (Sleeman, 1987). The system presents a problem for the student to solve. The problem is generated by the system or retrieved from a list of problems. The selection procedure of the problem is based on issues specified and the state of the student model. An issue, as stated by Kearsley (1988), is meant to be a method of transforming equations, whether a single transformation or the interaction of several transformations, and represents the skills to be acquired by the student. The transformation is applied to the current expression and results in a new current expression. This generates a tree from the current expressions. The student can backtrack through the tree and pick up other branches. The system automatically redisplays the updated tree after each transformation and analyzes the student's transformation choice. If the choice matches the system's preferred (system domain) choice, then it provides positive feedback. If the student's choice does not match the system's preferred choice, further analysis is required (Kearsley, 1988).

Critique of TSEARCH

Sleeman (1987) stated that TSEARCH has four shortcomings: (a) the major disadvantage of TSEARCH is its speed, (b) TSEARCH allows students to be very passive in learning because students can use the HELP facility for a prompt at each stage, (c) the task selection algorithm should make use of the information in the transformation matrix to select (appropriate) tasks for the user, and (d) the transformation matrix provides valuable information for the type of issue-based coach implemented in the WEST system (Burton & Brown, 1982). Such a coach could occasionally point out better solution paths than those chosen by the user.

The Design of MicroSEARCH

MicroSEARCH is a version of TSEARCH implemented on an IBM PC using Pascal. The following design changes were made between the TSEARCH and MicroSEARCH versions. (a) Instead of using all the rules for each type of task, only those known to be relevant are used. (b) The system now has two phases: an offline phase that creates the "complete" solution space ("complete" up to some predefined cutoff point), and an online phase that accesses the solution and interacts with the student.

Issues and Concerns Related to MicroSEARCH. Of the issues raised by Sleeman in the last section, the only one addressed to date by MicroSEARCH has been that of speed. As of today application of MicroSEARCH is limited to a very specific domain, as in algebra, where only the *simplification section* was programmed and marketed by Park Row. MicroSEARCH encourages students to do a depth-first search of the task space like TSEARCH (Sleeman, 1987).

In ICAI the most common instructional strategies have been discovery learning and gaming. Obviously, one discovers error as well as truth. Other approaches such as derived from Component Display Theory (Merrill, 1987) have not been implemented. More recently, there have been several systematic attempts to provide instructional information into the design of ICAI systems. Such attempts include the design of a new ICAI tutor (O'Neil, Slawson, & Baker, 1991) and the design of instructional strategies to improve existing ICAI programs (O'Neil & Baker 1991). However, neither of these efforts systematically evaluated the resulting "improved" ICAI programs.

We have chosen for the macrostrategy O'Neil et al.'s (1991) domain-independent instructional strategy to teach problem solving. *Domain* could legitimately refer to subject matter, application area, task, or performance outcome (O'Neil & Slawson, 1988). (In this chapter, *domain* refers to the subject matter of elementary algebra).

Independence can mean "other than" or "as well as" the target domain. *Domain-independent* instructional strategies could mean independent of the subject matter (i.e., strategies independent of math), or independent of the performance outcome (i.e., strategies appropriate both to concept learning and to problem solving), or both. The problem of domain independence, in other words, is a problem of degree of transfer or generalizability (O'Neil, 1987). In this chapter, *independence* means independent of subject matter. Thus, domain-independent strategies are, in effect, strategies to teach particular performance outcomes, that is, problem solving in the particular domain of algebra.

Gagné (1977) developed a set of instructional strategies for problem solving shown in Table 6.1.

O'Neil et al. (1991) extended this strategy (with Gagné's consulting assistance) to teach in general a strategy of diagnostic problem solving. They further applied this strategy in the area of electronics, particularly troubleshooting (see Tables 6.2 and 6.3).

An alternative view of teaching electronics troubleshooting is provided by Lesgold and Lajoie (1991); Kieras (1988); Frederiksen, White, Collins, and Eggan (1988); Towne and Munro (1988); and Winne (1989).

We modified and implemented in MicroSEARCH the domain-independent instructional strategies by revising the strategy in Tables 6.2 and 6.3, and extending their ideas into the teaching of algebra problem solving. Tables 6.4 and 6.5 provide the modifications into algebra.

In summary, the approach in this study was to synthesize and expand instructional strategies described from the following theoretical position: the domain-independent instructional strategies for problem solving provided by O'Neil et al. (1991) and component display theory by Merrill (1983, 1987).

Component display theory evolved from Merrill and Tennyson's earlier work on designing concept lessons (Merrill & Tennyson, 1977) and from their analysis and research to clarify the categories specified by Gagné. Using component display theory, a given presentation can be segmented into a series of discrete

TABLE 6.1
Domain-Independent Instructional Strategies (Learning Conditions) to Teach Problem-Solving Outcomes

1. Retrieval of relevant rules and concepts
2. Successive presentation of novel problem situations
3. Demonstration of solutions by student

TABLE 6.2
Domain-Independent Instructional Strategy to Teach Diagnostic Problem Solving

1. Define diagnostic problem-solving family to be taught by describing problem-solving characteristics or events pertaining to the family (e.g., "Electrical troubleshooting consists of checking current flow at input and output points.").

2. Communicate a description of the appropriate example device(s) as whole system(s), and the necessary concepts and principles of operation in the order prescribed in Table 6.3.

3. Confirm or teach subordinate skills (e.g., demonstrating how each check is made, how each exchange is done in the example device).

4. Describe and demonstrate appropriate diagnostic problem-solving task strategies to be taught for this application (e.g., select component to test based on malfunction probability).

5. Provide practice using a variety of novel problems requiring the strategies taught, and provide feedback and correction.

displays. Component display theory assumes that most cognitive instruction occurs through two modes, *telling* or *questioning,* and that these modes can be used with two instructional elements, generalities, or examples. In component display theory, learning outcomes are classified in two dimensions: the type of content involved (fact, concept, principle, procedure) and the task level (remember, use, find) required for that content. Nizamuddin (1988) provided extensive detail on the instructional design and its implementation in MicroSearch Plus.

TABLE 6.3
Domain-Independent Instructional Strategy to Teach Diagnostic Problem Solving (Part 2)

Communicate a Description of the Appropriate Example Device(s) as Whole System(s), and the Necessary Concepts and Principles of Operation in the Order Prescribed Here:

1. Present name and brief overall description of the device including operational controls of inputs and ways in which failures are indicated on the device with examples.

2. Present concepts of causal media in system (e.g., current flow if electrical system, forces if mechanical, etc.).

3. Present concepts of schematic representation and methods of illustrating physical/schematic mapping to be used with examples.

4. Present concept of replaceable units. Present names, locations, and functions of replaceable units using diagrams as needed for examples. Require the student to identify the parts by pointing to them.

5. Teach operation and function (how the system works in terms of inputs, controls, component functions, causal flows, and outputs) of major activating and intermediary components, with reference to schematics and physical layout diagrams, taught by tracing causal paths through components on schematics and referencing physical locations.

TABLE 6.4
Domain-Independent Instructional Strategy to Teach Algebra Problem Solving as Implemented in MicroSEARCH Plus

---

1. Define diagnostic problem-solving family to be taught by describing problem-solving characteristics or events pertaining to the family (e.g., "To solve 1st order linear equation," $ax + b = c$).

2. Communicate a description of the appropriate example as a whole problem, and necessary concepts and principles of operation in algebra as shown in Table 6.5.

3. Provide practice, using a variety of novel problems requiring strategies taught, and provide feedback and correction.

The instructional strategies were programmed in Pascal and integrated into the existing MicroSEARCH program. The ICAI algebra program MicroSEARCH was developed by Sleeman (1987) and was marketed by Park Row Software (1987). This program reflected the state of the art in cognitive science operating in a personal computer environment. Its predominant instructional strategy was that of a guided discovery approach. The instructional effectiveness of adding our strategies to an existent ICAI shell program was empirically tested.

AN EXPERIMENTAL STUDY

The altered ICAI program was compared with the existing package, with three different formats. Students were randomly assigned to each format, that is, the MicroSEARCH test group with only 2 examples and 17 test items, the Micro-

TABLE 6.5
Domain-Independent Instructional Strategy to Teach Algebra Problem-Solving as Implemented in MicroSEARCH Plus

---

Communicate a Description of the Appropriate Example as a Whole Problem, and Necessary Concepts and Principles of Operation in Algebra as Shown Here:

---

1. Present name and brief overall description of the problem including order of operations (e.g., "We are going to solve a lst order linear equation. For this problem-solving technique you need to separate the variables and constants of the given problem. That is, keep the variables on one side and constants on the other side, by the methods of combining the like terms, etc.").

2. Present concepts and principles of causal information (e.g., equation, solve, addition property of zero, etc.).

3. Present concepts and principles of symbolic representation with examples (e.g., $ax + b = c$, $x = c$, $5x = 10$, $x = 2$, $a + 0 = a$, etc.).

4. Teach procedure (how to solve the problem, e.g., side change, reciprocal, etc.) of major activating and intermediary steps.

SEARCH group with 48 problems, and the enhanced instructional design group (MicroSEARCH plus). It was expected that the experimental group (MicroSEARCH Plus) would perform better than the other groups.

Selection of the Sample

The sample was taken from a junior college in Southern California. The students were volunteered from beginning and intermediate algebra classes. We started with 140 subjects. For different reasons such as the student leaving early, computer problems, incomplete data, and so on, 37 students were dropped from the final analysis. A total of 103 valid subjects were entered into a computer that used a program from the Statistical Package for Social Sciences (Nie et al., 1975) to analyze the data.

This sample (n = 103), with an average age of 25.5 years (SD = 7.79), included 31 males and 72 females. Ethnic distribution as 78 Whites, 7 African Americans, 8 Latinos, 4 Native Americans, 4 Asians, and 2 other students. To check the homogene ty of the age difference in all three groups a one-way analysis of variance (ANOVA) was performed. The ANOVA was not statistically significant. Thus the three groups were statistically equivalent on age.

MICROSEARCH

The original MicroSEARCH was developed by Sleeman (1987) for one section of elementary algebra, called the *simplification section.* The current state of our MicroSEARCH Plus is for *solving linear equations,* which is another domain of elementary algebra.

Linear equations MicroSEARCH Plus has been created in different structures for different groups. The following are the brief descriptions for each group:

1. Two practice problems and 17 test items: The first 2 problems were given for practice. They were similar to the 17 test problems, with no feedback or help. But each subject was assigned a proctor to provide clear understanding of the procedures in MicroSEARCH and the problem itself.

After finishing the examples, then 17 test items were provided. During the test time, no proctorial help was given. Only two function keys were provided: F3 (NEXT)—leave the current problem and begin the next one; F9 (UNDO)—undo the previous transformation and return the problem to its most recent state.

2. Forty-eight practice problems: This set also was divided into two parts. The first part had 13 problems with advice messages. The second part consisted of 35 problems with no advice messages. Five function keys were available: F1—help; F3 (NEXT)—leave the current problem and begin the next one; F4 (BACK)—Leave the current problem and return to the previous one; F8 (TREE)—show solution tree (see Fig. 6.1); F9 (UNDO)—undo the previous

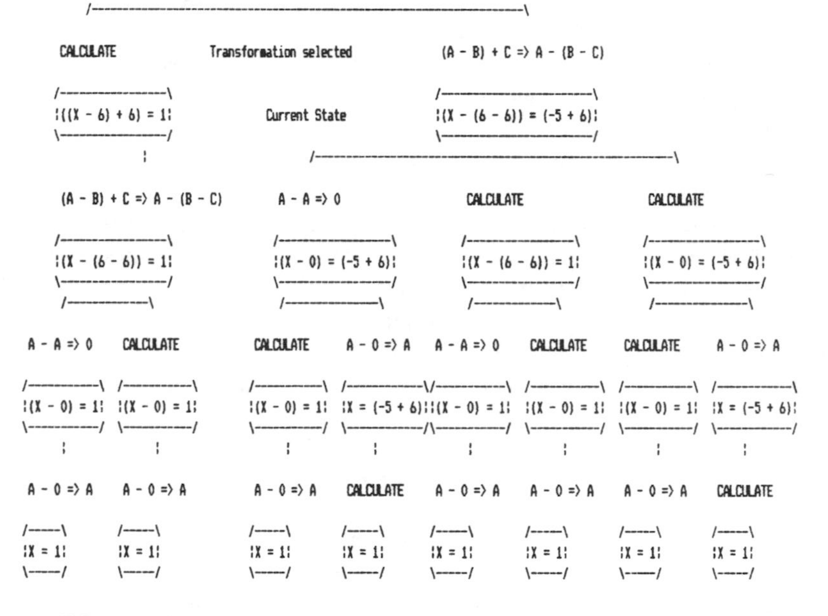

FIG. 6.1. Sample tree output from one MicroSEARCH practice problem. The initial state and current states are placed in the box. The selected transformations are shown without the box.

transformation and return the problem to its most recent state, one step backward at a time.

3. Instruction and practice problems: First instruction was provided, then practice problems for each category were provided. The instructional sequence of teaching old and new knowledge of concepts, principles, and procedures to solve an equation using the (a) addition, or the (b) multiplication property, or (c) both addition and multiplication properties is derived from the general model of teaching problem-solving skills (Aufmann & Barker, 1985). The following modules constitute the instruction:

Module 1. Teach prerequisite *concepts:*
1. Equation.
2. Solve an equation.

Module 2. Teach *prerequisite principle, the addition property of equation:*
1. Teach prerequisite concept, additive inverse.
2. Teach principle, the addition property of equations.

Module 3. Teach *procedure to solve an equation using the addition property of equations:*
1. Teach procedure to solve an equation using the addition property of equations.

Module 4. Teach *prerequisite principle, the multiplication property of equations:*
1. Teach prerequisite concept, reciprocal inverse.
2. Teach principle, the multiplication property of equations.

Module 5. Teach *procedure, to solve an equation using the multiplication property of equations:*
1. Teach prerequisite procedure, remove a coefficient.
2. Teach procedure, to solve an equation using the multiplication property of equations.

Module 6. Teach *procedure, to solve an equation using both the addition and the multiplication properties of equations.*

Module 7. *Integrated practice.*

Here no advice messages were given. The following learner control keys were given: F1—help; F3 (NEXT)—leave the current problem and begin the next one; F4 (BACK)—Leave the current problem and return to the previous one; F8 (TREE)—Show solution tree; F9 (UNDO)—undo the previous transformation and return the problem to its most recent state, one step backward at a time.

The overall control of the instruction is shown in Fig. 6.2.

Every participant in this research project was given an anxiety test before and after the instruction. The results of the anxiety test were not used in this chapter.

The following dependent variables were used: number of problems correctly answered on the test, total steps taken for the test, total time spent to take the test.

Seventeen equations were given to be solved. Any student starting from the initial state of a problem and reaching the goal state was considered to have the right answer. The right answer scored 1 point and the wrong scored 0 points. No partial credit scores were given. The program kept track of the total time and counted the number of steps for each individual on each problem.

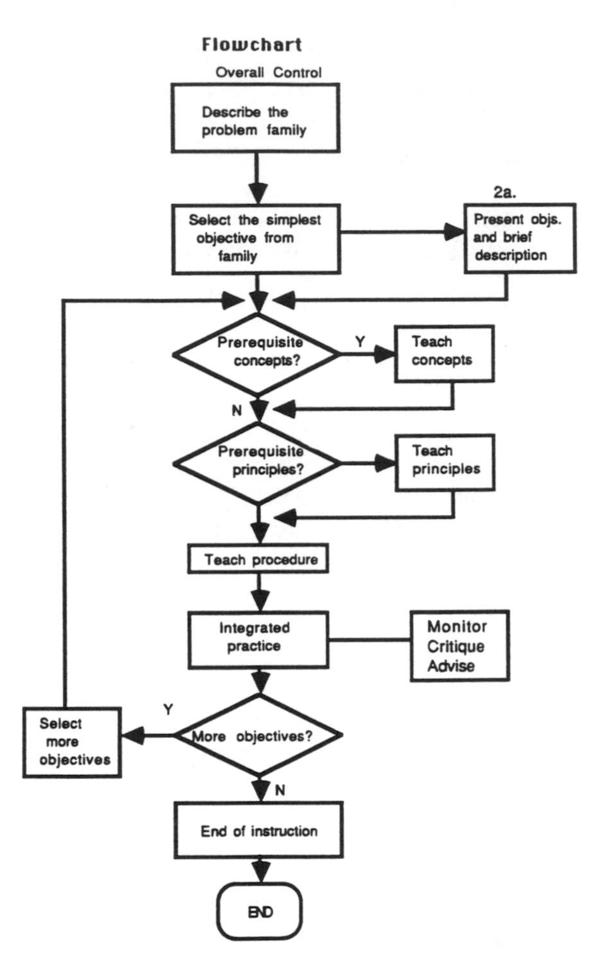

FIG. 6.2. Flowchart for domain independent instructional strategy to teach algebra problem-solving as implemented in MicroSEARCH Plus.

RESULTS

Computation Score

Out of 103 students, only 65 students' computation placement scores were found in the student record file; number of students in each group as follows: MicroSEARCH test group N=22, MicroSEARCH with multiple problems group N=22, and MicroSEARCH Plus with instructional enhancements group N=21. The means for Groups 1, 2, and 3 were 20.50, 20.55, and 20.24, and the

TABLE 6.6
Performance Measures

Results of Cognitive Test Data (Number of correct test items)	
MicroSEARCH test group	(X= 8.5; SD= 4.8; n= 32)
MicroSEARCH with multiple problems	(X = 10.2; SD = 4.7; n = 36)
MicroSEARCH Plus with instructional enhancements	(X= 12.3; SD= 3.6; n= 35)

standard deviations were 7.50, 5.37, and 5.47, respectively. The differences were not statistically different. Thus, the groups were matched on computational skills before the treatments were initiated.

Number of Correct Problems

As may be seen in Table 6.6 on the 17 test questions, the means for MicroSEARCH test group, MicroSEARCH with multiple problems group, and MicroSEARCH Plus with instructional enhancements group were 8.5, 10.2, and 12.3 respectively.

It was expected that the instructional design enhanced MicroSEARCH Plus group would exhibit significantly more correct answers than either the MicroSEARCH group with multiple problems and advice messages or the MicroSEARCH test group.

Groups were significantly different; $F\ (2,\ 102) = 6.26$, $p < 0.05$. The significant omnibus F-test was followed by the Newman-Keuls post hoc tests. A post hoc Newman–Keuls procedure concluded that the MicroSEARCH test only group and the instructional design enhanced MicroSEARCH Plus group, and the MicroSEARCH group with multiple problems and the instructional design enhanced MicroSEARCH Plus group all were significantly different at the .05 level. MicroSEARCH test only group and MicroSEARCH with multiple practice problems group were not significantly different. That means only advice messages with many problems did not significantly improve the problem-solving skills. On the other hand, instructional design enhanced MicroSEARCH Plus significantly improved problem-solving skills more than the other two groups.

Steps

To complete the 17 test questions the means for MicroSEARCH test group, MicroSEARCH with multiple problems group, and MicroSEARCH Plus group were 203.03, 195.06, and 199.43, and the standard deviations were 131.80, 122.05, and 98.64, respectively.

Time

The mean total times (in min) taken by the students in MicroSEARCH test group, MicroSEARCH with multiple problems group, and MicroSEARCH Plus group to complete the test were 46.10, 25.43, and 28.61, respectively. The standard deviations were 23.96, 11.53, and 19.90, respectively.

It was expected that the instructional design enhanced MicroSEARCH group would take less time than either the MicroSEARCH group with multiple problems and advice messages or a MicroSEARCH test group. Groups were significantly different; $F(2, 102) = 11.45, p < .05$. The significant F-test was followed by the Newman–Keuls post hoc tests. Results indicated that MicroSEARCH test only group was different from both MicroSEARCH with multiple problems group and MicroSEARCH Plus with instructional enhancements group. But MicroSEARCH with multiple problems group and MicroSEARCH Plus with instructional enhancements group did not differ significantly, which means both MicroSEARCH with multiple problems and MicroSEARCH Plus with instructional enhancements group took the same amount of time for the test.

It was expected that the instructional design enhanced MicroSEARCH group would generate significantly fewer steps than the MicroSEARCH group with multiple problems and advice messages or a MicroSEARCH test group. However the groups were not significantly different.

The following are important observations from the correlational studies. The total time to complete the test is directly related to the total steps required to finish the test ($r = .61, p = .01$). In other words, the total time depends on the number of steps required to finish the test, which is obvious—The more steps, the more time. Similar relationships also were found in total steps in examples and total time in examples ($r = .48, p = .01$).

A direct relationship also was discovered in students who took more steps and who consequently got more problems correct ($r = .43, p = .01$). Thus, it may be concluded that in a MicroSEARCH-style test, the more steps taken, the better chance there is to get the right answer; one reason may be the goal-oriented state of the system (i.e., variable = constant).

The outcomes of this experiment supported the major research assertion, that students in the enhanced MicroSEARCH Plus group would produce significantly more correct answers than either the MicroSEARCH with multiple problem and advice message or MicroSEARCH test only groups. It was expected that explicit training in problem solving would result in more efficient as well as effective learning.

The findings of this study suggest there is more room for improvements: (a) The data from the study could be used formatively to improve the existing enhanced MicroSEARCH Plus program, and (b) a full set of design ideas including other concepts, principles, and procedures that were not implemented, and more emphasis on common errors, could be added. In addition, other facets of component display theory (for example, more extensive use of secondary presentation forms) can be extended.

SUMMARY

This chapter reports the design, development, and evaluation of a set of domain-independent instructional strategies to teach problem-solving outcomes in algebra through Intelligent Computer-Aided Instruction (ICAI). The ICAI Algebra program, MicroSEARCH, was developed by Sleeman (1987).

At this time this program reflected the state of the art of cognitive science in a personal computer environment. Its predominant instructional strategy was that of a guided discovery approach. Sleeman's approach was augmented by us with two major theoretical positions: the domain-independent instructional strategy for problem solving (O'Neil et al., 1991) and component display theory by Merrill (1983, 1987). These instructional strategies were programmed in Pascal and integrated into the existing ICAI MicroSEARCH package.

The results indicated that the instructional design enhanced MicroSEARCH Plus with instructional enhancements group exhibited significantly more correct answers on the test than either the MicroSEARCH group with multiple problems or the MicroSEARCH test only group. The results in general supported the rationale that augmenting an ICAI program with explicit instructional design strategies will lead to improved performance. Shute's (in press) finding on a study of a microadaptive approach to tutoring, in general, supports the previous rationale.

There are some artificial intelligence-based software packages now on the market. We believe that most of these need some kind of instructional design to be more efficient. To make these packages more useful to the users, we need to combine more ingredients, such as instructional strategies, both at the macro-and microlevels. The state of the art in computer-aided instruction may in this manner be enhanced. The rationale that augmenting an ICAI program with explicit instructional design strategies will lead to improved performance is supported in this study.

ACKNOWLEDGMENTS

The research reported in this chapter was supported in part by a contract from the Defense Advanced Research Projects Agency (DARPA), administered by the Office of Naval Research (ONR), to the UCLA Center for the Study of Evaluation/Center for Technology Assessment. However, the opinions expressed do not necessarily reflect the positions of DARPA or ONR, and no official endorsement by either organization should be inferred. This research also was supported in part under the Educational Research and Development Center Program cooperative agreement R117G10027 and CFDA catalog number 84.117G as administered by the Office of Educational Research and Improvement, U.S. Department of Education. The findings and opinions expressed in this report do not reflect the position or policies of the Office of Educational Research and Improvement or the U.S. Department of Education.

REFERENCES

Anderson, R. J. (1981). Tuning of search of the problem space for geometry proofs. *Proceedings of IJCAI, 81,* 165–170.

Aufmann, R. N., & Barker, V. C. (1985). *Introductory algebra: An applied approach.* Boston: Houghton Mifflin.

Burton, R. R., & Brown, J. S. (1982). An investigation of computer coaching for informal learning activities. In D. Sleeman & J. S. Brown (Eds.), *Intelligent tutoring systems* (pp. 79–98). London: Academic Press.

Frederiksen, J. R., White, B. R., Collins, A., & Eggan, G. (1988). Intelligent tutoring systems for electronic troubleshooting. In J. Psotka, L. Massey, & S. Mutter (Eds.), *Intelligent tutoring systems: Lessons learned* (pp. 351–368). Hillsdale, NJ: Lawrence Erlbaum Associates.

Gagné, R. M. (1977). *The conditions of learning* (3rd ed.). New York: Holt, Rinehart & Winston.

Kearsley, G. (1988). Authoring systems for intelligent tutoring systems on personal computers. In D. Jonassen, (Ed.), *Instructional designs for microcomputer courseware* (pp. 381–396). Hillsdale, NJ: Lawrence Erlbaum Associates.

Kieras, E. D. (1988). What mental model should be taught: Choosing instructional content for complex engineered systems. In J. Psotka, L. Massey, & S. Mutter (Eds.), *Intelligent tutoring systems: Lessons learned* (pp. 85–112). Hillsdale, NJ: Lawrence Erlbaum Associates.

Lesgold, A., & Lajoie, S. (1991). Complex problem solving in electronics. In R. Sternberg & P. Frensch (Eds.), *Complex problem solving: Principles and mechanisms* (pp. 287–316). Hillsdale, NJ: Lawrence Erlbaum Associates.

Littman, D., & Soloway, E. (1988). Evaluating ITs: The cognitive science perspective. In M. Polson & J. Richardson (Eds.), *Foundations of intelligent tutoring systems* (pp. 209–241. Hillsdale, NJ: Lawrence Erlbaum Associates.

Merrill, M. D. (1983). Component display theory. In C. M. Reigeluth (Ed), *Instructional-design theories and models: An overview of their current status* (pp. 279–333). Hillsdale, NJ: Lawrence Erlbaum Associates.

Merrill, M. D. (1987). A lesson based on the component display theory. In C. M. Reigeluth (Ed)., *Instructional theories in action.* Hillsdale, NJ: Lawrence Erlbaum Associates.

Merrill, D., & Tennyson, R. (1977). *Teaching concepts: An instructional design guide.* Englewood Cliffs, NJ: Educational Technology Publications.

Nie, N. et al. (1975). *SPSS* (Instruction Manual). New York: McGraw-Hill.

Nizamuddin, K. G. (1988). *Role of instructional strategies in improving MicroSEARCH for intelligent computer aided instruction in algebra.* Unpublished doctoral dissertation, University of Southern California, Los Angeles, CA.

O'Neil, H. F. (1981). *Computer-based instruction: A state-of-the-art assessment.* New York: Academic Press.

O'Neil, H. F. (1987). *Description of activities and general findings of the domain independent instructional strategies: Review of the literature.* Unpublished monograph.

O'Neil, H. F., & Baker, E. L. (1991). Issues in intelligent computer-assisted instruction: Evaluation and measurement. In T. Gutkin & S. Wise (Eds.), *The computer and the decision making process* (pp. 199–224). Hillsdale, NJ: Lawrence Erlbaum Associates.

O'Neil, H. F., & Slawson, A. (1988, April). *Design of a domain-independent instructional strategies knowledge base.* Paper presented at the 1988 annual conference of the American Educational Research Association, New Orleans, LA.

O'Neil, H. F., Slawson, A., & Baker, E. L. (1991). Design of domain-independent problem solving instructional strategies for intelligent computer-assisted instruction. In H. Burns, J. Parlett, & C. Luckhardt (Eds.), *Intelligent tutoring systems: Evolutions in design* (pp. 69–103). Hillsdale, NJ: Lawrence Erlbaum Associates.

Park Row Software (1987). *MicroSEARCH: An artificial intelligence demonstration disk.* La Jolla, CA: Park Row Press.

Shute, V. J. (1993). A macroadaptive approach to tutoring. *Journal of Artificial Intelligence in Education, 4,* 245–271.

Simon, H. A. (1984). AI—the reality and the promise. In *AI—Opportunities and limitations in the 80's: Proceedings.* Coral Gables, FL.

Sleeman, D. (1987). Micro-SEARCH: A "shell" for building systems to help students solve nondeterministic tasks. In G. Kearsley (Ed.), *Artificial intelligence and instruction: Applications and methods* (pp. 69–82). Reading, MA: Addison-Wesley.

Towne, D. M., & Munro, A. (1988). The intelligent maintenance training system. In J. Psotka, L. Massey, & S. Mutter (Eds.), *Intelligent tutoring systems: Lessons learned.* Hillsdale, NJ: Lawrence Erlbaum Associates.

Wenger, E. (1987). *Artificial intelligence and tutoring systems: Computational and cognitive approaches to the communication of knowledge.* Los Altos, CA: Morgan Kaufmann.

Winne, P. (1989). Theories of instruction and of intelligence for designing artificially intelligent tutoring systems. *Educational Psychologist, 24*(3), 229–259.

7 Using Hypercard Technology to Measure Understanding

Eva L. Baker
David Niemi
Howard Herl
CRESST/University of California, Los Angeles

Great interest in developing alternative, truer measures of student knowledge has stimulated national educational policy development (National Council on Education Standards and Testing, 1992), state testing innovation (Baron, 1990), and visions for local educational reform (L. B. Resnick & D. P. Resnick, 1992). Although research has explored the use of technology in an assessment role, it has focused on computers primarily as a surrogate (Braun, chap. 11; Shavelson, Baxter, & Pine, 1991), or as an expert scoring system (Bennett, Rock, & Wang, 1991). Yet the power of technology in an assessment role will be fully realized only if we can unlock its potential to improve the validity, not just the efficiency, of our inferences about student accomplishments. Validity was the main focus of our approach to the application of technology to assessment. An additional constraint was to develop a strategy that used existing software rather than invest in a costly, time-consuming software development effort.

A dual context informed our research. First, we attempted to develop technology-sensitive outcome measures that might be more sensitive to experimental uses of computers in classrooms (Baker, Gearhart, & Herman, chap. 9). Second, we were interested in generating measures that would respond to calls for expanded validity standards (Linn, Baker, & Dunbar 1991; Baker, O'Neil, & Linn, in press). These new validity criteria, among others, include cognitive complexity, instructional sensitivity, transfer and generalizability, and fairness. The topic areas we selected for assessment were content in history and science; the cognitive task measured was the degree of understanding students possessed in these content areas. Although some research in our lab had used written explanations as direct measures of student knowledge (Baker, Freeman, & Clayton, 1991), we wished to explore whether students could demonstrate their understanding in alternate ways, ways that depended less on their language production skills. We wished to explore as directly as possible the way students represented their content knowledge.

KNOWLEDGE REPRESENTATION AS A COGNITIVE CONSTRUCT

Knowledge representation is a theoretical construct devised to help explain human competencies. Attributing cognitive representations to individuals is equivalent to describing classes of related competencies. Representing competencies with structured knowledge can help to illuminate extremely complex behavior patterns associated with learning and problem solving.

Knowledge structures comprise organized relational knowledge (Scriven, 1974; Skemp, 1976). These structures, called *schemas,* are thought to provide organizing frameworks for interpretation and action. Schemas have been conceived as organizing and relating both declarative and procedural knowledge as well as strategic knowledge (Gelman & Greeno, 1989; Messick, 1984). Schemas constitute a framework for comprehending and interpreting objects and events. Researchers believe that schemas have a determining effect on the acquisition of new knowledge (Messick, 1984) and guide knowledge storage and retrieval, generalization and interpretation of ideas, and the initiation and regulation of action (J. R. Anderson, 1990).

In the last 15 years or so, there has been a trend in psychological and artificial intelligence research toward understanding the organization and structure of knowledge. In artificial intelligence (AI) research, this focus was necessitated by the inability of early AI programs using search heuristics to outperform humans. Psychological theories based on search heuristics also failed to model human capabilities adequately. It became clear that search heuristics that did not use an organized knowledge structure were not very effective, so researchers shifted their efforts toward the development of theories that could account for the role of knowledge structures in cognition (Minsky, 1975; Rumelhart & Ortony, 1977).

Many researchers in cognitive science have focused on the so-called novice-to-expert shift (Chi, Glaser, & Rees, 1982); that is, they have tried to describe the difference between novice and expert knowledge structures in specific domains (Chi & Ceci, 1987). To achieve such descriptions, knowledge structures must be assessed: A number of well-known techniques exist for evaluating knowledge structures involving, for example, various kinds of cognitive, conceptual semantic maps (e.g., Goldsmith, Johnson, & Acton, 1991; Novak & Gowin, 1984, Shavelson, 1974; Shavelson & Geeslin, 1975). Other methods have included the documentation of misconceptions (Gentner & Stevens, 1983), analyses of perceived similarities among elements in a domain (Chi et al., 1982), and information-processing analyses of problem-solving strategies (Larkin, McDermott, D. P. Simon, & H. A. Simon, 1980). Although a plethora of evaluation techniques has been tested, there has been little systematic work on the question of what causes changes in knowledge structures.

In cognitive research, a common way to represent conceptual knowledge is in the form of nodes and links between them, nodes representing concepts or their attributes, and links the relations between concepts. Under this model, domain understanding develops by making connections (i.e., links) between ideas, facts, procedures, and other types of domain knowledge.

Views of memory suggest knowledge is organized in complex networks rather than in linear sequences (Rumelhart, Lindsay, & Norman, 1972; Rumelhart & Ortony, 1977). These semantic networks include conceptual, factual, and procedural knowledge components. In certain interpretive disciplines, such as the field of social studies and more particularly the area of history, there are fewer linear or unequivocal hierarchical relationships among relevant concepts, facts, and procedures (Newman, 1992; Voss, Greene, Post, & Penner, 1983; Voss, Tyler, & Yengo, 1983; Voss, Vesonder, & Spilich, 1980; Wineburg, 1991a, 1991b).

Representing knowledge as a network of nodes and links is consistent with semantic mapping techniques and recent versions of schema theory (e.g., J. R. Anderson, 1990; Chi & Ceci, 1987; Hiebert & Carpenter, 1992; Marshall, 1991), as well as related approaches to understanding that discuss the integration of skills and concepts (e.g., Gelman & Greeno, 1989).

The theoretical inspiration for the origins of cognitive structure can be traced back to the 1960s. Ausubel (1963) attributed success in the learning and retention of meaningful material to the cognitive structure that the learner possessed. The concepts contained in the learner's cognitive structure and the relationships between them are hypothesized to be primarily responsible for the integration of new material in the learner's existing cognitive structure—"an individual's organization, stability, and clarity of knowledge in a particular subject-matter field" (p. 26). Ausubel (1963) also stated that "the importance of cognitive structure variables has been generally underestimated in the past because preoccupation with noncognitive, rote, and motor types of learning has tended to focus attention on such current situational and interpersonal factors as practice, drive, incentive, and reinforcement variables. Cognitive structure is also, in its own right, the most significant independent variable influencing (facilitating, inhibiting, limiting) the learner's capacity for acquiring more new knowledge in the same field" (p. 27). Shavelson (1974) defined cognitive structure as "an assemblage of identifiable elements and the relationships between those elements" (p. 231) and as "the structure in a student's or teacher's mind, a hypothetical construct referring to the organization (relationships) of concepts in memory" (p. 232).

Since the 1970s the most prevalent methods for assessing students' cognitive structures have been word-association tasks (Preece, 1976a, 1976b, 1976c; Shavelson, 1972, 1974; Shavelson & Geeslin, 1975; Shavelson & Stanton, 1975;

Thro, 1978), card sorting and graph building tasks (Goldsmith, Johnson, & Acton, 1991; Preece, 1976a, 1976b, 1976c; Shavelson, 1972, 1974; Shavelson & Geeslin, 1975), and multidimensional scaling (Dansereau, Long, Evans, & Actkinson, 1980; G. M. Diekhoff, 1983; G. M. Diekhoff & K. B. Diekhoff, 1982; Fenker, 1975; Goldsmith et al., 1991; Jonassen, 1989; Shavelson, 1972; Wainer & Kaye, 1974).

For example, Thro (1978) gathered word-association data on each of 17 concept words in physics and employed the relatedness coefficient (Garskof & Houston, 1963) to raw distances for multidimensional scaling techniques. The digraph building approach to measuring text structure comprises diagramming every sentence of a course textbook into a digraph (Warriner & Griffiths, 1957). In digraph analysis, content structure is something that is created from the text itself, using digraph theoretical techniques (Goldsmith et al., 1991; Preece, 1976a, 1976b, 1976c; Shavelson, 1972, 1974; Shavelson & Geeslin, 1975). Given the sentence *Force is the product of mass and acceleration,* a digraph could be constructed with symmetrical relationships between force-product, product-mass, and product-acceleration. Nondirectional linking verbs and prepositions between concepts (*is*) result in symmetrical relationships; coordinating conjunctions between concepts (*and*) specify independent relationships (the absence of a mass-acceleration relationship). The distance between two concepts would be the number of arcs in the shortest path connecting the two concepts.

COGNITIVE MAPS

The cognitive map learning strategy approach is based on research on human memory. Early conceptual work (Quillian, 1968) was instrumental in advancing the notion that human memory may be organized as a network, comprising concepts (nodes) interconnected by different kinds of relationships (links). Quillian also offered the notion that there are certain types of nodes: *type* nodes, that lead directly to the meaning of its concept name, while interconnecting with other types of nodes, and *token* nodes, allowing for an indirect association with the concept. The physical representation of these nodes requires each type node to be placed in a different plane from the potentially many token nodes linked with it. The token nodes subsequently link to other token nodes located in the same plane. This memory model set forth by Quillian (1968) allows for various types of nodes to be used for eliciting content knowledge.

These early authors (T. H. Anderson, 1979; T. H. Anderson & Armbruster, 1981) credit the work of Hanf (1971) and Merrit, Prior, E. Grugeon, and D. Grugeon (1977) as precursors to concept mapping. Hanf (1971) suggested that a concept map necessarily must begin with the main idea (root node of a hierarchically constructed map), and subsequently lead to secondary and tertiary ideas. The concept map would finally contain the least important events concerning the content domain at the bottom. The hierarchical approach to constructing concept maps has also been described by Novak (1979, 1980) and Novak and Gowin (1984), who suggested a different protocol for this construction. The top of the map, according to Novak, would be the most useful place to position the most general and inclusive concepts, with more specific and less inclusive concepts below these higher level concepts.

Dansereau and Holley (1982, p. 26) stated: "Networking forms the basis for the primary strategies in the learning strategy system." In their research, students identified concepts and represented the relationships between them in the form of a concept map. Empirical research on the effects of concept mapping (Dansereau et al., 1979; Holley, Dansereau, McDonald, Garland, & Collins, 1979) found that students using the concept mapping strategy performed significantly better on text processing tasks than students using their own method. This early work also experimented with the categories and specific number of link labels used in concept maps. Initially, 13 links were provided, which proved to be somewhat unwieldy for students. Later work (Dansereau & Holley, 1982) settled on a six-link system, consisting of hierarchical, chaining, and clustering link types. The six links in the system were: (a) is part of, (b) is a type of (an example of, a kind of), (c) leads to (results in, causes), (d) is like (is similar to), (e) has (characterized by, is a property of), and (f) illustrates (supports, is evidence of).

Why should concept maps work? One argument relates to the use of cognitive resources. When constructing concept maps, the learner is free from tasks such as "writing everything down" (Hanf, 1971) and can concentrate on higher level cognitive processes. Keeping discourse to a minimum could potentially prove beneficial to student subpopulations with less language fluency. A second explanation for the potential power of concept maps is the focus they provide on spatial displays. Ault (1985) contended that "a concept map depicts hierarchy and relationships among concepts. It demands clarity of meaning and integration of details. Mapping exercises require one to think in multiple directions and to switch back and forth between different levels of abstraction" (p. 38). Novak, Gowin, and Johansen (1983) concluded that learning could be more meaningful if students "map" key concepts to reveal hierarchical levels and relationships. Jonassen (1984) went so far as to state that "the spatial distances between ideas (as measured by the number of intermittent links between ideas) are roughly equivalent to the semantic distances between concepts or schemata in memory" (p. 169).

Concept mapping research has been investigated as an instructional intervention in biology (Moreira, 1979; Novak, 1979, 1980, 1981; Novak et al., 1983; Stewart, Van Kirk, & Rowell, 1979), general science (Ault, 1985; Stewart,

1982), and geology (Holley et al., 1979). Previous research has shown significant differences in performance on main ideas, including close and essay measures, when students used concept mapping techniques to represent knowledge of a geology text (Holley et al., 1979). The inference stemming from that particular research study is that students constructing concept maps are acquiring and organizing main ideas and concepts.

In organizing or reorganizing semantic information, the grouping of concepts is almost always along the structural lines of superset, subset, similarity, part, proximity, consequence, and precedence (Collins & Quillian, 1972). It is important to note that these relations can be applied in different ways to the same set of concepts. Collins and Quillian (1972) presented various types of relations between concepts, and possible links (in parentheses) have been categorized into their various relational categories: (a) superset (is a, is a member of), (b) subset (consists of, contains), (c) similarity (is like, is not like), (d) part (part of), (e) proximity (is adjacent to, is next to), (f) consequence (leads to, influences, causes), and (g) precedence (prior to).

There has been other research investigating students' interconnections of pairs of concepts (nodes) via the use of relational links (Lambiotte, Dansereau, Cross, & Reynolds, 1989). There has been a growing consensus (Churcher, 1989; Duncan, 1989; Lambiotte et al., 1989) that links should be named, modifiable, directional, and represented by a canonical set. Lambiotte et al. (1989) presented the following list of link categories: (a) hierarchy (type), (b) chain (leads to), (c) cluster (characteristic), (d) procedural (next), (e) influences, and (f) part. Duncan (1989) offered the following set of link categories: (a) being (is a), (b) showing (is an example of), (c) causing (leads to, causes), (d) using (uses, can be used by), (e) having (has), (f) including (includes), and (g) similarity (is like).

CRESST EMPIRICAL RESEARCH

The intent of our research was to explore the utility of knowledge representation using a hypertext system as an alternative strategy to measure student understanding. The research we report is very much in progress. We describe our studies of expert representations in history topics and explorations in the assessment use of hypertext to measure history and science understanding of secondary school students. In these studies we used an adaptation of the Lambiotte et al. (1989) analysis. In a prior study (Baker, Niemi, Gearhart, & Herman, 1990) we used HyperCard as a vehicle for directly eliciting content knowledge representations from high school students. In this study, 28 11th-grade history students were given an assessment of their understanding of the Great Depression historical period. The students were taught to use HyperCard to construct their knowledge representations of the Great Depression. Specific relational links were to be used in the knowledge representation task: (a) is prior to, (b) influences, (c) leads to, (d) is like, (e) is not like, (f) is a type of, (g) is part of, (h) supports, (i) is an example, (j) is a property of, and (k) is used for. Prior knowledge, reading comprehension, and essays were administered. In an effort to explore construct validity, students completed additional topic-related measures. The results of this study indicated that the technique was feasible.

We were also interested in the expert/novice paradigm in our context. What are the characteristics of expert knowledge structures, including structural patterns, structural elements, and content details of their direct knowledge representations? How similar are expert-constructed knowledge structures in terms of conceptual and structural attributes? Are there common declarative elements, relational links, and structural patterns that are found in the direct knowledge representations of experts?

Experts represent their knowledge at a deeper, more conceptual level than novices. Previous studies and research have shown that experts use principle-based conceptual entities whereas novices' knowledge structures are syntactically or surface-feature oriented, leading to more superficial relationships between concepts (Chi, 1985; Chi, Glaser, & Farr, 1988; Chi, Glaser, & Rees, 1982; Chi, Hutchinson, & Robin, 1989). The first hypothesis is that history experts will construct more cohesive direct knowledge structures about U.S. history knowledge than will students from the broad high school population.

Can expert performance be used as a basis for setting standards for students' knowledge representation in history? In order to use expert knowledge representations as criteria to rate student work, there must exist a degree of similarity between experts' representations. Components of similarity should include link relations, complexity, and semantic content of organization of the knowledge base.

When experts represent their subject matter knowledge, they perceive large meaningful patterns in their domain (Chi et al., 1988; Gentner & Stevens, 1983). Experts not only have more content knowledge in a given domain but also have a superior ability to organize their knowledge bases.

An expert study in content knowledge representation of U.S. history was conducted with three PhD history students. Each doctoral student wrote six essays over a 2-day period covering four content areas of U.S. history, including the Revolutionary War, the Civil War, immigration, and the Great Depression. Each expert read each historical debate (Paine–Inglis, Henry–Inglis, Lincoln–Douglas, Pixley–Brooks, Simon–Graham, and Roosevelt–Long) and the respective writing prompts, and subsequently completed an explanation task for each prompt.

On the third day, the three doctoral students constructed HyperCard-stack concept maps for the Civil War and Great Depression topics. The HyperCard stacks contained the following relational links: (a) is prior to, (b) influences, (c) leads to, (d) is like, (e) is not like, (f) is a type of, (g) is part of, (h) supports, (i) is an example, (j) is a property of, and (k) is used for (Baker & Niemi, 1991;

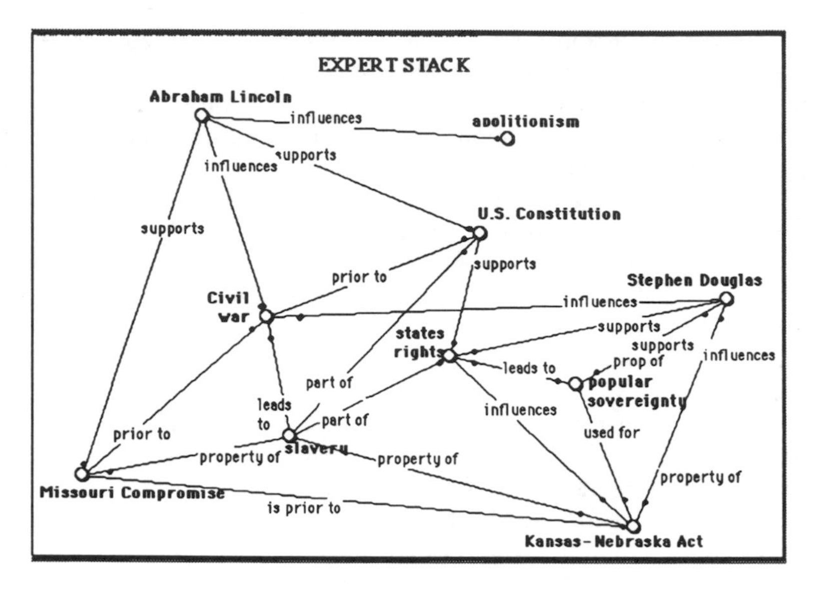

FIG. 7.1. Part of an expert concept map.

Baker, Niemi, Novak, & Herl, 1992). The PhD students generated the nodes, noting them as concepts, facts, or procedures, and labeled the relationships between pairs of nodes using the set of relational links. Figure 7.1 displays a concept map constructed from an expert's HyperCard stack.

Expert essays and concept maps were analyzed and some consistencies were discovered concerning both intra- and intertask comparisons. There was roughly 75% (50 out of 69) agreement between concepts used in the essay and nodes included in the concept map tasks. In both the Civil War and Great Depression topics, approximately the same number of nodes was used by the experts. The experts represented their views on the positions of the participants in the debates by relating concepts and principles to supporting facts. The experts used on average about 50% concept nodes and 50% fact nodes in their concept maps. The experts wove facts (Kansas-Nebraska Act, Missouri Compromise, and U.S. Constitution) and concepts (slavery, popular sovereignty, and states' rights) together by integrating both temporal and abstract aspects of their knowledge representations. One major difference between experts and novices was in the ability to correctly identify fact nodes and their relationships to more abstract ideas.

As with the expert studies, HyperCard provides a basic representational tool. Its basic unit consists of "a node, a link, and another node" (Churcher, 1989). Our work, related to Lambiotte et al. (1989) and Fischer (1989), requires the student to construct directly a structure in HyperCard. Thus the scoring of this open-ended task presents considerable challenge. Rather than developing totally arbitrary scoring schemes or using expert–novice comparisons, we have undertaken a series of research studies designed to explore the feasibility and validity of scoring dimensions using construct validity approaches.

CONSTRUCT VALIDITY STUDY

Subjects

Subjects for this study were 24 11th-grade and 21 12th-grade students in two classrooms participating in the Apple Classrooms of Tomorrow℠ (ACOT) project, an ongoing, multiyear investigation of the effects of high access to technology on educational outcomes and procedures (see Baker, Gearhart, and Herman, chap. 9, for a description of the ACOT environment). Most students had been enrolled in ACOT classrooms for at least 2 years. All had extensive experience with Macintosh computers and hypermedia environments.

Content Materials

Two topics in each subject area were tested: (a) primary texts from the pre-Civil War and Great Depression eras in U.S. history, and (b) descriptions of two types of analysis in chemistry, one involving tests to distinguish diet from regular soda[1] and the other a series of tests used to identify five different baking ingredients.

Tasks

Students were given texts to read as part of the assessment procedure (Baker et al., 1990, 1991). In this study we used the following texts: for the Civil War, the Lincoln–Douglas debates; for the Great Depression, speeches by Franklin D. Roosevelt and Huey Long; and for the two chemistry topics, descriptions of chemical analysis demonstrations performed by a high school teacher. The two chemistry texts were similar except for the structure of the analysis described. Each text took between 15 and 25 min to read. In the case of the chemical tests for sugar in sodas, any of the several tests described would be sufficient to identify the presence of sugar, that is, to distinguish diet from regular soda. In the case of quantitative tests to identify baking ingredients, results from several different chemical tests were needed to identify each of five different substances.

HyperCard Materials

Diskettes with specially modified HyperCard stacks were provided to students. These stacks contained built-in pull-down menus of link and node types. The link and node types were adapted for the science and history topics used in this study

[1]The soda task is a modification of a task developed by the Connecticut State Department of Education.

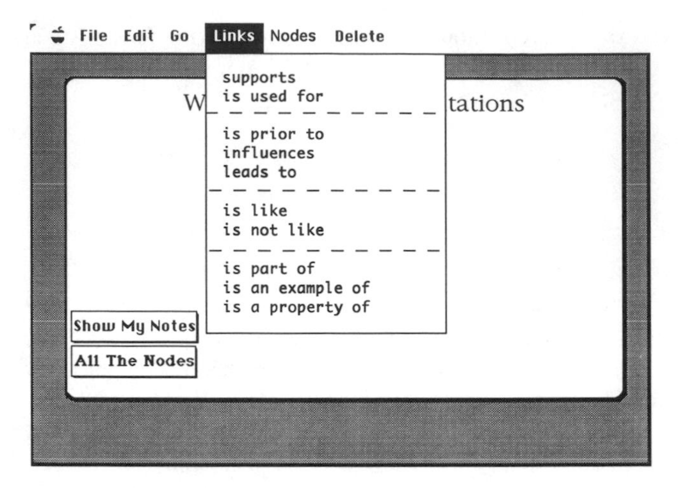

FIG. 7.2. Student card with pull-down link menu.

from semantic network and concept mapping literature (Lambiotte et al., 1989; Novak & Gowin, 1984). An example of a HyperCard screen is shown in Fig. 7.2.

Individual HyperCard cards served as nodes in the concept maps students generated, and links were represented as buttons on the cards. The node-type menu enabled students to label the cards as concepts, facts, or procedural nodes.

A menu of 10 relational links (see Table 7.1) was also provided to help students identify relations among the concepts, facts, and events they included in their HyperCard knowledge representations. This menu did not include the "type of" links used in the graduate student study.

Each student completed a sequence of assessment tasks, including one history topic and one science topic. It took the 11th-graders who participated in the study

TABLE 7.1
Relational Links in EXPERIMENTAL Knowledge Representation

Prior to
Influences
Leads to
Is like
Is not like
Is part of
Is used for
Supports
Is an example of
Is a property of

From Baker and Niemi (1991).

$9\frac{1}{2}$ class periods, or about $6\frac{1}{3}$ hrs spread over 5 days, to complete all tasks. The 12th-graders spent 7 class periods, or about $4\frac{2}{3}$ hrs over 4 days, to complete all tasks except the history essay. All tests and questionnaires were administered by a member of our research team.

Combining each history topic with each science topic yielded four topic sets. At the 11th-grade level, the order of the subject areas, history and science, was counterbalanced, and the four topic sets were also counterbalanced, producing eight possible topic orderings. Twelfth-graders took the science tests first, and topic orders were counterbalanced within the two subject areas. Thus, each topic set was given to about one-quarter of the students at each grade level.

Training in Knowledge Representation

Prior to undertaking the assessment tasks, all students received training in HyperCard knowledge representation. Students were given about 30 min of training in the task of using HyperCard specifically for knowledge representation purposes. The trainer modeled the use of representation using the prespecified links but a different topic: The area of music was chosen specifically because it was anticipated that students would have considerable background knowledge. Understanding of the links was assessed by a criterion test in which students were given 16 node pairs and asked to generate as many different links as possible. All students demonstrated that they could use at least nine link types correctly. Understanding of node types was tested by requiring students to label five nodes correctly.

After training, the following sequence of activities and time allocations were repeated for each subject area (science and history): (a) 20-item prior knowledge test, 10 min; (b) 5-item attitude measure, 5 min; (c) read texts, 20 min; (d) generate HyperCard stack, 40 min; (e) 5-item attitude measure, 5 min; (f) write essay, 40 min; (g) 20-item metacognitive measure, 10 min; (h) 5-item attitude measure, 5 min; (i) debriefing questionnaire, 15 min. Because of the schedule constraints, 12th-grade students were unable to complete the essay task. In this chapter, data are reported for prior knowledge, essay, and HyperCard elements.

Essay Data and Scoring

Students completed relevant essays following each representation using word processing software. Two trained raters scored all essays on five validated dimensions: general impression of content quality, number of principles and concepts, prior knowledge, proportion of detail from texts, and misconceptions (Baker, in press; Baker et al., 1991). Each dimension was scored on a 1-to-5-point scale, with 1 representing the lowest performance level. Subject (history and science) order was counterbalanced across the two raters, and within each subject area, the order of the essays was independently randomized for each rater.

Analyses and Results

One way to explore the utility of HyperCard representations is to compare them to other indicators of student competence. We posit that there should be some regular relationships between performance on our scored essays and elements of the HyperCard representation. We expect reasonable relationships because our essay scoring scheme does not explicitly credit expression and other felicitous verbal skills, but instead attends to the extent to which the student is judged to have elaborated understanding of the topic area, a competence presumed measured by the representation. We also collected questionnaire and transcript data as additional measures of competence.

HyperCard Elements

Our computer program automatically calculated the number of total nodes, node types, total links, and link types. Means and standard deviations are reported for history knowledge structure elements in Table 7.2 and for science knowledge structure elements in Table 7.3. Tables 7.2 and 7.3 show that procedural nodes

TABLE 7.2
Means and Standard Deviations for History Knowledge Structure Elements

	Long-FDR			*Lincoln-Douglas*		
	M	*SD*	*N*	*M*	*SD*	*N*
Total nodes	8.28	(5.64)	16	13.31	(7.71)	11
Facts	5.52	(4.48)		7.69	(6.34)	
Concepts	1.81	(2.52)		4.46	(6.35)	
Procedure	.66	(1.27)		1.00	(1.15)	
Other	.28	(.64)		.15	(.55)	
Total links	7.52	(6.84)		17.46	(13.51)	
Uses	.23	(.53)		2.00	(3.79)	
Supports	.71	(1.45)		3.62	(3.54)	
Prior to	.66	(1.11)		1.08	(1.75)	
Influences	1.14	(2.08)		2.31	(3.32)	
Leads to	2.28	(3.03)		1.92	(1.84)	
Like	.57	(1.59)		.69	(.75)	
Not like	.23	(.53)		2.07	(2.06)	
Part of	.95	(1.16)		2.23	(2.24)	
Example	.66	(1.15)		1.46	(1.39)	
Property	.04	(.21)		.38	(.65)	
Prior knowledge	18.91	(7.99)		19.25	(6.68)	

From Baker and Niemi (1991).

TABLE 7.3
Means and Standard Deviations for Science Knowledge Structure Elements

	Baking			*Soda*		
	M	*SD*	*N*	*M*	*SD*	*N*
Total nodes	13.12	(7.39)	17	13.37	(9.25)	19
Facts	5.65	(5.05)		4.10	(5.01)	
Concepts	1.76	(2.05)		3.57	(3.48)	
Procedure	4.29	(3.96)		5.42	(4.87)	
Other	1.41	(4.13)		.26	(.56)	
Total links	14.17	(12.95)		13.00	(10.76)	
Uses	2.17	(3.43)		2.26	(3.16)	
Supports	1.35	(1.97)		1.58	(2.22)	
Prior to	.70	(1.72)		.63	(1.25)	
Influences	1.41	(1.91)		.73	(1.44)	
Leads to	1.41	(1.37)		.94	(1.26)	
Like	.47	(.87)		.47	(.77)	
Not like	1.17	(1.94)		.57	(1.07)	
Part of	2.94	(4.72)		2.52	(2.87)	
Example	1.64	(2.08)		2.21	(2.99)	
Property	.88	(1.76)		.42	(.83)	
Prior knowledge	19.20	(8.70)		20.57	(9.23)	

From Baker and Niemi (1991).

are rarely used in students' history maps, compared with their science maps. Also, patterns of link use are different across the two subject areas; for instance, the "example" link occurs more frequently in science than in history maps.

In this set of experiments we also provided a pull-down menu of node types: facts, concepts, procedural nodes, and other (uncodable) categories (see Fig. 7.3). Our findings suggest that students clearly differentiated the uses of nodes by subject matter area. Table 7.4 displays the proportion of total nodes labeled by category for each of the task areas.

Facts are critical elements in all four tasks; however, they dominate in the history area. Concepts show relatively stronger frequency in the history area, but the major differences occur with the procedural node area where the science use averages more than four times the use in history. Such differences are expected, given the typical focus in history on declarative knowledge.

Different use patterns emerged as well for the types of links as a function of subject matter. Table 7.5 presents the link categories for four tasks by topic.

Clearly, the links "part of," "example," and "used for" were found to be appropriate to the science tasks and links such as "influences" more appropriate for the history task.

Another set of relationships useful for analysis is the average number of links per node. Higher averages suggest a more elaborated view of the topic. Table 7.6

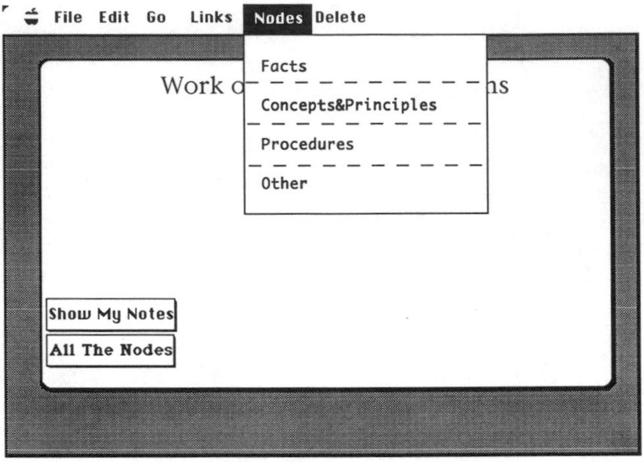

FIG. 7.3. Student card with pull-down node menu.

presents the average links per node calculated by student. These data differ somewhat from the results obtained by dividing total links by total nodes.

Qualitative Review of Stacks

Inspection of the HyperCard stacks suggested that many students possessed a low level of prior knowledge. This was supported by the students' low performance on the prior knowledge tests.

CONCLUSIONS

Our analytical approaches depended on exploratory methods—correlations among stack features, such as node frequencies and link types, with other measures, such as prior knowledge and essay scores. Most of these data have been

TABLE 7.4
Proportion of Node Types by Task

Node Type	*Long/FDR*	*Linc/Doug*	*Baking*	*Soda*
Facts	.66	.61	.41	.27
Concepts	.22	.30	.13	.29
Procedural nodes	.09	.07	.39	.41
Others	.03	.02	.07	.02
N	16	11	15	15

From Baker and Niemi (1991).

TABLE 7.5
Proportion of Node Types by Task

Link Type	*Long/FDR*	*Linc/Doug*	*Baking*	*Soda*
Used for	.04	.12	.16	.18
Supports	.08	.21	.08	.11
Prior to	.14	.05	.05	.06
Influences	.13	.10	.09	.04
Leads to	.30	.10	.12	.11
Not like	.03	.15	.08	.04
Part of	.14	.12	.17	.20
Example	.08	.11	.14	.17
Like	.06	.04	.04	.03
Property	.01	.01	.07	.03
N	15	11	13	15

From Baker and Niemi (1991).

reported in Baker et al. (1992). But the inferences from them are fundamentally unsatisfactory for a number of reasons. We have found in these studies that student knowledge in science and history, even in situations where they have been taught, is dismally low. This paucity of knowledge puts us in a difficult position. We have no range of student expertise against which to study the usefulness of this approach to the measurement of understanding.

Our next step, therefore, is to pursue systematically studies of expert representations in order to derive model structures against which student efforts may be compared. Dimensions of scoring to be explored include the consistency between experts on single topics, the stability of each expert across a variety of topics, and the determination of features that emerge as consistent predictors of expert understanding. We anticipate these to include both structural and semantic properties of maps. In the area of structure, we plan to explore depth, differentiation, and elaboration and in the semantics, we will look at the levels of content

TABLE 7.6
Average Links Per Node

	Long-FDR		*Linc-Doug*		*Baking*		*Soda*	
Average Links/Node	*M*	*SD*	*M*	*SD*	*M*	*SD*	*M*	*SD*
Node	1.59	2.07	1.00	0.57	1.14	0.65	1.47	1.14
N	15		11		13		15	

From Baker and Niemi (1991).

represented as well as its specificity. We believe such studies are prerequisite to the development of valid scoring rubrics for these potentially useful alternative measures.

ACKNOWLEDGMENTS

The research reported in this chapter was supported in part by a contract from the Defense Advanced Research Projects Agency (DARPA), administered by the Office of Naval Research (ONR), to the UCLA Center for the Study of Evaluation/Center for Technology Assessment. However, the opinions expressed do not necessarily reflect the positions of DARPA or ONR, and no official endorsement by either organization should be inferred.

The work reported herein has received partial support from the Apple Classrooms of Tomorrow[SM] Project, Advanced Development Group, Apple Computer, Inc., and from the Educational Research and Development Center Program, cooperative agreement number R117G10027 and CFDA catalog number 84.117G, as administered by the Office of Educational Research and Improvement, U.S. Department of Education. The findings and opinions expressed in this report do not reflect the position or policies of Apple Computer, Inc., the Office of Educational Research and Improvement, or the U.S. Department of Education.

REFERENCES

Anderson, J. R. (1990). The place of cognitive architectures in a rational analysis. In K. VanLehn (Ed.), *Architectures for intelligence* (pp. 1–24). Hillsdale, NJ: Lawrence Erlbaum Associates.

Anderson, T. H. (1979). Study skills and learning strategies. In H. F. O'Neil, Jr., & C. D. Spielberger (Eds.), *Cognitive and affective learning strategies* (pp. 77–98). New York: Academic Press.

Anderson, T. H., & Armbruster, B. B. (1984). Studying. In P. D. Pearson (Ed.), *Handbook on reading research* (pp. 657–679). New York: Longman.

Ault, C. R. (1985). Concept mapping as a study strategy in Earth science. *Journal of College Science Teaching, 15,* 38–44.

Ausubel, D. P. (1963). *The psychology of meaningful verbal learning.* New York: Grune & Stratton.

Baker, E. L. (in press). Learning-based assessments of history understanding. *Educational Psychology.*

Baker, E. L., Freeman, M., & Clayton, S. (1991). Cognitive assessment of history for large-scale testing. In M. C. Wittrock & E. L. Baker (Eds.), *Testing and cognition* (pp. 131–153). Englewood Cliffs, NJ: Prentice-Hall.

Baker, E. L., & Niemi, D. (1991, April). *Assessing deep understanding of science and history through hypertext.* Paper presented at the annual meeting of the American Educational Research Association, Chicago.

Baker, E. L., Niemi, D., Gearhart, M., & Herman, J. (1990, April). *Validating a hypermedia measure of knowledge representation.* Paper presented in the Technology-Sensitive Performance

Assessment Symposium at the annual meeting of the American Educational Research Association, Boston.

Baker, E., Niemi, D., Novak, J., & Herl, H. (1992). Hypertext as a strategy for teaching and assessing knowledge representation. In S. Dijkstra (Ed.), *Instructional models in computer-based learning environments* (pp. 365–384). Heidelberg, Germany: Springer-Verlag.

Baker, E. L., O'Neil, H. F., Jr., & Linn, R. (in press). Policy and validity prospects for performance-based assessment. *American Psychologist, 48*(12), 1210–1218.

Baron, J. B. (1990, April). *How science is tested and taught in elementary school science classrooms.* Paper presented at the annual meeting of the American Educational Research Association, Boston.

Bennett, R. E., Rock, D. A., & Wang, M. (1991). Equivalence of free-response and multiple-choice items. *Journal of Educational Measurement, 28,* 77–92.

Chi, M. T. (1985). Interactive roles of knowledge and strategies in the development of organized sorting and recall. In J. W. Segal, S. F. Chipman, & R. Glaser (Eds.), *Thinking and learning skills: Vol. 2. Research and open questions* (pp. 457–484). Hillsdale, NJ: Lawrence Erlbaum Associates.

Chi, M. T., & Ceci, S. J. (1987). Content knowledge: Its role, representation, and restructuring in memory development. *Advances in Child Development and Behavior, 20,* 91–143.

Chi, M. T., Glaser, R., & Farr, M. J. (1988). *The nature of expertise.* Hillsdale, NJ: Lawrence Erlbaum Associates.

Chi, M. T., Glaser, R., & Rees, E. (1982). Experts in problem solving. In R. Sternberg (Ed.), *Advances in the psychology of human intelligence* (Vol. 1, pp. 7–75). Hillsdale, NJ: Lawrence Erlbaum Associates.

Chi, M. T., Hutchinson, J. E., & Robin, A. F. (1989). How inferences about domain-related concepts can be constrained by structured knowledge. *Merril-Palmer Quarterly, 35*(1), 27–62.

Churcher, P. R. (1989). A common notation for knowledge representation, cognitive models, learning and hypertext. *Hypermedia, 1,* 235–254.

Collins, A., & Quillian, M. R. (1972). How to make a language user. In E. Tulving & W. Donaldson (Eds.), *Organization of memory* (pp. 309–351). New York: Academic Press.

Dansereau, D. F., & Holley, C. D. (1982). Development and evaluation of a text mapping strategy. In A. Flammer & W. Kintsch (Eds.), *Discourse processing* (pp. 536–554). Amsterdam: North Holland Publishing.

Dansereau, D. F., Long, G. L., Evans, S. H., & Actkinson, T. R. (1980). Objective ordering of instructional material using multidimensional scaling. *Journal of Structural Learning, 6,* 299–313.

Dansereau, D. F., McDonald, B. A., Collins, K. W., Garland, J. C., Holley, C. D., Diekhoff, G. M., & Evans, S. H. (1979). Evaluation of a learning strategy system. In H. F. O'Neil, Jr. & C. D. Spielberger (Eds.), *Cognitive and affective learning strategies* (pp. 3–44). New York: Academic Press.

Diekhoff, G. M. (1983). Testing through relationship judgments. *Journal of Educational Psychology, 75*(2), 227–233.

Diekhoff, G. M., & Diekhoff, K. B. (1982). Cognitive maps as a tool in communicating structural knowledge. *Educational Technology, 22*(4), 28–30.

Duncan, E. B. (1989). Structuring knowledge bases for designers of learning materials. *Hypermedia, 1,* 20–33.

Fenker, R. M. (1975). The organization of conceptual materials: A methodology for measuring ideal and actual cognitive structures. *Instructional Science, 4,* 33–57.

Fischer, K. (1989). SemNet. In R. McAleese (Ed.), *Hypertext: Theory into practice* (pp. 16, 19). Norwood, NJ: Ablex Publishing.

Garskof, B. E., & Houston, J. P. (1963). Measurement of verbal relatedness: An idiographic approach. *Psychological Review, 70,* 277–288.

Gelman, R., & Greeno, J. G. (1989). On the nature of competence: Principles for understanding in a domain. In L. B. Resnick (Ed.), *Knowing, learning, and instruction: Essays in honor of Robert Glaser* (pp. 125–186). Hillsdale, NJ: Lawrence Erlbaum Associates.

Gentner, D., & Stevens, A. L. (1983). *Mental models*. Hillsdale, NJ: Lawrence Erlbaum Associates.

Goldsmith, T. E., Johnson, P. J., & Acton, W. H. (1991). Assessing structural knowledge. *Journal of Educational Psychology, 83*(1), 88–96.

Hanf, M. B. (1971). Mapping: A technique for translating reading into thinking. *Journal of Reading, 14,* 225–230, 270.

Hiebert, J., & Carpenter, T. P. (1992). Learning and teaching with understanding. In D. A. Grouws (Ed.), *Handbook of research on mathematics teaching and learning* (pp. 65–97). New York: Macmillan.

Holley, C. D., Dansereau, D. F., McDonald, B. A., Garland, J. C., & Collins, K. W. (1979). Evaluation of a hierarchical mapping technique as an aid to prose processing. *Contemporary Educational Psychology, 4,* 227–237.

Jonassen, D. H. (1984). Developing a learning strategy using pattern notes: A new technology. *Programmed Learning and Educational Technology, 21*(3), 163–175.

Jonassen, D. H. (1989). Mapping the structure of research and theory in instructional systems technology. *Educational Technology, 29,* 7–10.

Lambiotte, J. G., Dansereau, D. F., Cross, D. R., & Reynolds, S. B. (1989). Multirelational semantic maps. *Educational Psychology Review, 1,* 331–367.

Larkin, J. H., McDermott, J., Simon, D. P., & Simon, H. A. (1980). Models of competence in solving physics problems. *Cognitive Science, 4,* 317–345.

Linn, R. L., Baker, E. L., & Dunbar, S. B. (1991). Complex, performance-based assessment: Expectations and validation criteria. *Educational Researcher, 20*(8), 15–21.

Marshall, S. P. (1991). The assessment of schema knowledge for arithmetic story problems: A cognitive science perspective. In G. Kulm (Ed.), *Assessing higher order thinking in mathematics* (pp. 155–168). Washington, DC: American Association for the Advancement of Science.

Merrit, J., Prior, D., Grugeon, E., & Grugeon, D. (1977). *Developing independence in reading*. Milton Keynes: Open University Press.

Messick, S. (1984). Abilities and knowledge in educational achievement testing: The assessment of dynamic cognitive structures. In B. S. Plake (Ed.), *Social and technical issues in testing: Implications for test construction and use* (pp. 156–172). Hillsdale, NJ: Lawrence Erlbaum Associates.

Minsky, M. (1975). A framework for representing knowledge. In P. Winston (Ed.), *The psychology of computer vision* (pp. 211–277). New York: McGraw-Hill.

Moreira, M. (1979). Concept maps as tools for teaching. *Journal of College Science Teaching, 8*(5), 283–287.

National Council on Education Standards and Testing (1992). *Raising standards for American education*. Washington, DC: U.S. Government Printing Office.

Newman, F. M. (1992). The assessment of discourse in social studies. In H. Berlak, F. Newman, E. Adams, D. Archbald, T. Burgess, T. Raven, & T. Romberg (Eds.), *Toward a new science of educational testing and assessment* (pp. 53–70). Albany, NY: State University of New York Press.

Novak, J. D. (1979). Applying psychology and philosophy to the improvement of laboratory teaching. *American Biology Teacher, 41*(8), 466–470, 474.

Novak, J. D. (1980). Learning theory applied to the biology classroom. *American Biology Teacher, 42*(5), 280–285.

Novak, J. D. (1981). Applying learning psychology and philosophy of science to biology teaching. *American Biology Teacher, 43*(1), 12–30.

Novak, J. D., & Gowin, D. B. (1984). *Learning how to learn*. Cambridge: Cambridge University Press.

Novak, J. D., Gowin, D. B., & Johansen, G. T. (1983). The use of concept mapping and knowledge vee mapping with junior high school science students. *Science Education, 67*(5), 625–645.

Preece, P. F. (1976a). Associative structure of science concepts. *British Journal of Educational Psychology, 46,* 174–183.

Preece, P. F. (1976b). The concepts of electromagnetism: A study of the internal representation of external structures. *Journal of Research in Science Teaching, 13*(6), 517–524.

Preece, P. F. (1976c). Mapping cognitive structure: A comparison of methods. *Journal of Educational Psychology, 68*(1), 1–8.

Quillian, M. R. (1968). Semantic meaning. In M. Minsky (Ed.), *Semantic information processing* (pp. 227–270). Cambridge, MA: MIT Press.

Resnick, L. B., & Resnick, D. P. (1992). Assessing the thinking curriculum: New tools for educational reform. In B. R. Gifford & M. C. O'Connor (Eds.), *Changing assessments: Alternative views of aptitude, achievement, and instruction* (pp. 37–75). Boston: Kluwer.

Rumelhart, D. E., Lindsay, P. H., & Norman, D. A. (1972). A process model for long-term memory. In E. Tulving & W. Donaldson (Eds.), *Organization of memory* (pp. 197–246). New York: Academic Press.

Rumelhart, D. E., & Ortony, A. (1977). The representation of knowledge in memory. In R. C. Anderson, R. J. Spiro, & W. E. Montague (Eds.), *Schooling and the acquisition of knowledge* (pp. 99–135). Hillsdale, NJ: Lawrence Erlbaum Associates.

Scriven, M. (1967). The methodology of evaluation. In R. W. Tyler, R. M. Gagne, & M. Scriven (Eds.), *Perspectives of curriculum evaluation* (AERA Monograph Series on Curriculum Evaluation, No. 1, pp. 39–83). Chicago: Rand McNally.

Shavelson, R. J. (1972). Some aspects of the correspondence between content structure and cognitive structure in physics instruction. *Journal of Educational Psychology, 63,* 225–234.

Shavelson, R. J. (1974). Methods for examining representations of a subject-matter structure in a student's memory. *Journal of Research in Science Teaching, 11*(3), 231–249.

Shavelson, R. J., Baxter, G. P., & Pine, J. (1991). Performance assessment in science. *Applied Measurement in Education, 4,* 347–362.

Shavelson, R. J., & Geeslin, W. E. (1975). A method of examining subject-matter structure in instructional material. *Journal of Structural Learning, 4,* 199–218.

Shavelson, R. J., & Stanton, G. C. (1975). Concept validation: Methodology and application to three measures of cognitive structure. *Journal of Educational Measurement, 12,* 67–85.

Skemp, R. R. (1976). Relational and instrumental understanding. *Mathematics Teaching, 77,* 20–26.

Stewart, J. (1982). Two aspects of meaningful problem solving in science. *Science Teaching, 66*(2), 731-749.

Stewart, J., Van Kirk, J., & Rowell, R. (1979). Concept maps: A tool for use in biology teaching. *American Biology Teacher, 41*(3), 171–175.

Thro, M. P. (1978). Relationships between associative and content structure of physics concepts. *Journal of Educational Psychology, 70*(6), 971–978.

Voss, J. F., Greene, T. R., Post, T. A., & Penner, B. C. (1983). Problem-solving skill in the social sciences. In G. H. Bower (Ed.), *The psychology of learning and motivation* (Vol. 17, pp. 165–213). New York: Academic Press.

Voss, J. F., Tyler, S., & Yengo, L. (1983). Individual differences in social science problem solving. In R. F. Dillon & R. R. Schmeck (Eds.), *Individual differences in cognitive processes* (Vol. 1, pp. 205–232). New York: Academic Press.

Voss, J. F., Vesonder, G. T., & Spilich, G. J. (1980). Text generation and recall by high-knowledge and low-knowledge individuals. *Journal of Verbal Learning and Verbal Behavior, 19,* 651–667.

Wainer, H., & Kaye, K. (1974). Multidimensional scaling of concept learning in an introductory course. *Journal of Educational Psychology, 66*(4), 591–598.

Warriner, J. E., & Griffiths, F. (1957). *English grammar and composition: Complete course*. New York: Harcourt Brace.

Wineburg, S. S. (1991a). Historical problem solving: A study of the cognitive processes used in the evaluation of documentary and pictorial evidence. *Journal of Educational Psychology, 83*(1), 73–87.

Wineburg, S. S. (1991b). On the reading of historical texts: Notes on the breach between school and academy. *American Educational Research Journal, 28*(3), 495–519.

8 A New Mirror for the Classroom: A Technology-Based Tool for Documenting the Impact of Technology on Instruction

Maryl Gearhart
Joan L. Herman
Eva L. Baker
John R. Novak
Andrea K. Whittaker
University of California, Los Angeles/CRESST

PROJECT BACKGROUND

Since 1987, UCLA's Center for Technology Assessment has been conducting a set of evaluation, research, and development activities at selected Apple Classrooms of Tomorrow℠ (ACOT) sites, with the goal of documenting the impact of technology access on K–12 environments (Baker, 1988; Baker, Gearhart, & Herman, 1990, 1991; Baker & Herman, 1988, 1989; Baker, Herman, & Gearhart, 1988; Baker & Niemi, 1990, 1991; Gearhart, Herman, Baker, Novak, & Whittaker, 1990; Gearhart, Herman, & Whittaker, 1991; Gearhart, Herman, Whittaker, & Novak, 1991; Herman, 1988). When Eva Baker and Joan Herman initiated the work with ACOT in 1987, the ACOT℠ project had been implemented in selected classrooms at five sites that were dispersed nationally and varied considerably in student characteristics and school context factors. Students and teachers in all classrooms were provided with high access to individual computer support both at home and at school, and ACOT's goal was to document how instructional innovations emerge in high access environments.[1] Since 1987,

[1]ACOT initially defined "high access" as one computer for each student and teacher both at school and at home. By the completion of our studies, however, both of the sites featured in this report had reconfigured their hardware. The elementary site provided fewer computers, greater diversity of computers, and some integrated multimedia technology; not every student was provided a computer at home. The secondary site continued assured access to any student at all times, but access at school was reorganized and supported by a greater diversity of hardware and integrated media.

the ACOT project has evolved to encompass more sites and has assumed a more directive role in the kinds of teacher support provided. It has shifted from a "bottom-up" exploration of the impact of technology access to a research-and-development laboratory for the construction of new technology tools for instruction and new tools for the assessment of instruction and instructional impact.

The work of the UCLA Center for Technology Assessment has evolved as well. From the outset, the center's goal for its work with ACOT has been to develop a model of technology assessment in K–12 environments by exploring the utility and applicability of existing measures and by developing new measures as needed. The shift in our work has been one of emphasis: As a result of continued confrontations with the limitations of existing measures, the development of new assessment tools has become our primary focus.

This chapter is a description of one of our new measures, a technology-based classroom observation instrument for documenting the impact of technology on classroom instruction. In the report that follows, we explain the need for a new observation tool sensitive to technology impact, and then illustrate the utility of the tool with samples of two of our current approaches to data analysis.

A Technology-Based Classroom Observation Tool

Our ongoing evaluation of the ACOT project required a method for documenting instructional impact and for providing "process" explanations for student and teacher outcomes. The instrument we had in mind would provide fairly comprehensive "snapshots" of classroom activities that would reveal variations in instructional practices related to uses of diverse resources. Based on data produced from informal observations, we needed a tool that could document instruction in different subject areas, determine how particular technology uses limit certain kinds of classroom organizations and support others, describe how teachers' roles may shift when technology is in use, document how the nature of students' work differs when technology resources are in use, and determine whether technology use has an impact on students' responses to instruction (e.g., their engagement with peers, or investment in their work). No existing observation instrument was available to provide us with data appropriate to our needs.

The Limits of Available Observation Instruments for Our Purposes

Many available classroom observation instruments focus on teachers' instructional roles during teacher–student interactions (see reviews by Cazden, 1986; Dunkin & Biddle, 1974; Evertson & Green, 1986). Two traditions are most prevalent. One approach commonly serves as a "process" partner in process–product analyses of functions of classroom talk believed to influence student outcomes (e.g., Flanders, 1970; Good & Brophy, 1984); observation schemes derived from this tradition vary in their underlying model of the cognitive functions of interaction in supporting students' learning. A second approach is derived from linguistic or sociolinguistic analyses of discourse (e.g., Green & Wallat, 1981; Sinclair & Coulthard, 1975). Schemes within this genre are used in investigations of the cultural context of teaching and learning, the functions of language in intellectual activities (e.g., Cazden, John, & Hymes, 1972), and the communicative requirements of classroom participation (e.g., Mehan, 1979). Across these traditions, observation methods include a considerable range of procedures: on-the-spot coding procedures using either time sampling or event sampling techniques, postobservation coding of video- or audiotape, and ethnographic examinations of selected case excerpts.

Although we viewed description of teacher–student interaction as important to our scheme, we considered the available tools inadequate on several counts. First, the varieties of instructional activities represented were incomplete: Within current constructivist interpretations of needed educational reforms, the underlying models of "good teaching" implicit in most classroom interaction instruments are too narrowly focused on the teachers' roles and on classroom talk, and are insufficiently attentive to description of students' activities. Second, the methods for representing instructional resources in these schemes did not reflect the technologies we would be observing. Third, few schemes offered methods of simultaneous coding that would enable us to explore relations among co-occurring contexts and events.

Closest in rationale, design, and content to the scheme we envisioned was a coordinated set of instruments developed by Stallings (Stallings, 1975, 1976; Stallings & Giesen, 1974; Stallings & Kaskowitz, 1974), later adapted by Giesen and Sirotnik (1979), and used for two highly regarded large-scale evaluations of school programs: A Study of Schooling (Goodlad, Sirotnik, & Overman, 1979) and Follow Through (Stallings, 1975; Stallings & Kaskowitz, 1974). The schemes included the Physical Environment Inventory, Daily Summary, Classroom Snapshot, and Five Minute Interaction. These multiple dimensions were helpful guides to our own efforts to design a scheme containing categories that could be cross-classified to produce a broad range of analyses. For example, the Classroom Snapshot captured relations among *activities* (such as demonstration, discussion, work on written assignments), *directors* (teacher, aide, student, group, class, independent), and *group size*. The Five Minute Inventory entailed event recording of classroom interactions: *persons* involved, *interactions* (e.g., Adult: direct questions, response, imperative, encouragement, monitor/observe; Student: directive, response, refusal, question), *context* (e.g., instruction, behavior, routines), and *means* (e.g., touching, with humor, with materials, negative affect). We adapted and integrated some of these categories in our own tool.

Because A Study of Schooling data were collected for each scheme at different times of the day, their procedures for observation were not directly useful to our goal for an integrated system. We revised the procedures to enable us to document as much as possible about what was happening at a given time, to permit us to examine relations among co-occurring aspects of classroom activities.

OUR TOOL

Our goal is to document the characteristics of instruction associated with use of technology resources. If teachers are lecturing, how is the class organized and what resources are in use to support the lecture? When computers are in use, how challenging are students' tasks, how are students working with the teacher and one another, and what proportion of them are engaged in productive interaction? If students are composing long texts or projects, what resources are they using to support their work, and what symbol systems are in use?

We developed a versatile, technology-based observation tool that could serve our needs for research and evaluation, and the needs of education professionals for an observation method that can be easily trained and that permits rapid analysis and display of results. In the observation scheme that resulted, instructional activities are the central organizing blocks. The emphasis of the scheme is on capturing the nature of instructional tasks, the roles of teachers, the nature of social relationships, the variety of resources, and the responses of students. The instrument's breadth of coverage is coordinated with qualitative techniques for collecting fine-grained descriptions of instructional content and process.

The instrument uses a time-sampling procedure to minimize rater bias, which is likely to be greater if raters sample events (because events are difficult to define when so many instructional characteristics are coded) or if raters make summary judgments over an entire class period. Therefore, with the exception of single-coded indices (the date, teacher observed, and subject area), the observation form is organized for recording in timed intervals. The form is machine scannable, which permits instant updating and rapid analysis of the resulting database.

Observers code a set of *activity descriptors* on a time-sampling schedule throughout the period (Gearhart & Herman, 1990). The activity descriptors are coded once during each 5-min (elementary) or 10-min (secondary) interval. During an observation period, our coders observe for 1 min at the start of each 5- or 10-min interval; they then code just what occurred within that prior minute, and use any remaining time to record field notes. The major categories and codes for the activity descriptors are listed here. Note that, for any given interval, multiple coding is permitted within all categories except classroom organization.

- *Classroom Organization:* teacher-led, independent work, group/cooperative, group/collaborative (jointly produced product), pair/cooperative, pair/collaborative, pair/tutoring, student-led

- *Instruction and Support Roles:*

  Directing instruction (codes that apply only to teacher-led classroom organizations): explain/provide information, question (for comprehension or examination), answer students' questions, direct students' work (step by step), correct/grade, test, read to students

  Facilitating instruction (codes that apply to independent, cooperative, and collaborative work): monitor/rove to help students at work, facilitate discussion, conference, joint problem-solve

  Management and Discipline: manage, discipline

  Not Present (with the group currently observed)

- *Symbol Systems Serving Key Instructional Functions* in the material the teachers make available to students: verbal, numeric, math symbols, graphic, chart, diagram, pictorial, model, map, puzzle/pattern, motor/action, music, objects

- *Instructional Intent* expected of students' work: low (emphasis on rote recall), medium (requiring inference or problem solution within a well-structured problem context), high (requiring inference and construction of a response in a less structured task context)

- *Length of the Responses* expected of students: repeat/copy (student replicates provided material exactly—e.g., spelling practice, cursive practice, keyboarding drill), select (multiple choice, true/false), short (no more than a sentence in length), medium (no more than a paragraph in length), long (multiparagraph)

- *Symbol Systems Students Use in Their Work:* verbal, numeric, math symbols, graphic, chart, diagram, pictorial, model, map, puzzle/pattern, motor/action, music, objects

- *Resources in Use:*

  Textual: textbooks (textbooks, assigned literature, workbooks/worksheets, tests), *print resources* (library books, reference books, periodicals, reference/help sheets), *materials* (paper, file cards, blackboard), *student's own work*

  Hands on materials

  Computer: instructional software (electronic worksheet; simulation/strategy) and *applications* (word processing, HyperCard, graphics, database, spreadsheet, programming, telecommunications)

  Other technology: laserdisc, scanner, film/video, slide/filmstrip, audio, robotics, class monitor, overhead, MIDI, calculator

- *Students' Responses to the Activities:*

  Appropriateness of students' behavior: a judgment of the percentage of students who are on task

  Students' focus and investment: a judgment on a 1 to 5 scale

Productive student-student interaction: a judgment of the percentage of students who are talking with one another about their work

Results of the time-sampled observations are scanned, analyzed, and displayed in graphic or tabular formats on a Mac II. Currently the resultant displays are catalogued for flexible retrieval using a menu-driven interface; a goal is to develop a user-friendly interface for real-time, online queries.

ILLUSTRATIVE USES

The instrument provides us with "snapshot" descriptions of classroom instruction that can serve multiple research and development functions. In this chapter we illustrate two of our current uses: documentation of commonly reported changes in high access classrooms, and model-driven descriptions of change.

Documentation of Reported Changes in High Access Classrooms

There is a clear need for empirical documentation of commonly reported changes in classroom practices in high access environments. Researchers and educators have made informal observations that computer use is associated with more challenging projects, less directed teaching and more teacher facilitation, more frequent group projects, more time on task, and more peer assistance (see, for example, Collins, 1991; Hawkins & Sheingold, 1986). However, there is little empirical documentation of these changes.

Based on observations collected from 1989 through 1991, we have produced preliminary findings bearing on others' informal reports. To preview the findings summarized here: Our analyses to date indicate certain associations between technology use and classroom activities that are consistent with informal reports. But some of our results are not consistent with what now appear to be overly general and overly romantic sketches of technology's impact. Our data suggest that teachers make motivated choices about resources and pedagogical methods based on subject area, and thus their classroom activities are not technology-driven in any simple way. Thus our findings serve to underscore the importance of documenting technology impact (a) within specific subject areas, (b) at particular levels of schooling (e.g., elementary vs. secondary), and (c) for specific uses of technology.

We must stress the illustrative nature of our results. Although observations were made of activities that observers and teachers agreed were representative of each teacher's instruction, the data reported here may represent a less than adequate sampling of teachers' instruction: At the elementary level, the database included 145 5-min intervals (12 hrs) in language arts and 73 5-min intervals (6.1 hrs) in mathematics; at the secondary level, the database consisted of 45 10-min intervals (7.5 hrs) in English.

The analysis strategy was based on a nested series of queries: We defined a set of resource contexts, beginning with a simple distinction between those where the computer was in use and those where it was not, and compared instructional patterns in those two contexts. We then made further refinements as questions for analysis emerged; for example, how did instruction differ when computers were used for applications (such as word processing) versus instructional courseware? Most analyses of instructional patterns were based on aggregations of individual codes. For example, when we examined instruction and support roles, we created two summary categories: *directing instruction* and *facilitating instruction*, representing the use of any of the roles in those two categories respectively.

Interobserver agreement was computed as percent agreement for the aggregated variables we report here. At the elementary level, agreement ranged from 60% to 100%, based on a subset of 83 co-observed 5-min intervals: Agreement was highest for instructional role variables (82%–93%) and classroom organization (89%–100%), and moderate for instructional intent (70%), length of response (67%), and productive peer interaction (60%). Reflecting the challenges of multiple coding when intervals are short, the coding disagreements for instructional intent and length of response were most frequently attributed to differences in "what I managed to notice" in each interval (rather than in the appropriate code); therefore our analyses pooled the observations of both raters for each interval. Interobserver agreement at the secondary level was high for all variables (81% to 100%), based on a subset of 27 co-observed 10-min intervals.

Illustrative Results: Language Arts and Mathematics at One Elementary Site

The results for language arts were more consistent with informal reports of instructional patterns in high access contexts than were the results for mathematics. (Note that, because multiple coding is permitted, totals within categories are often greater than 100%.)

- In language arts, computers were in use a bit less than 20% of the time, and uses were always for applications (100% of computer time) rather than for delivery of instructional courseware (0% of computer time). The application in use was a word processor. In mathematics, although computers were observed in use slightly more frequently (32%) than in language arts, there was a striking difference in type of use: Computers were used infrequently for applications (17% of computer time) and always for instructional courseware (100% of computer time).

• In language arts, use of the computer (always for word processing) was associated with independent student work rather than teacher-led work, and with a role for teachers as facilitators of students' work rather than as director and deliverer of information (Table 8.1); instruction without computer support was characterized by greater likelihood of teacher-led work and directive teaching. In mathematics, comparisons of instructional characteristics with and without computer support were similar to those for language arts.

• A comparison of mathematics instruction for applications versus instructional courseware revealed that teachers were more likely to be facilitating (rather than directing) students' work only when students were using instructional courseware (Table 8.2). Although based on a small number of observation intervals, the pattern does illustrate the importance of examining instructional characteristics in the context of specific uses of technology (Table 8.3).

Reports that technology use supports more challenging student work were supported only by our pilot data for language arts.

• In language arts, tasks were somewhat more challenging and students' responses were somewhat longer when computers were in use (for word process-

TABLE 8.1
Instructional Contexts in Two Elementary Subjects When Computers Were Versus Were Not in Use (Percentage of 5-min Intervals)

Subject Area	*Computers in Use*	*Computers Not in Use*
	Classroom Organizations	
Language arts *(N)*	*(23)*	*(122)*
Teacher led	.04	.69
Independent	1.00	.27
Cooperative	–	.05
Student led	–	–
Mathematics *(N)*	*(24)*	*(49)*
Teacher led	.17	.71
Independent	.46	.33
Cooperative	.38	.14
Student led	–	–
	Instructional Roles	
Language arts *(N)*	*(23)*	*(122)*
Direct	–	.48
Facilitate	.65	.32
Mathematics *(N)*	*(24)*	*(49)*
Direct	.17	.76
Facilitate	.38	.12

TABLE 8.2
Instructional Contexts in Elementary Mathematics for Two Uses of Computers
(Percentage of 5-min Intervals When Computers Were in Use)

Observation Category	*Instructional Software*	*Applications*
N	*(24)*	*(24)*
Classroom organizations		
Teacher led	.04	.69
Independent	1.00	.27
Cooperative	–	.05
Student led	–	–
Instructional roles		
Direct	.17	.50
Facilitate	.38	.50

ing). In mathematics, tasks were somewhat less challenging and students' responses were somewhat shorter on computer: Students were primarily using instructional courseware for practice of basic skills.

In summary, instructional patterns observed in these high access classrooms differed both by subject area and by the nature of computer use.

Model-Driven Descriptions of Instructional Change

Our instrument is designed to provide documentation of instructional practices associated with technology use and changes in instructional practices over time. The value of the descriptions we produce is markedly enhanced when descriptions are guided by a model of instructional change: If patterns change over time as predicted by a model, our results provide validation for the model; if patterns are inconsistent with a model of change, our results suggest needed revisions in the model.

In this section, our examples illustrate an approach we are taking to model-driven methods of data analysis. We have drawn from two frameworks to help us articulate our expectations for instructional impact of high technology access.

Toward a Model of Instructional Change: Two Key Frameworks. Dwyer, Ringstaff, and Sandholz (1990) proposed a model of ACOT teacher change based on analyses of ACOT teachers' regularly dictated audiotape records of their ACOT experience. Dwyer and his colleagues proposed a five-phase process of instructional change:

- Entry: The technology is implemented and a team of teachers is selected.
- Adoption: Basic instructional patterns are maintained, with technology support for drill and practice and for word processing.

TABLE 8.3
Task Characteristics in Two Elementary Subjects When Computers Were Versus Were Not in Use (Percentage of 5-min Intervals)

Subject Area	*Computers in Use*	*Computers Not in Use*
	Levels of Instructional Intent	
Language arts *(N)*	*(23)*	*(122)*
Low	.04	.33
Medium	.91	.39
High	.09	.03
Mathematics *(N)*	*(24)*	*(49)*
Low	..42	.12
Medium	.55	.61
High	–	.02
		–
	Product Item Lengths	
Language arts *(N)*	*(23)*	*(122)*
Repeat/Copy	.04	.11
Select	.04	.08
Short	.26	.47
Medium	.70	.02
Long	.04	–
Mathematics *(N)*	*(24)*	*(49)*
Repeat/Copy	–	–
Select	.25	.26
Short	.71	.55
Medium	–	.10
Long	–	–

- Adaptation: Teachers find that their instructional program is completed more rapidly and efficiently, freeing time for exploration of new curricula and pedagogy.
- Appropriation: Computer expertise enables experimentation.
- Invention: Teachers invent and implement fundamentally new forms for learning and teaching.

These phases of instructional change can be interpreted as phases in which "technology push" leads to a succession of newly emerging instructional goals (Baker, 1988). The phase descriptions do not point consistently to particular causes or contexts of change, however. For example, "efficiency" is cited in the transition from adoption to adaptation, but it is not clear how teachers recognize it or choose then to depart from traditional practices. Nor is a particular model of "new forms of learning and teaching" proposed for the Invention Phase.

To provide that model, we adapted ideas from Scardamalia and Bereiter (in press; Scardamalia, Bereiter, McLean, Swallow, & Woodruff, 1989). In their vision of technology-supported instructional environments, technology is a valued resource that can support "learning goals" rather than "task goals." Activities are organized across disciplines, and resources support active construction of understandings via multiple and flexible representations of content. Classroom work requires considerable initiative from the learner over many days if not weeks, and students' products are often lengthy. Learners use a variety of resources, often working cooperatively or collaboratively, and teachers are more often facilitating and supportively guiding students' efforts.

How might our instrument provide descriptions of instruction that could validate—or suggest revisions of—Dwyer et al.'s phases of instructional change? Table 8.4 is an outline of instructional characteristics that can be documented with our instrument and that fit the phases of Dwyer's model, including our Scardamalia-and-Bereiter-like interpretation of Dwyer's "invention" phase. We do recognize that our indices provide only indirect evidence for the phase characteristics. The challenge is to create the best "fit" of the instrument to the model to be investigated, and then to supplement the quantitative observation findings with coordinated qualitative data.

Illustrative Results. Comparisons between language arts instruction at our elementary site and English instruction at our secondary site illustrate how inferences can be made regarding the fit of our observations to various stages. The patterns we found suggested an association between school level and degree of instructional innovation: Compared with the secondary teachers, the elementary level teachers in our samples appeared to be considerably further from the visionary model of inventive, instructional inquiry environments sketched previously.

Subject Area. At the elementary school level, only one core subject—science—was ever double-coded with language arts; field notes indicate that students were engaged in science writing 19% of the time. In contrast, at the secondary site, English was judged as integrated with another subject—social studies—66% of the time.

Resources in use. At the elementary level, the resources in use tended to be textual and not technology. Computers were in use 16% of the time. Computers were used exclusively for applications; constructive writing tools—word processing—were the applications in use. There were no observations of software providing other forms of representation (e.g., graphics) or multirepresentational technologies such as laserdisc, video, or audio. Because children were observed to be engaged in drawing and other art and even music activities

TABLE 8.4
Best Fit of the Observation Tool to Dwyer et al.'s (1990) Phases of Instructional Change

OBSERVATION CATEGORY	*ENTRY (Implementation of Technology Selection of a Team of Teachers)*	*ADOPTION (Traditional Instruction Instructional Courseware Word Processing)*	*ADAPTATION (More Rapid Completion of Instruction Time Freed for Exploration)*	*APPROPRIATION (Experimentation with New Curriculum and Technology Supported Pedagogy)*	*INVENTION (Learning as Inquiry Knowledge-Building Communities Supported by Technology)*
Subject areas	Isolated	Isolated	Isolated Consideration of interdisciplinary possibilities	Experimentation with interdisciplinary work	Integration of subjects interdisciplinary work
Resources	Traditional texts	Traditional texts Instructional courseware Word processing	Traditional texts Instructional courseware Word processing Local experimentation with other applications and simulations	Declining reliance on texts and instructional courseware Word processing Increasing use of other applications and simulations Experimentation with multimedia Increasing used of print and media resources	Print and media resources Applications software Integrated, interactive multimedia Telecommunications

Task characteristics	Low or moderate challenge Multiple-choice or short answer responses	Low or moderate challenge Multiple-choice or short answer responses	Low or moderate challenge Multiple-choice or short answer responses Written compositions of increasing length	Decreasing assigning of basic skills and multiple-choice or short answer tasks Written compositions of increasing length Experimentation with more challenging and lengthier projects	Frequent opportunities for challenging, open-ended, lengthy projects
Classroom organization	Teacher led Independent	Teacher led Independent	Teacher led less frequent Independent Experimentation with cooperative work	Teacher led less frequent Independent Experimentation with cooperative and collaborative work	Cooperative and collaborative work quite common
Instruction and support roles	Directing Facilitating limited to students' independent work	Directing Facilitating limited to students' independent work	Directing less frequent Facilitating more frequent, and increasingly extended to students' independent writing	Directing less frequent Facilitating more frequent, with experiments in specific techniques such as conferencing	Facilitating roles most frequent, and include conferencing and joint problem solving Use of telecommunications to support interchange with people outside the classroom

associated with their language arts curriculum, what we found is that teachers were not yet exploiting the potential of technology to support these same activities.

At the secondary site, the resources in use were also more often textual than technology. Computers were in use here 36% of the time, again exclusively for applications. Here, however, there was some variety in type of applications—word processing (81% of computer time), HyperCard (56% of computer time), and graphics (62% of computer time). In addition, occasional use of interfacing multirepresentational technologies was noted—audio (6% of computer time) and scanners (69% of computer time). Thus at the secondary site we did observe some technology-based tools for multirepresentational activities.

Classroom Organization. At the elementary level in language arts, classrooms were generally organized for independent work, and teachers utilized computers heavily as support for independent work (Table 8.5). Cooperative work was very rare, and although truly collaborative projects were observed

TABLE 8.5
Instructional Contexts for English/Language Arts at Two School Levels When Computers Were Versus Were Not in Use (Percentage of Intervals)

Level	*Computers in Use*	*Computers Not in Use*
	Classroom Organizations	
Elementary *(N)*	*(23)*	*(122)*
Teacher led	.04	.69
Independent	1.00	.27
Cooperative	–	.05
Student led	–	–
Secondary *(N)*	*(16)*	*(29)*
Teacher led	.06	.86
Independent	.81	–
Cooperative	.62	–
Student led	.12	.13
	Instructional Roles	
Elementary *(N)*	*(23)*	*(122)*
Direct	–	.48
Facilitate	.65	.32
Secondary(*N)*	*(16)*	*(29)*
Direct	.06	.90
Facilitate	.81	–

Note. Observations were recorded every 5 min at the elementary level, and every 10 min at the secondary level.

(jointly produced products), these activities were not technology supported. At the secondary level in English, classrooms were generally organized for independent work with computer use, and teacher-led instruction off computer. Although cooperative activities were not uncommon on computer, none of these was a collaborative activity.

Instruction and Support Roles. At both the elementary and the secondary levels, teachers were predominantly facilitating instruction when students were on computers, directing instruction when off computer (Table 8.5). Students were engaged in productive peer interaction more often with computer support (Table 8.6).

Nature of Students' Work. At the elementary level, the language arts tasks were rated predominantly as either medium or low in instructional intent. Thus, teachers tended to assign well-structured activities with teacher-defined criteria for completion (Table 8.7). Although teachers were utilizing word processing as support for students' writing, activities in which students participated substantively in planning and coordinating their work were rarely observed. Similarly, students' responses were generally either short or medium in length, and whereas task length tended to be longer with computer support, it was rarely judged as long in any resource context.

In contexts of computer support at the secondary level, although well-structured activities with teacher-defined criteria for completion were most common, ill-structured activities (high) were not uncommon (Table 8.7). Similarly, students' responses were observed to vary in length, including long. In contexts without computer support, the very low frequency of any recorded observation for instructional intent or response length reflects the finding that students in the

TABLE 8.6
Percentage of Students Engaged in Task-Related Peer Interaction During English/Language Arts at Two School Levels When Computers Were Versus Were Not in Use (Estimates Averaged Over Observed Intervals)

Level	*Computers in Use*	*Computers Not in Use*
Elementary *(N)*	*(23)*	*(120)*
Independent work	.43	.36
Cooperative work	–	.63
Secondary *(N)*	*(16)*	*(29)*
Independent work	.52	.20
Cooperative work	.50	–

Note. Observations were recorded every 5 min at the elementary level, and every 10 min at the secondary level.

TABLE 8.7
Task Characteristics for English/Language Arts at Two School Levels When Computers Were Versus Were Not in Use (Percentage of Observed Intervals)

Level	*Computers in Use*	*Computers Not in Use*
	Levels of Instructional Intent	
Elementary *(N)*	*(23)*	*(122)*
Low	.04	.33
Medium	.91	.39
High	.09	.03
Secondary *(N)*	*(16)*	*(29)*
Low	.56	.24
Medium	.69	–
High	.44	–
	Product Item Lengths	
Language arts *(N)*	*(23)*	*(122)*
Repeat/Copy	.04	.11
Select	.04	.08
Short	.26	.47
Medium	.70	.02
Long	.04	–
Mathematics *(N)*	*(16)*	*(29)*
Repeat/Copy	.81	.24
Select	.69	.21
Short	.69	–
Medium	.69	–
Long	.69	–

Note. Observations were recorded every 5 min at the elementary level, and every 10 min at the secondary level.

secondary classrooms were rarely producing any assigned product without computer support.[2]

Interpretation: A Role for Subject Matter Expertise in Teaching. Why might secondary teachers be more able to create opportunities for technology-supported, constructive student work? To provide a possible explanation for the results, and therefore a possible explanation for instructional change as described by a model like Dwyer et al.'s phase model, we return again to work of Scardamalia and Bereiter.

Scardamalia and Bereiter (in press) argued that students engaged in constructive inquiry must be provided with resources representing multiple kinds of expertise. The kinds of expertise articulated—subject matter, curriculum, and pedagogical—can be distributed among teachers, students themselves, and in-

[2]Note that only *observable* student work was coded for instructional intent or response length. We did not consider listening, reading, watching, or taking notes to be codable for these variables.

structional materials. Thus, although teachers are not seen as solely responsible for providing expertise, as contributors to the design of instructional environments, their expertise certainly helps them to know what is needed to support a given project. Moreover, their own engagement in building personal scholarship—subject matter expertise—provides a model to students of knowledge-building activities.

Scardamalia and Bereiter did not address directly how kinds of expertise can support constructive uses of technology. It is reasonable to assume, however, based on their arguments, that understandings of a subject's concepts and methods enable teachers to envision how technology might support inquiry within that discipline. If so, then the differences we found in technology use between the elementary- and secondary-level teachers are not surprising given typical differences in subject area training and specialization for teachers at each level. Elementary teachers are curricular and pedagogical generalists within a tradition where curriculum has been defined as a set of discrete facts and concepts not typically based on disciplinary expertise. The secondary teachers are likely to have somewhat greater subject matter knowledge by virtue of the training required of them for certification. Secondary teachers also focus their curriculum development efforts within one subject area. It is likely, then, that subject matter expertise, together with an instructional focus within one subject area, supported ACOT secondary teachers' appropriation of technology's capabilities to support knowledge building and inquiry.

Both sets of teachers, however, have yet to exploit the full potential of technology for fostering deep understanding of subject matter content. There was evidence of some instructional innovation at the secondary level, but the patterns tended to suggest local experimentation (adaptation/appropriation) rather than comprehensive revision (invention). Further work is needed to understand how subject matter expertise, among a range of other factors, plays a role in teachers' construction of new conceptions of instructional environments.

FUTURE DIRECTIONS

Our larger goal is to develop methods to document the emergent impact of technology on classroom instruction and on student, teacher, and parent outcomes. In this chapter, we described one new tool, our classroom observation instrument, and we demonstrated its value for documenting instruction. We provided two illustrations of its potential uses: documentation of commonly reported observations of instruction in high access classrooms, and validation of models of the role of technology use in instructional change.

The ultimate usefulness of our instrument depends both on its coordination with other kinds of qualitative data gathering and on its validation through planned contrasts, either with classrooms utilizing technology in very different ways or with the ACOT sites themselves over time. Accordingly, we "triangulate" our observations with detailed field notes, teachers' reflections on their instruction in questionnaires and in interviews, and curriculum documentation through analysis of students' and teachers' portfolios. Validity is inferred from comparative analyses of these data sources, from comparisons of ACOT observations collected over time, and from observations of technology from observations of contrasting sites (Gearhart & Herman, 1989, 1991; Herman, Gearhart, & Baker, 1988) where there are differences in both degree and organization of technology access (Herman, Gearhart, & Valdes, 1991).

Through its "snapshot" representations of classroom activities, the instrument holds considerable promise as a tool for teachers' professional development as well as for research. ACOT teachers who have piloted the current scannable paper version find it is not difficult to learn to use, and they report that the process of observing with our tool has a positive impact on their understandings of their teaching. The challenge now is to facilitate the rapid translation of teachers' observations into graphs and tables. Using a Macintosh Powerbook as a platform, Dwyer and his colleagues at Apple (Dwyer, Reilly, & Yocam, 1992) are currently adapting the observation tool for teachers' observations of their peers. The outcome will be a tool that helps to bridge the worlds of teachers and researchers, a tool that enhances the likelihood of instructional documentation that can inform improvements in methods of teaching.

ACKNOWLEDGMENTS

This chapter is based on presentations for the June 1990 Open House, Apple Classrooms of Tomorrow, Cupertino, CA, and the September 1990 Technology Assessment Conference, UCLA. The work reported in this chapter was supported in part by the Advanced Development Group of Apple Computer, Inc. and in part by a contract from the Defense Advanced Research Projects Agency (DARPA), administered by the Office of Naval Research (ONR), to the UCLA Center for the Study of Evaluation/Center for Technology Assessment. However, the opinions expressed in this report are solely those of the authors and do not necessarily reflect the positions of Apple Computer, DARPA, or ONR, and no official endorsement by those organizations should be inferred. This research also was supported in part under the Educational Research and Development Center Program cooperative agreement R117G10027 and CFDA catalog number 84.117G as administered by the Office of Educational Research and Improvement, U.S. Department of Education. The findings and opinions expressed in this report do not reflect the position or policies of the Office of Educational Research and Improvement or the U.S. Department of Education.

Our thanks to the teachers who have permitted us to observe in their classrooms and to our associates who have provided helpful feedback during the research: Laurie Desai, Sharon Dorsey, David Dwyer, Margaret Rogers, Robert Tierney, and Keith Yocam.

REFERENCES

Baker, E. L. (1988, April). *Sensitive technology assessment of ACOT.* Paper presented at the annual meeting of the American Educational Research Association and the International Association for Computing in Education, New Orleans.

Baker, E. L., Gearhart, M., & Herman, J. L. (1990). *The Apple classrooms of tomorrow: 1989 UCLA evaluation study (Report to Apple Computer).* Los Angeles: UCLA Center for the Study of Evaluation.

Baker, E. L., Gearhart, M., & Herman, J. L. (1991). *The Apple classrooms of tomorrow: 1990 UCLA evaluation study (Report to Apple Computer).* Los Angeles: UCLA Center for the Study of Evaluation.

Baker, E. L., & Herman, J. L. (1988). *Implementing STAR: Sensible technology assessment/research (Report to Apple Computer).* Los Angeles: UCLA Center for the Study of Evaluation.

Baker, E. L., & Herman, J. L. (1989, April). *The ACOT report card: Effects on complex performance and attitude.* Paper presented at the annual meeting of the American Educational Research Association, San Francisco.

Baker, E. L., Herman, J. L., & Gearhart, M. (1988). *The Apple classrooms of tomorrow: 1988 UCLA evaluation study (Report to Apple Computer).* Los Angeles: UCLA Center for the Study of Evaluation.

Baker, E. L., & Niemi, D. (1990, April). *Validating a hypermedia measure of knowledge representation.* Paper presented at the annual meeting of the American Education Research Association, Boston.

Baker, E. L., & Niemi, D. (1991, April). *Assessing deep understanding of history and science through hypertext.* Paper presented at the annual meeting of the American Education Research Association, Chicago.

Cazden, C. B. (1986). Classroom discourse. In M. C. Wittrock (Ed.), *Handbook of research on teaching* (pp. 432–463). New York: Macmillan.

Cazden, C. B., John, V. P., & Hymes, D. (Eds.). (1972). *Functions of language in the classroom.* New York: Teachers College Press.

Collins, A. (1991, September). The role of computer technology in restructuring schools. *Phi Delta Kappan, 73*(1), 28–36.

Dunkin, M., & Biddle, B. (1974). *The study of teaching.* New York: Holt, Rinehart & Winston.

Dwyer, D. C., Reilly, B., & Yocam, K. (1992). *Implementation of the UCLA/ACOT observation tool on a Mac PowerBook.* Personal communication.

Dwyer, D. C., Ringstaff, C., & Sandholtz, J. (1990, April). *The evaluation of teachers' instructional beliefs and practices in high-access-to technology-classrooms.* Paper presented at the annual meeting of the American Educational Research Association, Boston.

Evertson, C. M., & Green, J. L. (1986). Observation as inquiry and method. In M. C. Wittrock (Ed.), *Handbook of research on teaching* (pp. 162–213). New York: Macmillan.

Flanders, N. (1970). *Analyzing teaching behavior.* Reading, MA: Addison-Wesley.

Gearhart, M., Herman, J. L., Baker, E. L., Novak, J. L., Whittaker, A. W. (1990, April). *A new mirror for the classroom: The effects of technology on instruction.* Paper presented at the annual meeting of the American Education Research Association, Boston.

Gearhart, M., & Herman, J. L. (1989). *Belridge DACOTT 21/20 Project: 1988–89 Evaluation Report. Report to Belridge School District.* Los Angeles: UCLA Center for the Study of Evaluation.

Gearhart, M., & Herman, J. L. (1990). *The UCLA/ACOT classroom observation tool: Manual.* Unpublished manuscript, Center for the Study of Technology Assessment, University of California, Los Angeles.

Gearhart, M., & Herman, J. L. (1991). *Belridge DACOTT 21/20 Project: 1989–90 Evaluation Report. Report to Belridge School District.* Los Angeles: UCLA Center for the Study of Evaluation.

Gearhart, M., Herman, J. L., Whittaker, A. K., & Novak, J. R. (1991, April). The effects of high access on instruction. In D. Dwyer (Chair), *The impact of technology on classroom activities and interactions: Restructuring instruction?* Symposium conducted at the annual meeting of the American Educational Research Association, Chicago.

Giesen, P., & Sirotnik, K. A. (1979). *The methodology of classroom observation in a study of schooling* (A study of schooling in the United States (Tech. Rep. No. 5). Los Angeles: University of California, Graduate School of Education.

Good, T., & Brophy, J. (1984). *Looking in classrooms* (3rd ed.). New York: Harper & Row.

Goodlad, J. I., Sirotnik, K. A., & Overman, B. C. (1979). A study of schooling: Some findings and hypotheses. *Phi Delta Kappan, 64,* 465–470.

Goodlad, J. I., Sirotnik, K. A., & Overman, B. C. (1983). A study of schooling: An overview. *Phi Delta Kappan, 61,* 176–178.

Green, J., & Wallat, C. (1981). Ethnography and language in educational settings. Mapping instructional conversations. In J. Green & C. Wallat (Eds.), *Ethnography and language in educational settings.* Norwood, NJ: Ablex.

Hawkins, J., & Sheingold, K. (1986). The beginning of a story: Computers and the organization of learning in classrooms. In J. A. Culbertson & L. L. Cunningham (Eds.), *Microcomputers and education* (pp. 40–57). Chicago: University of Chicago Press.

Herman, J. L. (1988, April). *The faces of meaning: Teachers', administrators', and students' views of the effect of ACOT.* Paper presented at the annual meeting of the American Educational Research Association and the International Association for Computing Education, New Orleans.

Herman, J. L., Gearhart, M., & Valdes, R. (1991, April). *The effects of technology in bilingual classrooms.* Paper presented at the 1991 annual meeting of the American Educational Research Association, Chicago.

Herman, J. L., Gearhart, M., & Baker, E. L. (1988). *Belridge DACOTT 21/20 Project: 1988 Evaluation Report. Report to Belridge School District.* Los Angeles: UCLA Center for the Study of Evaluation.

Herman, J., Heath, T. M., Valdes, R. M., & Brooks, P. E. (1990). *Los Angeles Unified School District Information Technology Division: Model Technology Schools Project—Bell Complex. 1989–90 Research and Evaluation Report.* Los Angeles: University of California, Center for the Study of Evaluation.

Mehan, H. (1979). *Learning lessons.* Cambridge, MA: Harvard University Press.

Scardamalia, M., & Bereiter, C. (in press). Higher levels of agency for children in the zone of proximal development: A challenge for the design of new knowledge media. *Journal of the Learning Sciences.*

Scardamalia, M., Bereiter, C., McLean, R. S., Swallow, J., & Woodruff, E. (1989). Computer-supported intentional learning environments. *Journal of Educational Computing Research, 5*(1), 51–68.

Sinclair, J. M., & Coulthard, R. M. (1975). *Towards an analysis of discourse.* London: Oxford University Press.

Stallings, J. A. (1975). Implementations and child effects of teaching practices in Follow Through classrooms. *Monograph of the Society for Research in Child Development, 40,* (7–8).

Stallings, J. A. (1976). How instructional processes relate to child outcomes in a national study of Follow Through. *Journal of Teacher Education, 27,* 43–47.

Stallings, J., & Giesen, P. A. (1974, April). *A study of confusability in codes in observational measurement.* Paper presented at the annual meeting of the American Educational Research Association, Chicago.

Stallings, J., & Kaskowitz, D. (1974). *Follow Through classroom observation evaluation 1972–1973.* Palo Alto, CA: Stanford Research Institute.

9 Evaluating the Apple Classrooms of Tomorrow[SM]

Eva L. Baker
Maryl Gearhart
Joan L. Herman
University of California, Los Angeles/CRESST

BACKGROUND

The Apple Classrooms of Tomorrow[SM] (ACOT[SM]) project was initiated in classrooms at five school sites in 1985 as a program of research on the impact of interactive technologies on teaching and learning. Originally conceived as a program to study what happens when "tomorrow's" resources are routinely available in classrooms, ACOT provided students and teachers an Apple computer both at school and at home. Sites were selected by ACOT staff to represent a range of student, school, and community characteristics. Elementary sites were established in northern California's Silicon Valley, a Tennessee suburb, an urban Tennessee community, and a rural Minnesota location; the secondary site is located within a major city in Ohio. The process of site selection differed across sites, although all sites and their participating teachers were required to demonstrate their interest and willingness to participate.

Although the project has expanded over time to encompass a larger and more diverse set of efforts, key components at all sites have been the provision of high technology access, site freedom to develop technology-supported curriculum and pedagogy as appropriate to site goals, and the resulting study of what happens when technology support is readily available to students and teachers. ACOT has encouraged instructional innovation, emphasizing to participating teachers the potential of computers to support student initiative, long-term projects, access to multiple resources, cooperative learning, and instructional guidance rather than stand-up teaching.

From 1987 through 1990, UCLA conducted a series of evaluation studies focused on the five original ACOT sites (Baker, Gearhart, & Herman, 1990,

1992, 1993; Baker, Herman, & Gearhart, 1988, 1989). Assessment of ACOT presented a continual challenge to what is meant by "formative evaluation," requiring ongoing attention to new goals, new modes of instructional transaction, and new outcomes as they evolved. ACOT's evolutionary character required both close-up interaction with sites to understand the changes that were occurring and new tools that could capture these changes and their outcomes.

Our approach to the study of ACOT effectiveness was one of triangulation. Recognizing the imperfections of existing measures and the constraints on the real-world laboratories in which ACOT was implemented, we employed a strategy to assess progress based on a range of measures and multiple benchmarks. Comparisons of ACOT students' basic skills performance to nationally reported norms were one approach; comparisons of student progress and achievement over time were another; comparisons of ACOT classrooms with demographically similar classrooms were still another information point; gathering data on classroom practices and parents' background characteristics to help explain student outcomes was yet another. Our strategy was inherently developmental. We started with standard measures and then developed an expanded set of measurement tools to capture ACOT as it evolved. Creating alternative indices of classroom process and student outcomes was a key component in our assessment strategy.

Thus, key attributes of the UCLA evaluation were:

- Collection and analysis of a broad range of potential student outcomes.
- Collection and analysis of such information over time.
- Linking outcome data with information on instructional process to provide explanatory power for findings.
- Linking multiple indicators of key outcomes to strengthen the validity of findings.
- Combining the strengths of both quantitative and qualitative methodologies.
- Using the known characteristics of existing measures as a means of developing and validating new measures.
- Providing uniform data collection strategies and measures across the diverse ACOT sites, but reserving places for interests, measures, and effects unique to each site.

Four basic questions guided the work:

1. What is the impact of ACOT on students?
2. What is the impact of ACOT on teachers' practices and classroom processes?

3. What is the impact of ACOT on teachers professionally and personally?
4. What is the impact of ACOT on parents and home life?

This chapter summarizes the findings of our core evaluation from 1987 through 1990. (Reports of substudies focused on the design of new measures are referenced in our conclusions.) Our inferences have been challenged by the concurrent evolution of ACOT goals, the need for development of new measures, the resistance of comparison classrooms to participation, and year-to-year changes in project organization at some of the sites.

METHODS

Overview

Data collection was initiated in the spring of 1988 with the administration of a range of existing student outcome measures with well-known characteristics. Student outcomes assessed in the initial year included (a) achievement on standardized tests, (b) performance in written composition, and (c) student attitudes. Results were used to provide a baseline for comparison with subsequent administrations in 1989 and 1990. Results also provided a basis for evaluating the usefulness of the information these kinds of measures can produce, and various of the student measures contained in the initial baseline battery were later replicated, revised, replaced, or supplemented as we gained understanding of ACOT outcomes and their appropriate measurement.

Comparison groups were identified by the fall of 1988 for most classrooms at most sites, but because the criteria for their selection varied as a function of site-specific constraints and because participation was often problematic, interpretation of comparison data required utmost caution. Table 9.1 contains the distribution of ACOT and comparison grade levels.

To provide evidence of ACOT impact on teachers and instruction and on parents and home activities, teacher and parent surveys were administered in the spring of both 1989 and 1990. Using a quantitative classroom observation method developed in 1988–1989, classrooms were observed at two sites in 1989–1990 (and in 1990–1991, as a follow-up to our core evaluation). Both the survey and observation data provided an explanatory context for the student outcome results.

Student Achievement

Iowa Tests. The Iowa Tests of Basic Skills were selected as the norm-referenced tests because, compared with other norm-referenced instruments, they best allowed us to compare students' performances across the many grade

TABLE 9.1
Distribution of ACOT and Comparison Sites by Year and Grade Level

		Year					
		1988		*1988-1989*		*1989-1990*	
Site	*Comparison*	*ACOT*	*Comparison*	*ACOT*	*Comparison*	*ACOT*	*Comparison*
A	Same district	1-3	–	1-4	3-4	1-4	1-4
B	Same district	4S[a]-4	–	4S-4	4S-4	4	4
C	Same district	5-6	–	4-6	4-6	4-6	5-6
D	Similar district	5-6	–	5-6	5-6	5-6	–
E	Same school	9-10	–	9-11	9-10	9-12	–

[a]4S was a special education fourth-grade class. In 1988, no data were collected from this class.

levels of ACOT. At the elementary level, we focused on four subtests that reflected core emphases at most sites: Vocabulary, Reading Comprehension, Mathematics Concepts, and Work-Study Skills/Visual Materials. At the secondary level, we chose two subtests, Vocabulary and Social Studies. Four sites agreed to administer the Iowa Tests, although at some sites only selected ACOT grade levels completed them, limiting our potential for analysis. Beginning with the spring of 1988, tests were administered to ACOT and comparison students in the fall (incoming students) and spring.

Writing. Students responded to writing prompts that asked for either narrative, descriptive, persuasive, or expository writing. In 1988 and 1988–1989, students provided samples of three genres at each site. In 1990, the sites specified the genres most emphasized at each grade level. The writing prompts were derived from those used in the International Association for the Study of Educational Achievement (IEA) Study of Written Composition (Baker, 1987).

Because the IEA study included national samples of students in Grades 6 and 10, ACOT students' essays in Grades 5 and up were rated on analytic scales employed in the IEA study, and results were compared with IEA national samples. Beginning in the fall of 1988, the essays of the youngest ACOT students (Grades 2–4) were rated with an analytic rubric developed by a southern California district for third- and fifth-grade narrative writing; the scales were derived from the same sources as the IEA scales. Results for ACOT students were compared with results from students in this southern California district.

Student Attitudes

The normed measures were administered on the same schedule as the Iowa Tests (mentioned earlier). All surveys were administered in the spring. The following five approaches were used to assess student attitudes:

1. Normed measures: School Attitude Measure (*SAM*) is a survey instrument published by Scott-Foresman consisting of five scales: Motivation for Schooling; Academic Self-Concept, Performance-Based; Academic Self-Concept, Reference-Based; Sense of Control; and Instructional Mastery. SAM is normed for Grades 4–12 and was administered to grades within this range. Self-Concept and Motivation Inventory (SCAMIN) is a self-report survey instrument published by Person-O-Metrics, Inc. (Dearborn Heights, MI) consisting of four scales at the early elementary level (Achievement Needs, Achievement Investment, Role Expectations, and Self-Adequacy). It is normed for K–12 and was administered to grades below fourth.
2. UCLA Student Questionnaire (spring 1990 only): Closed- and open-ended item content addressed a range of possible affective outcomes, some containing specific reference to technology impact, and others not.
3. Student attendance and mobility patterns were examined for sites that were able to provide us these data.
4. Teacher questionnaire and interview items were analyzed for teachers' perceptions of students' attitudes.
5. Parent questionnaire and interview items were examined for parents' perceptions of students' attitudes.

Teachers' Practices, Perceptions, and Attitudes

Questionnaires. UCLA-designed surveys were administered to ACOT teachers in the spring of both 1989 and 1990 and adapted for administration to comparison teachers. The 1989 questionnaire focused on curricular practices, perceptions of students' achievement, and perceived professional growth and stress. In 1988 teachers were also asked to complete the Occupational Stress Inventory (Psychological Assessment Resources, Lutz, FL). The 1990 teacher questionnaire focused on changes in curriculum and teaching practices, sources of influence on educational practice, perceptions of students' achievement, and perceived stress. The rate of return varied markedly by site and group.

Classroom Observations of Instructional Practice. The observation scheme was designed in 1988 to capture the nature of instructional tasks, the roles of teachers, the nature of social relationships, the variety of resources, and the responses of students (Gearhart, Herman, Baker, Novak, & Whittaker, chap. 8).

Major categories of the scheme include subject area of instruction, classroom organization, teachers' instructional roles, symbol systems in use, length of students' responses, the level of challenge of students' work, the variety of resources in use, and students' responses to the activities (appropriateness of behavior, focus and investment, productivity of peer interaction). The observations are recorded in timed intervals (5 min for elementary level, 10 min for secondary level) and supplemented with field notes.

Impact on Parents and the Home

UCLA-designed surveys were administered to ACOT parents in the spring of both 1989 and 1990 and adapted for administration to comparison parents. Both closed- and open-ended items addressed parents' perceptions of the impact of ACOT on their children, parental aspirations, and uses of the home computer. The rate of return varied considerably by site and group, and response by comparison parents was particularly weak. In 1990, only two sites agreed to distribute the questionnaires to comparison parents.

FINDINGS

To accommodate limitations on chapter length, we have adopted three strategies for reporting results. First, we provide an overview of the results for all measures employed in the core evaluation. Second, we illustrate specific findings that readers of our reports have found particularly interesting or unique. Third, in our conclusions we provide readers with references to companion research and development projects focused on the design of new assessments and evaluation methods.

Constraints

Firm conclusions about the effects of ACOT on student and other outcomes are constrained by a number of factors:

- ACOT was implemented in a relatively small number of classrooms, typically only one at a particular grade level, dispersed over an intentionally diverse set of school sites; thus ACOT effects were confounded by district requirements, teachers' influences, curriculum selection, school ambiance, and the characteristics of students, among other factors.
- Identification and participation of comparison classrooms were problematic.
- There were occasional site requests for adaptations of our instrumentation (particularly for the 1989–1990 year), adaptations that challenged meaning-

ful comparisons with national samples and interpretation of longitudinal comparisons.

- Finally, at some sites there were changes made from year to year in classroom and/or grade level ACOT participation that rendered longitudinal comparison inappropriate.

Nonetheless, we felt that some inferences were possible.

Student Outcomes

Summary. The ACOT program appeared as effective in promoting commonly measured student outcomes as the more typical instructional programs provided by the comparison sites. ACOT students had at least maintained their performance levels on standard measures of educational achievement in basic skills and had sustained positive attitudes. We drew these conclusions from measures addressing the traditional activities of schooling: standardized achievement tests, writing assessments, normed student attitude instruments, and archival data on student attendance.

There were several variations on this overall theme:

- There was evidence of *site-specific impact.* For example, in 1990, of the three sites that year with comparison students, only one site showed ACOT students' performance on achievement tests higher on some subtests; at a different site, ACOT students' performance was lower than that of comparison students for some subtests.
- There was evidence of *domain-specific ACOT impact across sites.* Where we had comparison classrooms, there were indications that ACOT enhanced students' writing abilities at one site in 1988–1989 and at three sites in 1989–1990 (for a total of three sites across the 2 years). Impact in other domains of student achievement was negligible or nonexistent.
- There was evidence that *project maturity* may have mediated more consistent cross-site ACOT impact on students' attitudes. Compared with the results of 1988–1989, the 1989–1990 results for ACOT student attitudes were more positive and more consistent across sites. In 1990 the attitudes of most ACOT children were at or above the national median for our normed measures, and at one of our two sites with comparison students (for these measures), there was evidence of improvement over time for ACOT students only.

Selected Results: Writing. Because so many ACOT teachers and students reported enthusiasm for word processing and an increased emphasis on writing instruction, we had reason to expect project impact on students' writing performance. Subsequent meta-analyses of research on use of word processors indicates a small but significant effect (Bangert-Drowns, 1993). We have therefore selected for presentation key results from our analyses of student writing performance, drawn from the final evaluation year (1989–1990). The complex task of interpretation is well-illustrated by the findings to be discussed.

We had several goals for this component of our evaluation: (a) follow students' growth from 1989 to 1990; (b) focus on assessment of the genres most emphasized at each site; and (c) continue exploration of an experimental "writing process" version of the assessment that permits students to rewrite their essays on a second day. To accomplish goals (a) and (b), at each cycle of data collection students were assigned to write on particular genres (narrative, descriptive, persuasive, or expository); for any given genre, no student wrote on exactly the same topic more than once. To accomplish our third goal, students at the secondary site were provided the opportunity to revise their essays, and both the first and second drafts were scored.

All student essays were scored by one or two raters. A 6-point analytic scale was used for essays in Grades 2–4, enabling comparison with Grade 3 students from a school district in Southern California. A 5-point IEA analytic scale was used for essays in Grades 5–12, enabling comparison with results from a national sample of students in Grades 6 and 10. Indices of interrater agreement were excellent for both rubrics. We report results only for General Competence (Grades 2–4) and Overall Impression (Grades 5–12).

There were five approaches to data analysis. ACOT group means were (a) judged against the rubrics' definitions of competence, (b) compared with district or national samples, and (c) when possible, contrasted with comparison group means. In addition, (d) longitudinal comparisons were examined for those students who wrote on a genre on two or more occasions, and (e) first and second draft ratings were compared.

Judgments of Competence. Across sites, the mean spring 1990 ratings of many participating ACOT classrooms were equal to or greater than the rubrics' definitions of competence (3.5 for the six-point scale; 3 for the five-point scale) (Table 9.2). Exceptions were younger students at Site 1, students from Site 3—an urban, impacted minority site—and the descriptive writing of students at Site 4. Interpretation of the particularly high performances of students at Site 5 was compromised by the site's requested collaboration with us in the design of each writing prompt.

Comparisons of ACOT with District or National Samples. Most ACOT classrooms fared as well or better than our district and national samples. Although the narrative scores of Grade 3 students at Site 1 (3.21) did not quite achieve the means of the comparison district students (3.41), the narrative, descriptive, and persuasive essays of Grade 6 students at Sites 3 and 4 were rated

TABLE 9.2
Means and Standard Deviations for Writing Tasks: Spring 1990

		Genre			
Site	*Grade*	*Narrative*	*Descriptive*	*Persuasive*	*Expository*
Six-point scale (competence = 3.5)					
1	B	2.40 (36) .62			
	C	3.21 (64) .87			
	D	4.02 (28) 1.02			
2	A	3.55 (46) .99			
3	A	2.61 (23) 1.07	3.13 (24 .83		
Five-point scale (competence = 3)					
3	B	2.62 (26) .55			
	C			2.85 (21) .76	
4	A	3.04 (28) .76	2.67 (35) .94		
	B	3.26 (42) .68	2.66 (43) .88		
5	A	3.43 (27) .74			
	B	3.65 (13) .69			3.17 (14) .47
	C				3.01 (30) .59
	D				3.74 (21) .32

Note. Writing of students in Grade 4 and below was scored on a six-point rubric. All other students' writing was scored with the five-point IEA rubric.

at levels the same as or higher than the IEA Grade 6 sample, and the narrative and expository essays of Site 5 10th-graders were rated at levels the same as or higher than the IEA Grade 10 students (Table 9.3).

Contrasts of ACOT with Comparison Students. Contrasts of ACOT and comparison students at three sites produced trends suggesting possible enhancement of writing competence associated with ACOT participation. At Site 1, students in Grade D (all of whom were second- or third-year ACOT) were performing at a slightly higher level than comparison students (Table 9.4), although this difference was not significant. There were no differences between these groups in growth over time (Table 9.5). (Note that at Site 1 ACOT's request that we limit the testing burden on individual children substantially reduced the number of students participating in the repeated measures analyses). At Sites 2

TABLE 9.3
Means and Standard Deviations for Writing Tasks: Comparisons of Spring 1990 ACOT Results With IEA Means (Five-point scale)

		Genre			
Grade	*Site*	*Narrative*	*Descriptive*	*Persuasive*	*Expository*
6	3			2.85 (21) .76	
	4	3.26 (42) .68	2.66 (43) .88		
	IEA	2.92 (1489) .82	2.68 (293) .73	2.10 (635) .78	
10	5	3.65 (13) .69			3.17 (14) .47
	IEA	3.46 (1291) .82			2.92 (1195) .88

Note. IEA tasks were administered in the fall or early winter.

and 3, ACOT students were outperforming comparison students in the spring (Tables 9.4 and 9.6), but only one grade level at Site 3 showed greater progress over time for ACOT students (Table 9.5).

Comparisons of ACOT First and Second Drafts. Supported by the ease of revision with word processing, the secondary site was particularly invested in our piloting a process version of the assessment. Whereas students' second drafts of their spring 1990 narratives were not different from their first (Grade 9: 3.56 vs. 3.43; Grade 10: 3.73 vs. 3.65), the second drafts of the expository essays of students in Grades 10 and 11 were more highly rated (Grade 10: 3.63 vs. 3.17, $p = .0086$; Grade 11: 3.40 vs. 3.01, $p = .0027$; Grade 12: 3.88 vs. 3.74).

Thus, overall, patterns of findings indicating ACOT impact on writing competency were present but inconsistent across sites and grade levels. Data were limited by site insistence on limiting the testing burden, collaborative design of some writing prompts, and spotty participation of comparison classrooms.

Selected Results: Students' Views of ACOT. Out attitude questionnaire included several open-ended items. Tables 9.7 and 9.8 contain the results: (a) elementary sites (*Are you glad to be an ACOT student? Why?*) and (b) secondary sites (*What's the best thing about being an ACOT student? What's the worst thing about being an ACOT student?*).

Across sites, students were likely to share positive feelings about ACOT participation (Table 9.7). Many responses showed appreciation for computer access, for the opportunity to become computer literate, and, for secondary students at Site 5, for ACOT's contributions to preparation for the future. How-

TABLE 9.4
Means and Standard Deviations for Writing Tasks: ACOT and Comparison Students
(Six-point scales)

	Narrative		*Descriptive*		*Persuasive*
Site and Grade	*Fall*	*Spring*	*Fall*	*Spring*	*Fall*
Site 1[G,GG]					
Grade B					
ACOT	1.69 (38)	2.40 (36)			
	.50	.62			
Comparison[C]	1.89 (77)	2.84 (91)			
	.48	.71			
Grade C					
ACOT	2.30 (60)	3.21 (65)			
	.64	.87			
Comparison		3.43 (67)			
		.80			
Grade D					
ACOT		4.02 (28)			
		1.02			
Comparison		3.54 (62)			
		.84			
Site 2					
Grade A					
ACOT[A]	2.50 (44)	3.55 (46)			2.51 (46)
	.65	.99			.69
Comparison	2.62 (27)	2.98 (25)			2.46 (28)
	.63	1.21			.75
Site 3					
Grade A					
ACOT[A]			2.61 (23)	3.13 (65)	
			1.07	.83	
Comparison			2.56 (45)	2.54 (32)	
			.84	.78	

[G]The mean ratings of grades participating at this time were significantly different; $p = .0001$.
[GG]The differences between ACOT and comparison students varied significantly among grade levels; p values ranged from .0004 to .0005.
[C]Comparison students' scores were higher than those of ACOT students; $p = .0420$.
[A]ACOT students' ratings were greater than those of comparison students; p values ranged from .0361 to .0086.

ever, by no means were students' views limited to the availability of computers: With the exception of Site 4, it was not uncommon for students to mention appreciation for learning a lot, their teachers, or unique methods of instruction. The climate that emerged in ACOT's school-within-a-school appeared to have special import for secondary level students at Site 5.

Secondary students at Site 5 were quite open with their critique of ACOT participation (Table 9.8). There were almost no complaints about technology use, although the scheduling of rooms to accommodate computer use was frustrating for some. Some students felt isolated from the rest of their high school classmates. The curriculum was more difficult than some had anticipated.

TABLE 9.5
Repeated Measures for Writing Tasks: ACOT and Comparison Students

		Time		
Site and Genre	*Grade and Group*	*Spring 1989*	*Fll 1989*	*Spring 1990*
Site 1	Grade C[T]			
Narrative[a]	ACOT	1.89		3.06
	Comparison	1.99		3.38
	Grade D[T]			
Narrative[a]	ACOT		2.00	3.75
	Comparison		2.44	3.53
Site 2	Grade A[T]			
Narrative[a]	ACOT		2.50	3.54
	Comparison		2.64	3.08
Site 3	Grade A			
Descriptive[a]	ACOT [TA]		2.41	3.12
	Comparison		2.60	2.50
Persuasive[b]	Grade C			
	ACOT	2.38		2.52
	Comparison	1.92		1.83

[a]Writing scored with six-point rubric.
[b]Writing scored with five-point IEA rubric.
[T]Students' scores increased over time: $p = .0001$.
[TA]Only ACOT students' scores increased over time: $p = .0406$.

TABLE 9.6
Means and Standard Deviations for Writing Tasks: ACOT and Comparison Students at Site 3
(Five-point IEA Scales)

	Narrative		Persuasive	
Grade and Group	*Fall*	*Spring*	*Fall*	*Spring*
Grade B				
ACOT[A]	2.23 (25) .49	2.62 (26) .55		
Comparison		2.08 (43) .47	1.52 (49) .52	
Grade C				
ACOT[A]			2.48 (21) .79	2.85 (21) .76
Comparison	2.40 (40) .43			1.73 (36) .61

[A]ACOT students' scores were higher than those of comparison students; $p = .0001$.

TABLE 9.7

ACOT Students Questionnaire Responses to "Are You Glad to be an ACOT Student" Why?: Percent of Students Sampled

	Site 1			Site 2	Site 3			Site 4		Site 5[1]			
Response	*Grade B*	*Grade C*	*Grade D*	*Grade A*	*Grade A*	*Grade B*	*Grade C*	*Grade A*	*Grade B*	*Grade A*	*Grade B*	*Grade C*	*Grade D*
(N)	(37)	(66)	(23)	(43)	(26)	(25)	(19)	(43)	(37)	(28)	(26)	(24)	(18)
Glad to be in ACOT	97	95	92	100	100	100	100	93	97	–	–	–	–
Why?													
No technology mention													
Positive/learning ("Learning a lot")	8	20	22	14	23	12	16	7	8	7	15	8	0
Pride/ACOT	3	5	0	0	4	4	5	9	5	7	8	17	0
Positive/ACOT ("Love ACOT")	32	15	4	26	27	16	32	12	24	4	4	8	17
Teachers/instruction	0	6	0	16	35		16	2	0	4	27	13	33
Climate	0	0	0	0	0	8	0	0	0	4	15	17	33
Student quality	0	0	0	0	4	4	0	0	0	0	0	0	0
Technology mention													
Positive/computers ("Love using computers")	41	36	48	44	19	32	20	44	47	32	15	21	11
Computer literacy	0	12	17	23	23	12	0	19	11	11	12	8	33
Preparation for the future	0	0	0	5	0	12	5	9	8	25	8	17	11
Computer games	0	6	0	2	4	8	5	5	0	0	0	0	0
Word processing	0	5	0	2	31	0	5	4	3	4	0	0	0
Ease of learning on computer	3	5	0	7	0	12	0	2	0	0	0	8	0
Home computer	0	6	0	0	4	20	0	0	3	11	12	4	6

[1]Question not asked at Site 5. The question "What is the best thing about being an ACOT student?" was substituted.

TABLE 9.8
ACOT Students' Questionnaire Responses to "What is the Worst Thing About Being an ACOT Student?: Percent of Students at Site 5

Response	*Grade A*	*Grade B*	*Grade C*	*Grade E*
(N)	(28)	(26)	(24)	(18)
No technology mention				
Negative feelings unspecified	11	8	4	6
Relationships with non-ACOT students	21	23	42	33
Program difficulty	25	35	38	38
Scheduling of periods and room changes	36	8	17	22
Teacher quality or methods	11	8	0	17
Visitors	0	8	0	0
Research demands	0	8	8	0
Technology mention				
Software too limited	4	4	0	0
Technical problems	4	0	0	6
Too much time on computers	4	0	8	0

Inferences Across Student Outcome Measures. The most reasonable interpretation of our complex findings was that ACOT enabled students to maintain their performance in core skill areas while they explored new areas. We viewed this result positively. First, the ACOT environment required both teachers and students to adapt to a host of new technological options. Student time spent in learning word processing and other software was time that otherwise would have been spent on traditional school subjects. Similarly, the time teachers needed to acquire technology skills and familiarity with software appropriate to individual and/or grade level needs or particular curricular objectives might have resulted in less time spent in curriculum planning. Time too may have been lost to occasional technical failures. Any of these short-term problems could have resulted in less-than-expected student academic growth or a temporary undermining of students' motivation and attitudes. Yet negative consequences on student outcomes were not in evidence.

Second, the ACOT experience appeared to be resulting in significant new learning experiences requiring higher level reasoning and problem solving (see instructional impact discussion later). Because more time in long-term, constructive activities may translate into less time in basic skills instruction, some decrement in basic skills test performance also might have been expected. From both these vantage points, then, maintenance of expected performance levels could be viewed as an accomplishment.

Effects on Teachers and Instruction

Our goal was to examine how characteristics of teachers and contexts interacted with ACOT's impact on teachers and instruction. From 1988 to 1989, our investigation relied on teacher questionnaires supplemented with field notes from site visits. Revised in 1989–1990, our second questionnaire focused on changes in practices, and an observation instrument was developed to document classroom activities in two sites.

Results from all measures indicated that the ACOT experience affected instruction and influenced teachers personally and professionally. At each site, ACOT represented a different pattern of opportunities for technology access, professional development, and restructuring of collegial roles and relationships, and our results reflected the impact of these site-specific implementations. However, in the summary to come, our results are reported as "broad brush" portraits of impact. Discussion of sites is precluded by space limitations; interpretation of sites was in any case made difficult by variation in survey returns and the virtual nonparticipation of comparison teachers.

Instructional Impact. Based on 1989 and 1990 surveys, ACOT teachers' reports of their classroom practices indicated fairly typical subject matter emphases and pedagogical methods, along with occasional experimentation with the use of technology to support innovative practices such as cooperative group work or long-term student projects. In 1990, teachers' self-descriptions of instructional change were consistent with many changes encouraged by ACOT: Teachers reported increases in classroom organizations and teaching methods that support student initiative and independence, decreases in traditional stand-up teaching and reliance on published teachers' guides, and changes in their uses of technology toward less frequent use of published instructional software and more frequent use of applications as well as computer-supported activities of their own design. There was evidence of influence other than ACOT as well, however: For instruction in core subject areas, there were site differences in use of state and district instructional guidelines that appeared to reflect variation in local pressures on student achievement. In addition, teachers acknowledged an impact of both computer access and national interest in writing instruction: Teachers reported teaching students more types of writing and a writing process approach.

Our quantitative observations provided us a direct view of technology's functions in instructional practice. Our results suggested effects mediated by teachers' prior practices and expertise (Gearhart, Herman, Baker, Novak, & Whittaker, chap. 8; Gearhart, Herman, Whittaker, & Novak, 1991). In one set of analyses, instructional patterns at an elementary ACOT site differed both by subject area and by the nature of computer use (e.g., use of instructional software vs. use of applications such as word processing). Our data suggested that the ACOT teachers were making motivated choices about resources and pedagogical methods based on subject area, and thus their classroom activities were not "technology-driven" in any simple way. In a second set of analyses, we found an association between school level and degree of instructional innovation: Compared with secondary ACOT teachers, the elementary-level ACOT teachers in our samples appeared to be considerably less innovative in technology-supported instruction.

Interpretation focused on the possible role of secondary-level teachers' greater subject matter expertise in instructional change.

Views of Project Impact. ACOT teachers were reasonably satisfied with their students' progress and generally positive in their views of the values of computer use for student learning. Nevertheless, ACOT teachers appeared to feel that computers alone do not assure student engagement or meaningful learning. For example, a number of teachers were not convinced that computer use helps students stay on task, or that students cheat less when using instructional software than when working in a workbook. Similarly, at a site with comparison teachers, ACOT teachers were less likely than comparison teachers to believe that computer use helps students grasp concepts easily or encourages students to think more. ACOT teachers' critiques of the ACOT project were diverse. Many teachers remarked favorably on the value of ACOT collegial relationships and the positive impact of computer use on productive student–teacher roles in the classroom. When describing weaknesses of the project, teachers focused most often on concerns about the productivity of staff relationships (both within ACOT teams and with other teachers in school), concerns for adequate curriculum coverage, need for better coordination of teacher planning, and lack of clarity of project goals. Compared with 1989 responses, critiques in 1990 were more distinctive reflections of each site's emphasis and project progress, suggesting that emerging clarity of project goals enabled increasingly differentiated project critiques. Table 9.9 illustrates the diversity of views expressed for one item, *What is your view of the strengths of the ACOT project?*

Views of Personal Impact. The project had considerable personal and professional impact on teachers, with reports of challenge and growth on the one hand and stress and demand on the other. Teachers remarked on a variety of benefits of the ACOT experience, for themselves as professionals and for their students, and appeared to be constructing new interpretations of their own and their students' abilities. Secondary teachers in particular appeared to be most actively revising their notions of students' roles in their own learning.

Effects on Parents and the Home

Parents' Perceptions of ACOT Impact. The ACOT parents who responded to our surveys reflected the diversity of parental backgrounds among the sites. Despite these differences in parents' education and occupation, and despite differences in ACOT project emphases, parents across sites were generally supportive of many aspects of the ACOT project and satisfied with their children's progress. Table 9.10 illustrates these patterns for parents' responses to an open-ended item, *What are the benefits of ACOT?* Parents felt that ACOT had benefited their children's knowledge of computers, attitudes toward learning, and achievement in some areas. There were some concerns about possible trade-offs

TABLE 9.9
ACOT Teachers' Views of ACOT's Strengths: Percent of Respondents

View	*Site 1*	*Site 2*	*Site 3*	*Site 4*	*Site 5*
(N)	(6)	(3)	(2)	(5)	(7)
Personnel strengths					
Teachers	0	67	0	40	28
Coordinators	0	0	0	20	0
ACOT colleague support	17	33	0	0	14
Other support	0	33	0	0	14
Enrichment of teaching content					
Curriculum	17	33	0	20	14
Teacher/student roles	0	0	0	20	28
Technology use	50	0	100	60	14
Student benefit					
Academic skills	17	0	0	0	0
Socioemotional growth	0	0	0	0	0
Peer learning	0	0	0	20	28
Computer skills	17	0	0	40	14

in curriculum coverage and, at the secondary site, students' isolation from the larger school community. Table 9.10 illustrates these responses for an item on ACOT drawbacks. Suggesting that parents' concerns about educational practice evolve as their children advance in school, parents' critiques of ACOT were more differentiated for students in upper elementary and secondary grades.

TABLE 9.10
ACOT Parents' Views of the Benefits and Drawbacks of ACOT: Percent of Respondents

View	*Site 1*	*Site 2*	*Site 3*	*Site 4*	*Site 5*
N	(109)	(32)	(9)	(128)	(51)
Benefits					
School performance	24	16	33	20	16
Attitudes	29	47	22	16	14
Context for learning	14	22	11	10	22
Social relationships	11	0	0	1	2
Computer knowledge	53	34	11	37	53
No benefit	0	0	0	0	0
Drawbacks					
School performance	11	6	0	11	16
Attitudes	4	0	0	2	0
Context for learning	23	13	11	21	33
Social relationships	1	0	0	2	22
Post-ACOT transmition	0	25	0	3	0
No drawback	46	31	55	36	33

Note. The categories of "No benefit" and "No drawback" indicate a parent's explicit mention of this view.

Use of the ACOT Home Computer. ACOT's provision of a home computer provided us with the unique opportunity to document family uses. Selected results from our 1990 survey are contained in Table 9.11. (Although the rate of return in 1989 was higher, the results from both surveys are similar.) There were site-specific patterns associated with level (elementary vs. secondary). Games, for example, were popular but dropped off in the upper grades at Site 5, perhaps because homework responsibilities were demanding. Similarly, use of word processing and graphics software—required for homework—were highest at Site 5, whereas use of instructional courseware was lowest.

At some sites ACOT parents reported that their children spent less time in play or watching TV than did children of comparison parents, but these results, if valid, may have reflected the kinds of families who applied for ACOT participation. ACOT home computers were used mostly by the ACOT children themselves, although, at an urban site where few homes would otherwise have had a computer, the computers were also used often by other family members and neighbors. Interest in computer use was generally maintained over time. Most family members used the computers for a variety of functions, including published software (games, instructional drill, computer literacy training, keyboarding) and applications (e.g., word processing, graphics); for ACOT children, the range of applications in use widened at the secondary level. Family interactions involving the computer were generally positive, although parents of upper-elementary and secondary-level students were more apt to feel unable to participate, unable to assist, and unable to understand what their children were doing.

THE CORE EVALUATION: IMPLICATIONS OF THE RESULTS

While we had hoped that the 1990 data collection would provide definitive findings, the following factors intervened to weaken our interpretations:

- The 1989–1990 data collection was designed to provide us repeated measurement of progress for many ACOT and comparison students. But the unexpectedly spotty 1989–1990 participation of comparison classrooms left us with empty data cells and limited understandings.
- Participating teachers were uncomfortable with certain of our core measures and requested revisions for the 1989–1990 data cycle. Expressing increasing confidence in the goals for the ACOT project at their sites, teachers were concerned about potential mismatches between their goals and our assessments. We were as invested in the design of assessment alternatives as they, but we recognized that changes in our measures put at risk our planned, 3-year, longitudinal evaluation design. To compromise, we reduced the testing burden on a site-by-site basis by limiting the number

TABLE 9.11
ACOT Children's Most Frequent Uses of the ACOT Home Computer: Percent of Parents Who Reported Having a Computer

	Site 1	Site 2	Site 3	Site 4	Site 5			
Use	*Grade C*	*Grade A*	*Grades Combined*	*Grade B*	*Grade A*	*Grade B*	*Grade C*	*Grade D*
(N)	(39)	(14)	(3)	(41)	(11)	(8)	(6)	(9)
Word processing	.31	.50	.00	.56	.54	.88	.83	.78
Games	.46	.64	.67	.68	.64	.62	.17	.22
Instructional activities	.46	.36	.67	.15	.18	.00	.00	.00
Drawing	.38	.14	.00	.27	.45	.38	.50	.44
Database	.05	.00	.33	.02	.09	.12	.00	.11
Spreadsheet	.02	.00	.00	.00	.00	.00	.33	.11
Electronic mail	.02	.00	.00	.02	.00	.00	.00	.00
Calendar	.02	.00	.00	.00	.00	.00	.00	.00

Note. Parents were asked to indicate the two most frequent uses.

of grade levels tested and accepting local district test results. In addition, we selected writing prompts based on site emphases on particular genres and topics. Although comparison among sites was never one of our objectives, comparisons over time within sites and to national norms were, and both of these were jeopardized by our design compromises.

There emerged from our results site-specific patterns in the outcome measures that begged for interpretation in the context of each site's particular focus and project thrust. But in the context of inadequate data, interpretations were more appropriately recast as questions for further study relating to school technology projects in general.

How Does the Organization and Focus of a Technology Project Affect the Process of Instructional Change?

A number of factors of possible relevance emerged in our study. *Organizational factors* included:

Scheduling. Longer or flexible class periods were helpful to student projects and interdisciplinary work.

Opportunity for team collaboration and planning. The more often that teachers could work together, the better it seemed for the coherence of the program.

School and district support. A district investment in instructional innovation or in technology appeared to ease technology-supported innovation within ACOT.

Physical plant. Technology was more readily utilized when access was easy; innovation appeared to be facilitated when settings could be reorganized for multiple purposes and groupings.

Differences in *project focus* included:

Curriculum area. A selective focus seemed to foster thoughtful implementation; efforts across the curriculum appeared overly ambitious and shallow (e.g., stand-alone use of off-the-shelf software).

Instructional goals. A focus on improving basic skills led to use of computer-based instructional software; an interest in enrichment resulted in "problem-solving" software or student choice of software; a focus on use of computer resources for authentic engagement in productive work required applications such as word processors, graphics programs, databases, and spreadsheets.

Because these factors varied unsystematically across ACOT sites and also interacted with local contexts, firm conclusions were inappropriate.

How Do Teachers' Knowledge and Beliefs Contribute to Instructional Uses of Technology Resources?

Across sites and classrooms, we found considerable variation in instructional uses of technology—variation in implementation across curricular areas, in uses for traditional (e.g., skill practice) versus nontraditional (constructive projects) student work, in choices among the many technology options available. In addition to the organizational factors already mentioned, differences among the teachers in their expertise and understandings of educational practice appeared to influence their technology implementation. For example, technology-supported innovation and experimentation appeared more likely among teachers who had not only technology skills but also—and quite critically—subject matter knowledge, curriculum knowledge (understandings of new methods of teaching a particular subject area), and competence with nontraditional pedagogy (e.g., cooperative grouping, student collaboration, long-term projects). Sound educational practice requires well-informed, solidly grounded rationale.

Why Do Students Vary in Their Affective Responses to Technology?

We found site-specific patterns of impact on students' attitudes, and, where students remained in ACOT for more than 1 year, suggestive evidence that positive impact, for some students, was limited to the first ACOT year only. It will be important to understand how technology use can contribute to sustained, productive student engagement.

How Should We Interpret the Results of Our Core Measures?

Here we confront complex and intertwined questions regarding (a) the meaning and validity of our measures, (b) the appropriateness of our core measures to ACOT goals, and (c) the effectiveness of the ACOT projects. Beyond the limitations of our data are judgments based on values that transcend any evaluation design. Certainly the core measures do not reflect well many of ACOT's goals. But what *do* they reflect, and are the competences assessed by traditional measures important outcomes for any school program? If traditional achievement measures can be interpreted as valid indices of basic skills, should we be concerned that our study produced little evidence of ACOT contribution to performance? It is difficult to ignore the test results for sites where students are performing consistently and well below the national median; it is also difficult to ignore results when they show a decline (as we found at one site). These results do suggest that ACOT programs must continue to strive to enhance certain basic skills. Nevertheless, at the same time we must move forward in the design of assessments that reflect the complex outcomes emphasized by ACOT's constructivist philosophy (Herman, in press).

Our work with ACOT was undertaken in the early phases of what has become a paradigm shift in views on the forms and functions of assessment—away from reliance on quantitative achievement indices representing aggregates of mastered skills and concepts, and toward performance-based measures that are intended to reflect the kinds of work valued in the workplace and community. Our questions about the fit of existing measures to ACOT teachers' objectives were to be answered by triangulating the results of different assessment approaches and by viewing the utility of any measure for the assessment of technology impact as a question for research. We knew that the design and investigation of new methods would take time. But we soon discovered that we were not alone in our quest for good measures. Our evaluation efforts corroborated the worries and resistance of teachers and administrators who were disenchanted with information produced from existing measures.

Thus ACOT, and the challenging assessment questions it has posed, stimulated the collaborative development of promising new measures and provided a context that fostered the exploration of instructional and assessment possibilities. By the spring of 1990, our focus shifted from evaluation to research and development. Two lines of development have been particularly promising.

Hypermedia Assessment. Since 1989, we have been developing a new hypermedia measure of knowledge representation. Implicit in this work is a recognition that students may display competence by a range of strategies and behaviors, and that present testing methodologies may seriously underrepresent the abilities of many students. It seemed clear to us that computational support might provide a means of overcoming some of the feasibility and cost problems associated with alternative measurement of complex learning outcomes such as deep understanding, explanation, and problem solving. Our hypermedia assessment project was an outgrowth of a long-term, U.S. Department of Education-funded study of the assessment of deep understanding through the use of extended student essays (Baker, Aschbacher, Chang, Niemi, & Weinstock, 1991; Baker, Freeman, & Clayton, 1991).

To investigate whether HyperCard representations could provide a more direct measure of students' understanding, the ACOT assessment study used HyperCard as a knowledge representation tool for two studies, one involving 11th-grade students (Baker, Niemi, & Novak, 1991) and the other 11th- and 12th-graders (Baker, Niemi, & Herl, chap. 7). Students used specially designed stacks to construct concept maps of history and chemistry knowledge before writing essays on given topics. Scoring systems, some of them automated, for analyzing these HyperCard products have been developed with the goal of exploring the possibility that hypertext might supplement or substitute for essay measures of deep understanding. Results suggest that one can make valid inferences about the structure of students' knowledge from HyperCard stacks and there may be students whose knowledge is more validly represented in hypertext than in essays or standardized test items.

Portfolio Assessment. When we designed our core evaluation, there existed no method of assessing the quality of ACOT students' long-term writing and multimedia projects. Therefore, we initiated a collaboration with ACOT teachers to develop portfolio methods for assessing students' compositions (Baker, Gearhart, Herman, Tierney, & Whittaker, 1991). At one elementary-level ACOT site, students began collecting their work in both a "working" portfolio and a smaller, student-selected "showcase" file. The showcase portfolios provided the context for an integrated set of activities: student self-assessment (prompted by sentence frames), teacher–student conferencing, informal parent–child conferencing, and parent assessment (responses to open-ended questions).

There were two, somewhat disappointing, outcomes of the initial 1989–1991 phase of the portfolio project. First, in the classroom, although the portfolio activities did enhance students' and teachers' interest in writing and multimedia composition, we nevertheless documented little change in teachers' assessment practices. Teachers viewed the portfolio process as a means of encouraging student investment and pride, and a context for communicating with parents. Second, outside the classroom, we found the portfolios to have, at best, limited potential for large-scale assessment of students' writing competency. We asked raters experienced in the assessment of traditional writing samples to judge the quality of children's portfolio collections (Gearhart, Herman, Baker, & Whittaker, 1992; Herman, Gearhart, & Baker, in press). Although ratings were achieved with high levels of agreement and yielded the expected grade-level differences in students' competence, raters were able only to assign a single, holistic score. Because they could not assign scores for any of the analytic subscales to the mixed collections of stories, summaries, letters, and poetry, there emerged a need to create a well-motivated match between portfolio contents and rubrics for assessment.

Therefore in 1991–1992 we began the systematic development of genre-based assessments for collections of children's compositions. By working with grade-level teams (K–1, 2–3, and 4–6) as well as a schoolwide steering committee, our goals are to develop agreement at the school level on standards that constitute writing competence and methods to track student's progress toward those standards (Dietel, Gearhart, & Herman, 1992; Gearhart, Herman, Baker, Wolf, & Whittaker, 1992; Gearhart, Herman, Wolf, & Baker, 1992).

SUMMARY

Our evaluation studies of five Apple Classrooms of TomorrowSM sites have documented the challenges of assessing the effects of technology access on teaching and learning. In the context of evolving ACOT goals and site-specific project strategies, our strategy was to employ a coordinated set of standard measures as we developed additional tools to capture emerging modes of instruction and unanticipated outcomes.

Although not conclusive, our work uncovered patterns of effects that suggest new lines of inquiry. We close with two examples. First, findings that ACOT may have had selective positive impact on writing and on student attitudes, particularly as projects matured, made evident the need to examine the impact of specific instructional uses of technology on specific outcomes. Second, findings that changes in practice were consistent with ACOT goals, such as increased use of cooperative groups and decreased "stand-up" directing teaching, did not reveal the particular role of technology in these changes. These emergent questions affirm the critical importance of measures sensitive to particular technology project designs and contexts.

ACKNOWLEDGMENTS

We are grateful for the cooperation of ACOT site coordinators and the teachers, principals, parents, and students at ACOT and comparison schools. Warm thanks to our talented research staff: John Novak, Andrea Whittaker, David Niemi, Howard Herl, Darlene Galluzzo, and Patricia Mutch.

The research reported in this chapter was supported in part by the Advanced Development Group of Apple Computer, Inc. and in part by a contract from the Defense Advanced Research Projects Agency (DARPA), administered by the Office of Naval Research (ONR), to the UCLA Center for the Study of Evaluation/Center for Technology Assessment. However, the opinions expressed in this report are solely those of the authors and do not necessarily reflect the positions of Apple Computer, DARPA, or ONR, and no official endorsement by these organizations should be inferred. This research also was supported in part under the Educational Research and Development Center Program cooperative agreement R117G10027 and CFDA catalog number 84.117G as administered by the Office of Educational Research and Improvement, U.S. Department of Education. The findings and opinions expressed in this report do not reflect the position or policies of the Office of Educational Research and Improvement or the U.S. Department of Education.

REFERENCES

Baker, E. L. (1987, September). *Time to write: Report of the US-IEA Study of Written Composition*. Paper presented at the IEA General Assembly, Teachers College, New York.

Baker, E. L., Aschbacher, P., Chang, S. C., Niemi, D., & Weinstock, M. (1991, April). *Validating measures of deep understanding of history scored by teachers*. Paper presented at the annual meeting of the American Educational Research Association, Chicago.

Baker, E. L., Freeman, M., & Clayton, S. (1991). Cognitive assessment of history for large-scale testing. In M. C. Wittrock & E. L. Baker (Eds.), *Testing and cognition* (pp. 131–153). Englewood Cliffs, NJ: Prentice-Hall.

Baker, E. L., Gearhart, M., & Herman, J. L. (1990). *The Apple Classrooms of TomorrowSM: 1989 Evaluation study* (Report to Apple Computer, Inc.), Los Angeles: University of California, Center for the Study of Evaluation/Center for Technology Assessment.

Baker, E. L., Gearhart, M., & Herman, J. L. (1992). *The Apple Classrooms of TomorrowSM: 1990 Evaluation study* (Report to Apple Computer, Inc.). Los Angeles: University of California, Center for the Study of Evaluation/Center for Technology Assessment.

Baker, E. L., Gearhart, M., & Herman, J. L. (1993). *The Apple Classrooms of TomorrowSM: The UCLA evaluation study* (CSE Tech. Rep. No. 353). Los Angeles: University of California, Center for the Study of Evaluation/Center for Technology Assessment.

Baker, E. L., Gearhart, M., Herman, J. L., Tierney, R., & Whittaker, A. K. (1991). Stevens Creek portfolio project: Writing assessment in the technology classroom. *Portfolio News, 2*(3), 7–9.

Baker, E. L., Herman, J. L., & Gearhart, M. (1988). *The Apple Classrooms of TomorrowSM: 1988 Evaluation study* (Report to Apple Computer, Inc.). Los Angeles: University of California, Center for the Study of Evaluation/Center for Technology Assessment.

Baker, E. L., Herman, J. L., & Gearhart, M. (1989, April). *The ACOT report card: Effects on complex performance and attitude.* Presentation at the 1989 annual meeting of the American Educational Research Association, San Francisco.

Baker, E. L., Niemi, J., & Novak, J. (1991, July). *Hypertext as a strategy for teaching and assessing knowledge representation.* Paper presented at the NATO Advanced Research Workshop, Enschede, The Netherlands.

Bangert-Drowns, R. L. (1993). the word processor as an instructional tool: A meta-analysis of word processing in writing instruction. *Review of Educational Research, 63*(1), 69–93.

Dietel, R., Gearhart, M., & Herman, J. L. (1992). *Portfolio assessment and high technology* (Video). Los Angeles: University of California, Center for the Study of Evaluation.

Gearhart, M., Herman, J. L., Baker, E. L., & Whittaker, A. K. (1992). *Writing portfolios at the elementary level: A study of methods for writing assessment* (CSE Tech. Rep. No. 337). Los Angeles: University of California, Center for the Study of Evaluation.

Gearhart, M., Herman, J. L., Baker, E. L., Wolf, S. A., & Whittaker, A. K. (1992, April). *Portfolios: An approach to the assessment of technology-supported composition.* Paper presented at the annual meeting of the American Educational Research Association, San Francisco.

Gearhart, M., Herman, J. L., Whittaker, A. K., & Novak, J. R. (1991, April). *The effects of high access on instruction.* Paper presented at the annual meeting of the American Educational Research Association, Chicago.

Gearhart, M., Herman, J. L., Wolf, S. A., & Baker, E. L. (1992, April). *Writing portfolios at the elementary level: A study of methods for writing assessment.* Paper presented at the 1992 annual meeting of the American Educational Research Association, San Francisco.

Herman, J. L. (in press). Issues in assessing the effects of technology in school reform. In B. Means (Ed.), *Technology's role in school reform.* San Francisco: Jossey-Bass.

Herman, J. L., Gearhart, M., & Baker, E. L. (in press). Assessing writing portfolios: Issues in the validity and meaning of scores. *Educational Assessment.*

10 Assessing Programs That Invite Thinking

Susan R. Goldman
James W. Pellegrino
John Bransford
Vanderbilt University

INTRODUCTION AND OVERVIEW

Our goal in this chapter is to discuss issues of evaluation that have arisen in the context of a problem-solving series that has been developed by the Cognition and Technology Group at Vanderbilt's Learning Technology Center. The research and development of the series, called "The Adventures of Jasper Woodbury," began as an effort to offer an alternative to traditional classroom contexts where students often fail to see the relevance of what they are learning to real life (e.g., Cognition and Technology Group at Vanderbilt, CTGV, 1990). A major goal of the series is to generate excitement about mathematics and science among middle school students (Grades 5, 6, 7) and help them develop powerful skills of mathematical problem formulation and problem solving. A second goal is to help students see how content domains that are traditionally taught as separate "subjects" are actually integrated in the real world (CTGV, 1991a, 1991b, 1993). Solving real problems often involves using math, science, geographic, and economic concepts together. The Jasper problem-solving series provides opportunities for students to experience such interdependence. A third goal of the series is to motivate students to become proficient in the "basic skills" of mathematics. We say more about each of these goals in subsequent sections of the chapter.

The introduction of the series as part of the regular classroom curriculum has brought to the forefront critical assessment and evaluation issues. As evidenced by the other chapters in this volume, there is considerable interest in implementing new technologies in instructional settings and assessing the effects they have on instructional outcomes. What remains less clear is how to classify the various dimensions along which these technology implementations vary and their resultant impacts. This will be critical for sorting out ways in which new technologies can and should be implemented and for realistic expectations about the outcomes that can or should be assessed. For example, a technology can be implemented to improve instructional management, or as a new way to deliver a current set of curricular materials, or as a means of providing new curricular content, or for meeting new curricular objectives. The extent to which a technology is designed to substitute for, enhance, or change the extant curriculum will very much determine how we assess its impact. The Jasper series is designed to have the potential to relate to extant curricula in all three of these ways. As a result, the assessment issues we discuss are directly related to the purposes for which the technology is used.

Just as a new technology can be implemented for multiple purposes, it is important to recognize that typical forms of assessment do not fall into a single functional category. Rather, they reflect multiple objectives, including (a) instructional management and monitoring, (b) program evaluation and accountability, and (c) selection and placement functions (L. B. Resnick & D. P. Resnick, 1991). Because different objectives may demand different forms of instrumentation, the situation becomes complex very quickly if "double duty" is demanded of an assessment instrument originally designed to meet only a single objective. For example, there is the increasing realization that assessment for purposes of program evaluation and accountability has come to drive the nature of the curriculum and modes of instruction (e.g., Fredericksen & Collins, 1989; L. B. Resnick & D. P. Resnick, 1991). In response to this realization, the argument is made that curriculum reform can be brought about by changing the "accountability" assessments. The curriculum will change in response to changes in what the tests test. This realization suggests a fourth function for assessment: as an instrument of instructional reform. However, to accomplish curricular reform in this way, attention must also be directed at instructional management and monitoring issues.

Although we touch on each of these issues in this chapter, our main focus is the nature of the challenges we face in designing assessments that map onto new curricular goals, such as emphasizing complex thinking and problem-solving skills and integrating concepts across curricular areas. The challenges exist for both the instructional management and monitoring functions as well as the program evaluation and accountability functions. In short, even when the curricular materials and model are developed and implemented it is no simple chore to design a reasonable and workable set of assessment instruments. Yet it is critical that we provide some measures of student learning. We have found that the Jasper activities themselves suggest several useful evaluation paths.

To place our ideas in context, we first briefly review the inadequacies of traditional mathematics problem-solving instruction and traditional forms of assessment. We then describe the Jasper series, the types of assessment challenges it raises, and our ideas about some possible solutions. We conclude the chapter by proposing an approach to assessment that we call SMART Assessment (Scientific and Mathematical Arenas for Refining Thinking) and describing a pilot test of the concept.

The Need to Reassess Mathematics Curricula and Assessment

It is useful to consider whether it is necessary to introduce an alternative mathematics curriculum, especially if that alternative creates the need to alter assessment and evaluation practices. There are multiple sources of evidence that there is indeed a need to reassess and modify current mathematics curricula, particularly for problem solving. As a nation, we face the problem that the mathematical and scientific literacy of our students is falling short of what is needed for today's technological world. The National Science Board Commission on Precollege Education argues that the "basics" for the 21st century must go beyond reading, writing, and arithmetic and must include communication, higher problem-solving skills, and scientific and technological literacy. In addition, the commission emphasizes that these new basics are needed by all students, "not only the few for whom excellence is a social and economic tradition" (see also Shakhashiri, 1989). Results from national studies reinforce the need to increase achievement in mathematics and science (e.g., Fourth National Assessment of Educational Progress in Mathematics; National Assessment of Educational Progress, NAEP, 1983; Kouba et al., 1988). In addition, business leaders with whom we have discussed these issues agree that the "new basics" are needed for all our students, not simply a select few.

Along with the perceived need to increase levels of mathematics and science literacy, recent reports published by the National Council of Teachers of Mathematics (NCTM, 1989) and other professional organizations (American Association for Advancement of Science, AAAS, 1989; National Research Council, 1989) call for changes in the way mathematics is taught. These reports base their recommendations on a number of factors, including (a) projected demographic changes in the nation's student population—the population from which tomorrow's workers will be drawn; (b) changing economic and technical needs of our society; (c) results from National Assessment of Educational Progress (1983) studies and cross-cultural comparisons that show serious deficiencies in the mathematical abilities of U.S. school children (Dossey, Mullis, Lindquist, & Chambers, 1988; McKnight et al., 1987); and (d) a change in our views of how children learn mathematics.

For example, there is now clear evidence that when learning takes place in meaningful contexts the result is knowledge that is longer lasting and more accessible than knowledge learned in nonmeaningful settings (see for discussion Bransford et al., 1988; CTGV, 1990; Sherwood, Kinzer, Bransford, & Franks,

1987a). Furthermore, learning seems to take place best in familiar contexts and through active involvement on the part of the learner (CTGV, 1992b; L. B. Resnick & Klopfer, 1989; Scardamalia & Bereiter, 1991). The Jasper series anchors complex mathematical problem solving in narratives that depict real people and real problems whose solution requires mathematical problem solving. The Jasper series stands in sharp contrast to the materials used for topics in traditional mathematics problem-solving instruction.

Problems With Traditional Approaches to Mathematics Problem Solving

Traditional approaches to teaching problem solving in mathematics involve the use of standard word problems such as those typically found in textbooks. There are several problems with these approaches. One was captured by Gary Larson in his *Far Side* cartoon series. He created the concept of "Hell's Library" and populated it with nothing but book after book of mathematical story problems. Many students agree with his assessment and, as former students, many teachers do, too.

A second problem with traditional word problems is related to the fact that many students do not see them as real. The problems often seem contrived and arbitrary and have nonrealistic goals. For example, one written problem we saw recently involved a trip to a haunted house. The setting seemed interesting. The problem posed to the students was: "There are 3 cobwebs on the first floor and 4 on the second floor. How many are there altogether?" This is hardly the kind of concern one would have when visiting a haunted house!

Data suggest that traditional word problems do not help students think about realistic situations. Instead of bringing real-world standards to their work, students seem to treat word problems as abstract situations and often fail to think about constraints imposed by real-world experiences (e.g., Charles & Silver, 1988; Silver, 1986; Van Haneghan & Baker, 1989). For example, Silver (1986) noted that students who were asked to determine the number of buses needed to take a specific number of people on a field trip divided the total number of students by the number that each bus would hold and came up with answers like $2\frac{1}{3}$. The students failed to consider the fact that one cannot have a functioning $\frac{1}{3}$ bus. Research also indicates that students have great difficulty with problems involving two or more steps and with problems that require reasoning skills (Kouba et al., 1988).

An additional problem with traditional word problems is that they *present* problems to be solved rather than help students learn to *generate and pose* their own problems. For example, imagine the task of going from one's house to a breakfast meeting at 8:30 a.m. in a new restaurant across town. What time should one leave? To answer this question, one has to generate subproblems such as "How far away is the meeting?", "How fast will I be able to drive?", and so on. The ability to generate the subproblems to be solved is crucial for real-world mathematical thinking (e.g., Bransford & Stein, 1984; Brown & Walter, 1990; Charles & Silver, 1988; Porter, 1989; Sternberg, 1986). Word problems typical of textbooks do not develop such generative skills.

The problem of nonmotivating and relatively ineffective materials for teaching mathematical problem solving has consequences that are particularly damaging during the middle school years. Educational experiences at this age may have important effects on students' interests and decisions about the kinds of courses to take in high school, which in turn affect career choices.

Problems with Traditional Approaches to Assessment

There are concomitant problems with traditional approaches to assessing mathematics and there is a growing consensus regarding the need for new procedures for assessing thinking in content areas such as mathematics and science (e.g., AAAS, 1989; NCTM, 1989). This concern is partially grounded in the understanding that educational reform and procedures for assessment are intimately linked (e.g., Bransford, Goldman, & Vye, 1991; Frederiksen & Collins, 1989; L. B. Resnick & D. P. Resnick, 1991). This is manifested by the reality that tests frequently control (and limit) the nature of what is taught as well as how it is taught. For example, most standardized tests used to compare schools, districts, and states focus primarily on factual knowledge and isolated subskills. Teachers work to help students prepare for these tests, but the procedures for doing this frequently focus on the acquisition of isolated facts and procedures such as the memorization of (a) content-specific vocabulary and formulas (e.g., endoskeleton, acute angle), (b) decontextualized steps in scientific inquiry (e.g., hypothesis generation, hypothesis testing, etc.), and (c) key proofs that are likely to show up on various standardized mathematics exams (see Schoenfeld, 1985, 1989).

In addition, the existing tests provide models for teachers who may try to construct their own formative assessments for purposes of improving their instruction. This tends to proliferate a specific objectives approach to instruction. Furthermore, because most tests are so highly dependent on language and reading skills (e.g., verbally presented word problems and descriptions of science phenomena), they often mask the potential of many individuals, especially minorities, who may have considerable potential for mathematics and science (e.g., Shavelson et al., 1991). In recent commentaries on typical testing approaches, the claim has been made that tests are therefore quite possibly harmful to children (e.g., Mokros, 1991), they engender an increasingly negative set of attitudes on the part of many students as they progress through school (e.g., Paris, Lawton, Turner, & Roth, 1991), and they are impediments to restructuring efforts designed to produce authentic student achievement (e.g., Newmann, 1991). Overall, typical approaches to assessment promote the kinds of teaching and learning that are incompatible with new curricula and instructional objectives reflecting a constructivist point of view (e.g., CTGV, 1990, 1992c; Papert, 1980; Piaget, 1952; L. B. Resnick & Klopfer, 1989). Many now agree with the following quotation from L. B. Resnick and D. P. Resnick (1991), which summarizes this general dissatisfaction: "The very idea of using test technology as it has developed over the past century may be fundamentally inimical to the real goals of educational reform" (p. 37).

THE ADVENTURES OF JASPER WOODBURY: AN ALTERNATIVE TO TRADITIONAL MATHEMATICAL PROBLEM-SOLVING INSTRUCTION

With the concerns about traditional mathematics problem-solving instruction and assessment in mind, we set out to create a context for mathematical problem solving that would be meaningful, realistic, and motivating to students. The Jasper Woodbury series provides that context and is based on design principles that evolved over a 5-year period of research and development (e.g., Bransford, Franks, Vye, & Sherwood, 1989; Bransford, Sherwood, Vye, & Rieser, 1986; Bransford, Sherwood, & Hasselbring, 1988; Bransford et al., 1988; CTGV, 1990; Sherwood et al., 1987a; Sherwood, Kinzer, Hasselbring, & Bransford, 1987b; Sherwood et al., 1987c; Young et al., 1989). Over the course of that time period, we have expanded the instructional functions for the Jasper series beyond complex mathematical problem solving. The Jasper series has evolved into a flexible instructional environment that can function on two additional levels:

- As an expandable curriculum in math, providing motivation and opportunities for anchoring component skills practice to a real problem.
- As a production tool for creating links across the curriculum to other subject areas such as geography, science, history, reading, and writing.

The Jasper series is video based and can be used at several levels of technological sophistication. At the high technology end, the adventures are on videodiscs and the videodisc player is controlled via a microcomputer. This level of technology enables all three instructional functions mentioned earlier. One step down involves videodisc-based adventures with the player controlled by a hand-held remote controller or by a bar code reader. This level enables two instructional functions (complex problem solving and extensions in math).

Seven Design Principles for Adventures That Invite Thinking

The design principles for the Jasper problem-solving series were selected because they enable teachers to create the kinds of mathematical problem-solving experiences for students that are recommended in the NCTM curriculum standards (1989). The NCTM document contains a number of important suggestions for changes in the types of classroom activities and mathematical content to be emphasized in mathematics classes. Suggestions for changes in classroom activities include more emphasis on complex, open-ended problem solving; communication and reasoning; more connections of mathematics to other subjects and to the world outside the classroom; more uses of calculators and powerful computer-based tools such as spreadsheets and graphing programs for exploring relationships (as opposed to having students spend an inordinate amount of time calculating by hand). The design principles for our videos were developed to make it easier for teachers to provide such opportunities. National Council of Teachers of Mathematics has also published standards for assessment that complement the curriculum standards (NCTM, 1989). So too with the Jasper series: Our challenge has been to design assessment contexts that measure the complex mathematics problem-solving activities that the adventures are designed to develop.

We describe seven design principles. Although they can each be described separately, in practice they mutually influence one another and operate as a Gestalt rather than as a set of independent features of the materials. Similar sets of design principles are applicable in many curricular domains, including science and literacy (CTGV, 1990, 1992a; McLarty et al., 1990).

1. Video-Based Presentation Format. Although some excellent work on applied problem solving has been conducted with materials that are supplied orally or in writing (e.g., Lesh, 1981), we decided to use the video medium for several reasons. First, it is easier to make the information more motivating because characters, settings, and actions can be much more interesting. Second, the problems to be communicated can be much more complex and interconnected using the video medium than they can be in the written medium—this is especially important for students who are below par in reading. Modern theories of reading comprehension focus on the construction of mental models of situations; students can more directly form a rich image or mental model of the problem situation when the information is displayed in the form of dynamic images rather than text (McNamara, Miller, & Bransford, 1991; Sharp et al., 1992). Teachers who have worked with our pilot videos have consistently remarked that our video-based adventures are especially good for students whose reading skills are below par. In addition, because there is a great deal of rich background information on the video, there is much more of an opportunity to notice scenes and events that can lead to the construction of additional, interesting problems that involve connections to other content areas (e.g., Bransford et al., 1988; CTGV, 1993). Note that the use of video, in and of itself, does not detract from students' motivation to acquire reading skills. In fact, video can be used quite effectively to enhance literacy skills (e.g., CTGV, 1991a; McLarty et al., 1990; Sharp et al., 1992).

2. Narrative Format. A second design principle is the use of a narrative format to present information. One purpose of using a well-formed story is to create a meaningful context for problem solving (for examples of other programs that use a narrative format, see Lipman, 1985; Bank Street College of Education, 1984). Stories involve a text structure that is relatively well understood by middle school students (Stein & Trabasso, 1982). Using a familiar text structure as the context for presentation of mathematical concepts helps students generate an overall mental model of the situation and lets them understand authentic uses of mathematical concepts (e.g., Brown, Collins, & Duguid, 1989).

3. Generative Learning Format. The stories in the Jasper series are complete stories with one exception. As with most stories, there is setting information, a slate of characters, an initiating event, and consequent events. The way in which these stories differ is that the resolution of the story must be provided by students. (There is a resolution on each disc, but students see it only after attempting to resolve the story themselves.) In the process of reaching a resolution, students generate and solve a complex mathematical problem. One reason for having students generate the ending—instead of guiding them through a modeled solution—is that it is motivating; students like to determine for themselves what the outcome will be. A second reason is that it allows students to actively participate in the learning process. Research findings suggest there are very important benefits from having students generate information (Soraci et al., 1994; Slamecka & Graf, 1978; Soraci, Bransford, Franks, & Chechile 1987).

4. Embedded Data Design. An especially important design feature of the Jasper series—one unique to our series and instrumental in making it possible for students to engage in generative problem solving—is what we have called *embedded data* design. All the data needed to solve the problems are embedded somewhere in the video story. The mathematical problems are not explicitly formulated at the beginning of the video and the numerical information that is needed for the solutions is incidentally presented in the story. Students are then able to look back in the video and find all the data they need (this is very motivating). This design feature makes our problem-solving series analogous to good mystery stories. At the end of a good mystery, one can see that all the clues were provided, but they had to be noticed as being relevant and put together in just the right way. The numerical information includes whole and mixed numbers and different forms of symbolic representation of quantity. The four basic arithmetic operations are required to solve the problem. Hence, in the context of a meaningful and complex problem, students understand the need for proficiency in adding, subtracting, multiplying, and dividing. Among students for whom those skills are weak, we assume that discovering the usefulness of basic arithmetic skills is an important source of motivation to practice those very skills. (There is a real need for research on this issue.)

5. Problem Complexity. The Jasper videos pose very complex mathematical problems. For example, the first episode in the series contains a problem comprised of more than 15 interrelated steps. In the second episode, multiple solutions need to be considered by students in order to decide the optimum one. The complexity of the problems is intentional and is based on a very simple premise: Students cannot be expected to learn to deal with complexity unless they have the opportunity to do so (e.g., Schoenfeld, 1985). Students are not routinely provided with the opportunity to engage in the kind of sustained mathematical thinking necessary to solve the complex problem posed in each episode. The video makes the complexity manageable. We believe that a major reason for the lack of emphasis on complex problem solving (especially for lower achieving students) is the difficulties teachers face in communicating problem contexts that are motivating and complex yet ultimately solvable by students.

6. Pairs of Related Videos. The sixth design principle involves the use of *pairs* of related problem-solving contexts. The cognitive science literature on learning and transfer indicates that concepts acquired in only one context tend to be welded to that context and hence are not likely to be spontaneously accessed and used in new settings (e.g., Bransford, Franks et al., 1989; Bransford & Nitsch, 1978; Bransford, Sherwood, et al., 1986; Brown, Bransford, Ferrara, & Campione, 1983; Brown et al., 1989; Gick & Holyoak, 1980; Salomon & Perkins, 1989; Simon, 1980). In the Jasper series the content of each pair of episodes is similar. For example, the first two episodes deal with trip planning and require the use of distance, rate, and time concepts and their interrelationships, although the specific circumstances of the trips are quite different. A second pair of episodes deals with gathering, evaluating, and assembling data into a defensible "business" plan for a project. Being able to apply principles learned in the first episode of each pair to the second allows students to experience the fact that problem solving gets easier the second time around. Students can also be helped to analyze exactly what they were able to carry over from one episode to another and what was specific to each and not generalizable (e.g., Goldman & CTGV, 1991; Goldman et al., 1991; Goldman et al., in prep.).

7. Links Across the Curriculum. Each narrative episode contains the data necessary to solve the specific complex problem posed at the end of the video story. As well, the narration provides many opportunities to introduce topics from other subject matters. For example, in the trip planning episodes, maps are used to help figure out the solutions. These provide a natural link to geography, navigation, and other famous trips in which route planning was involved, for example, Charles Lindbergh's solo flight across the Atlantic. We return to the topic of links across the curriculum in our subsequent discussion of the Jasper classroom.

Complex Mathematical Problem Solving in the Trip Planning Adventures

Perhaps the best way to understand the design principles and the assessment issues they pose is to "walk" through the pair of episodes on trip planning. Each video has a main story that is approximately 17 min in length. The "end" of each video narration features one of the characters (Jasper in the first episode; Emily in the second) stating the problem that has to be solved; it is posed as a challenge and the students are to figure out the solution. (Note that a worked out solution is appended to the video story but students are not shown this until after they have solved the problem.) Please note that the verbal descriptions of these adventures fail to capture the excitement in them. In this case, a video is truly worth a thousand words.

Journey to Cedar Creek. This episode opens with Jasper Woodbury practicing his golf swing. The newspaper is delivered and Jasper turns to the classified ads for boats. Jasper sees an ad for a'56 Chris Craft cruiser and decides to take a trip to Cedar Creek where it is docked. He rides his bicycle to the dock where his small "row" boat, complete with outboard motor, is docked. We see Jasper as he prepares for the trip from his dock to Cedar Creek: He is shown consulting a map of the river route from his home dock to the dock at Cedar Creek, listening to reports of weather conditions on his marine radio, and checking the gas for his outboard. As the story continues, Jasper stops for gas at Larry's dock. Larry is a comical looking character who knows lots of interesting information. For example, as he hands Jasper the hose on the gas pump, he just happens to mention all the major locations where oil is found. When Jasper pays for the gas, we discover the only cash he has is a $20 bill. As Jasper makes his way up river, he passes a paddle-wheeler, a barge, and a tug boat, and some information is provided about each of these. Next, Jasper runs into a bit of trouble when he hits something in the river and breaks his sheer pin. He has to row to a repair shop where he pays to have the pin fixed. Later, Jasper reaches the dock where the cruiser is located and meets Sal, the cruiser's owner. She tells him about the cruiser and they take the boat for a spin. Along the way, Jasper learns about its cruising speed, fuel consumption, fuel capacity, and that the cruiser's temporary fuel tank only holds 12 gallons. He also learns that the boat's running lights don't work so the boat can't be out on the river after sunset. Jasper eventually decides to buy the old cruiser, and pays with a check. He then thinks about whether he can get to his dock by sunset. The episode ends by turning the problem over to the students to solve.

It is at this point that students move from passive televisionlike viewing to the active generation mode discussed earlier. They must solve Jasper's problem. Students have to generate the kinds of problems that Jasper has to consider in order to make the decision about whether he can get the boat home before dark without running out of fuel. The problem looks deceivingly simple; in reality it involves many subproblems. But all the data needed to solve the problem were presented in the video. For example, to determine whether Jasper can reach home before sunset, students must calculate the total time the trip will take. To determine total time, they need to know the distance between the cruiser and Jasper's home dock and the boat's cruising speed. The distance information can be obtained by referring to the mile markers on the map Jasper consulted when he first began his trip. The time needed for the trip must be compared to the time available for the trip by considering current time and the time of sunset, information given over the marine radio. The problems associated with Jasper's decision about whether he has enough fuel to make it home are even more complex. As it turns out, he does not have enough gas and he must plan for where to purchase some—at this point money becomes a relevant issue. In this manner, students identify and work out the various interconnected subproblems that must be faced to solve Jasper's problem.

Rescue at Boone's Meadow. The second Jasper episode on trip planning is equally complex and involves planning for a rescue. The story revolves around Emily, a friend of Jasper and Larry. Emily is learning to fly an ultralight; her instructor is Larry. When the story begins, we see Larry describing the plane. He tells Emily about the weight limitations of the plane, its fuel consumption, fuel capacity, airspeed, and so forth. Some days later, Emily makes her first solo flight, after which she, Jasper, and Larry celebrate over dinner. While eating, Jasper tells them of his plans to hike into the wilderness to go fishing. The next scene shows Jasper at this remote fishing area. The tranquillity of the scene is disturbed by the sound of a gunshot. Upon investigating, Jasper finds that an eagle has been shot and wounded. Jasper immediately radios Emily for help.

Again, at this point in the story students move from passive televisionlike viewing to an active generation mode. They must decide the fastest way for Emily to get the eagle to a veterinarian. There are multiple vehicles, agents, and routes that can be used, subject to the constraints introduced by the terrain and capacities of the various vehicles and available agents. Like Jasper's river trip problem, the solution involves a multistep, distance-rate-time problem. It thus allows students to use the general schema of the Journey to Cedar Creek episode. In addition, the rescue problem involves generating multiple rescue plans and determining which is the quickest.

The episodes in the Jasper series involve students in planning complex problem solutions (including problem formulation and problem posing); information search, retrieval, and organization; and monitoring and evaluation processes. These cognitive activities are those mentioned in conjunction with critical thinking skills (e.g., Bransford et al., 1991; L. B. Resnick & Klopfer, 1989). It should be clear that testing students' acquisition of these skills requires dramatically new forms of assessment.

Additional Instructional Functions for the Jasper Adventures

In addition to its function as a context for engaging in complex mathematical problem solving, the Jasper episodes can be extended to other areas in the mathematics curriculum and to other curricular areas such as English, science, and social studies. For example, in the context of the trip planning videos, we have developed materials that anchor practice on measurement concepts to the Jasper episodes. To develop fluency with units of measurement, students are shown various objects and people who were seen in the episode and they are asked to estimate the size. The task involves discriminating among common units of measurement, for example, pounds, ounces, tons; inches, feet, weight. To develop proficiency by applying the Jasper problem solution, the parameters can be changed. For example, by changing the fuel capacity of the temporary fuel tank, Jasper may be able to make it home without refueling. To develop proficiency with trip planning, there are available a number of "perturbed" miniadventures that utilize the trip-planning schema as well.

The Jasper episodes were also designed to provide natural contexts for exploring science-related concepts such as (a) the density of metals (when determining materials for building boats and planes); (b) density of liquids (when considering the amount and effects of payloads); (c) exploring advances in communication and weather prediction (for boating, flying, and exploration) (CTGV, 1992a). We focused on the general issue of planning for trips (e.g., going down the river or flying to rescue the wounded eagle) because general "trip planning schemata" are applicable to a wide range of topics such as Lindbergh's flight across the Atlantic, Admiral Byrd's exploration of the Antarctic, the NASA space flight to the moon, and so forth. To capitalize on these linkages across content areas, we have a prototype version of "Publisher" software that makes use of hypermedia (CTGV, 1991b).

Hypermedia can be defined as the linkage of text, sound, video, graphics, and the computer in such a way that access to each of these media is virtually instantaneous. Through hypermedia, fundamental thinking and learning activities such as elaboration and flexible coding are facilitated because multiple modalities and symbolic systems can be represented and multiple connections among information can be established. The "Publisher" software provides easy access to hypermedia databases and calculating tools that allow students to explore interesting facts, ideas, and concepts in these domains and to understand how mathematics relates to these other areas.

The databases constructed with the "Publisher" provide students with an opportunity to explore scientific, geographical, and historical information related to the Jasper adventures and to use this information to solve real-world problems that people such as explorers and others throughout history have had to solve. As a simple illustration, the database for Episode I includes historical information relevant to life during the times of Mark Twain. When studying Mark Twain's world, it is very instructive for students to see how plans to go certain distances by water in Journey to Cedar Creek would be different if the mode of travel were steamboat or raft. A 3-hour trip for Jasper by motorboat would have taken the better part of a day on Huckleberry's raft. This means that drinking water, food, and other necessities would need to be included in one's plans.

It is noteworthy that students like to find their own problems and issues and add this information to the database. Their contributions can contain information about who submitted them, so students can be published in the school (or state or national) database. Our decision to begin the Jasper series with an emphasis on general principles of trip planning makes it easier to extend the mathematical thinking to a variety of domains (e.g., space explorations, historical expeditions such as Admiral Byrd's trip to Antarctica, Lindbergh's flight to Europe, etc.). We encourage students to explore specific segments on other videodiscs, such as those produced by National Geographic, that chronicle historic expeditions and other adventures that show evidence that the adventurers had to plan in similar ways to the characters in the Jasper adventures.

ASSESSMENT CHALLENGES

It is evident from the variety of ways in which Jasper can be used in the classroom that there are multiple assessment challenges to be addressed. The most appropriate assessment techniques can be expected to vary with the instructional function being evaluated. Add to this the issue of the purpose for which the assessment is undertaken and the complexity of the assessment challenges becomes clear.

From observations, anecdotes, and personal reports we know that reaction to the Jasper series is extremely positive. When children work with Jasper their involvement and enthusiasm are evident. Indeed, attitude data we have collected indicate that students of all ability levels enjoy solving the Jasper problems and would like to solve additional ones (Pellegrino, Heath, Warren, & CTGV, 1991; Van Haneghan et al., 1992). Teacher reports indicate that children are excited by the adventures and interested in solving them (CTGV, 1992c). Teachers have also been extremely enthusiastic about the cross-curricular links. They see many ways to extend the Jasper episodes into many areas of the curriculum. For example, at a recent training institute, two dozen teachers worked with the Jasper Publisher and created cross-curricular links. Each group of two came up with a different extension. How to systematically capture and measure such effects is a major assessment challenge. In the remainder of the chapter, we discuss our current thinking about how to approach these assessment challenges. We have organized the discussion around the three instructional functions the Jasper adventures may play. For each function, we discuss assessment for purposes of characterizing student learning in research contexts and in classroom contexts. We conclude by proposing an alternative assessment model that we have recently pilot tested.

Assessment of Complex Mathematical Problem Solving

We noted earlier that a major goal of the Jasper series is to help students learn to pose, formulate, and solve complex problems that are similar to those often encountered in everyday settings. Each Jasper adventure ends with such a problem and we have also developed sets of analogs that provide extra practice for each adventure (see CTGV, 1992c). Clearly, in order to assess the effects of this aspect of the curriculum on students' thinking, we need to measure the degree to which they transfer to new types of problem-solving tasks. For purposes of our research, the field of cognitive science provides useful information about ways to assess complex problem solving—at least for individuals. Verbal protocols are often regarded as benchmark measures of these processes. Empirical investigations conducted under controlled conditions indicate that solving the first Jasper adventure does indeed improve children's complex problem-solving skills (CTGV, 1990; Goldman et al., 1991; Van Haneghan et al., 1992; Young et al., 1990). In those studies we have used verbal protocols from individual interviews with children. We regard these as benchmarks against which to evaluate other forms of assessment. The challenges are to (a) develop surrogates of the interviews that are less time consuming to administer yet maintain the validity and reliability of the interviews and (b) to determine cognitive process measures that are appropriate to group problem solving.

A major reason for attempting to develop surrogates of our verbal protocol interview tests is that the latter are not feasible to administer under normal classroom conditions. This presents a potential problem because measures of student mastery of the processes involved in complex mathematical problem solving are critical to instructional management and monitoring. If teachers do not have some measure of how well students are doing in complex problem solving, they will not be able to evaluate their own teaching strategies and whether they need to change them, or the degree to which additional instructional time is needed and for whom.

One approach that we have taken in this regard is to attempt to develop paper-and-pencil measures that provide data that are consistent with our interview measures. Because one of the major goals of our interviews is to measure problem formulation or generation, we cannot simply administer multiple choice tests such as "Which of the following questions does Jasper need to ask himself in order to make his decision: When is sunset? How fast is the boat? How wide is the river? etc." The ability to *recognize* relevant questions is not the same as the ability to *generate* them on one's own. Therefore, there are many constraints on the nature of the tests that we can create.

At present we are experimenting with a paper-and-pencil test that involves a generative component (students must write down relevant questions to be solved) and an explanatory component (students must explain why someone who was attempting to solve Jasper's problem had carried out certain calculations). (Preliminary reports of the results of these procedures can be found in Pellegrino et al., 1991, and CTGV, 1992d). Following instruction on a Jasper adventure (when we try to assess without instruction we run into floor effects), the same students are being given a verbal protocol interview test and the paper-and-pencil test, with order of testing counterbalanced. Data such as these will allow us to measure the relative comparability of each type of test.

Assessing the complex mathematical problem-solving skills of students is most useful for purposes of formative assessment and instructional management. Verbal protocols and surrogate tests of problem solving such as those we have described in this section can be used to assess *mastery* of the problem-solving processes relevant to a specific Jasper adventure as well as *transfer* to new problems. A major goal of these assessments is to identify children who need more work before progressing further in the Jasper series. For transfer assessment we have devised tests that involve new complex problems that systematically differ from specific Jasper adventures. These Jasper problem "analogs" are also one of the ways in which the Jasper adventures extend into other areas of the math curriculum and are discussed more fully in that section.

Measures of Group Problem Solving

We are also attempting to assess the effects of using Jasper adventures in the context of group problem solving. Here we encounter a number of theoretical and methodological issues that have important implications for the assessment strategies to be used.

Consider the question of whether group problem solving using Jasper is superior to individual problem solving. If we show students a Jasper adventure and then ask them to solve it either individually or in groups, the groups almost always do better (e.g., Barron, 1991; Rewey, in prep.). Many other studies show similar effects (e.g., D. Johnson, Maruyama, R. Johnson, Nelson, & Skon, 1981; Slavin, 1984). But what do these results mean? Work being conducted by a member of our center, Brigid Barron, is designed to test several models of why groups may perform better than the average of a group of individuals. One class of models describes group performance by one member's level of performance. There are two possibilities here: the *most* competent member model and the *least* competent member model. According to these models, group performance is either as good, or as bad, as the strongest, or the weakest, member of the group. A second class of models holds that the performance of the group exceeds what any individual member of the group could achieve. The pooling of abilities model is one example of this type of model: Individual group members solve different portions of the problem and "pool" their efforts for the complete solution. An additional model in this class is the synergistic model. This model assumes that exchanges among group members promote thinking in ways that would not have occurred had the individual worked alone. This exchange process helps all components of the problem-solving process (Barron, 1991).

In order to assess the effects of group problem solving on individual students, it is necessary to test the abilities of individuals to solve new problems. A relatively small number of studies have addressed this question (e.g., Larson et al., 1985) but several members of our center are currently exploring it. For example, Barron (1991) found that high achieving mathematics students who worked in groups were better able to solve the Journey to Cedar Creek challenge than high achieving math students working alone; the former also showed better transfer on subsequently administered individual tests. For average achieving students, there was more individual variability in the effects of groups on problem solution and transfer. Rewey (in prep.) is looking at the effects of "scripting" group interactions on the nature of the group problem-solving process and on the effects on both group and individual problem solving. An important finding of Rewey's work concerns effects of groups on affect: In contrast to the attitudes of students who worked in groups, students who had to work alone did not like the Jasper challenge problem.

It seems clear that each of the models of group problem solving that were discussed earlier (e.g., the most or least competent member model, synergistic model, etc.) may be operative under some circumstances. For example, empirical studies that have compared heterogenous with homogenous ability groups (e.g., Webb, Ender, & Lewis, 1986) indicate that outcomes are mediated by the nature of the interactions that occur in the group. This being so, instructional management and monitoring purposes are best served by assessment techniques that enable teachers to characterize the group interaction, coupled with instructional techniques, such as scripting, for directing those interactions.

Assessment of Extensions to Other Areas of the Math Curriculum

The Jasper adventures can serve as anchors for work on aspects of the math curriculum not directly involved in solving the specific problem posed by a particular adventure. One important aspect of the math curriculum is the need to develop fluency with basic concepts and procedures. There is a strong need for greater theoretical consistency regarding the concept of fluency, especially in different skill areas, and in the linkages between fluency on component skills and complex thinking and problem solving.

Clearly, an emphasis on the importance of fluency is not new. In the area of reading, for example, LaBerge and Samuels (1974) argued that accuracy in reading words should not be confused with fluent access to their pronunciation. The same is true in the mathematics domain (e.g., Goldman & Pellegrino, 1991;

Kaye, 1986). Despite the importance of fluency in the theoretical literature, many curricula do not emphasize it. Instead, students are often introduced to new ideas for a short period of time; instruction then shifts to other ideas and there is little chance to become fluent at accessing basic concepts and skills. Although practice exercises are a common classroom activity, the emphasis is usually on accuracy and not on fluency. If instructional planning decisions are made only on the basis of accuracy, there may seem to be no need for further practice.

From a research perspective, we know how to measure fluency of basic concepts (e.g., 5 + 7 = 12) and we know that increased fluency on component skills can be achieved via practice (Goldman, Mertz, Pellegrino, 1989; Goldman, Pellegrino, & Mertz, 1988; Hasselbring, Goin, & Bransford, 1988). We also know that if students practice procedural algorithms, such as those used in long division, their accuracy and efficiency improve (Sherwood, Hasselbring, Marsh, & Mertz, 1990). We have yet to examine the development of fluency with complex problem-solving procedures. The Jasper adventures can function as an anchor for fluency training in all three areas of mathematics. For example, they can serve as an anchor for practice with the basic concepts introduced in the video, such as units of measurement and conversions among them (e.g., inches, feet, yards) as well as equivalences among different symbolic representations for quantities (e.g., decimals, fractions, mixed numbers, percentages). Procedural algorithms for specific calculations are used in the Jasper problem solutions; students may be motivated to become more proficient with these procedures when they see them used to solve a meaningful problem.

The importance of focusing on fluency in the area of mathematics is illustrated by data from a cross-sectional study of math-delayed and normally achieving students (Hasselbring, Goin, & Bransford, 1988; Hasselbring, Goin, Alcantara, & Bransford, 1990). The study assessed students' abilities to add specific facts such as 5 + 8 = ? Figure 10.1a shows that when accuracy is measured, math-delayed and normally achieving students perform at similar levels by about age 9 (roughly fourth grade). In contrast, Fig. 10.1b shows the results for fluency: The gap between the two groups increases with age.

In related work, we have also found that the traditional practice activities associated with many curricula involve work on specific skills and procedures in isolation or outside of contexts where the information might be needed. For example, the Mastering Fractions videodisc program (Systems Impact Inc., 1985) involves a series of lessons that helped students become very proficient at working with fraction problems such as $\frac{1}{2} + \frac{1}{4} = ?$, $\frac{1}{3} \times \frac{1}{4} = ?$ (e.g., Sherwood et al., 1990). Nevertheless, when students were asked to use their knowledge of fractions to solve word problems, they did poorly and no better than a control group. (Sherwood et al., 1990). Basically, the students' knowledge of fractions remained inert. We assume that the opportunity to move back and forth between Jasper problem-solving environments and fluency exercises on basic skills will promote the kinds of knowledge representations that appear to underlie expert

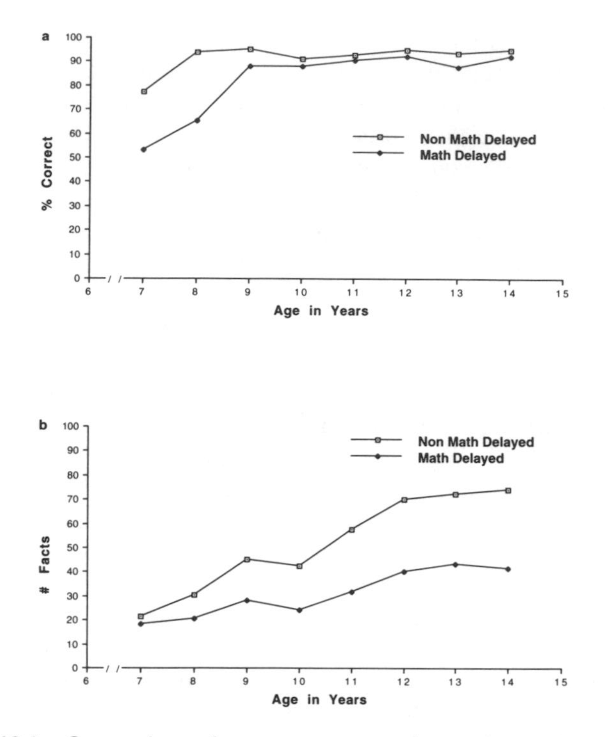

FIG. 10.1. Comparison of response accuracy by age for math-delayed and nondelayed students (a) and of the number of fluent facts by age for math-delayed and nondelayed students (b).

performance and that avoid the inert knowledge problem (e.g., see Bransford & Vye, 1989; Chi, Bassok, Lewis, & Glaser, 1989). In addition, if students achieve levels of proficiency that free attentional resources from the "basics," they can reallocate these to more complex thinking required for solving real-world problems.

We can also use the Jasper adventures to anchor practice with complex problem-solving procedures by creating variants of the problem presented in the video. For example, a second complex problem can be easily created by altering the original problem constraints, for example, the cruiser travels at a slower (or faster) rate or the time of sunset changes, and so on. Students need to use the same sets of planning and solution procedures but the specific calculations are different; sometimes changing the constraints also makes some steps unnecessary. We are working on paper-and-pencil as well as video-based analogs and are developing assessments of these that focus on problem generation and solution explanation skills. Performance on these Jasper isomorphs can serve practice and instructional purposes as well as serving as assessment techniques in their own right. Such performance-based assessment provides an index of student learning useful for instructional management and monitoring purposes and may hold promise for program evaluation and accountability purposes.

Fluency in the sense of rapid and accurate information access is needed at traditional "basics" levels as well as at procedural, qualitative reasoning, and planning levels. The assessment challenges with respect to fluency are (a) to measure both the speed of accessing concepts and skills as well as the degree to which students understand such concepts and are able to relate them to real-world problem-solving situations, and (b) to deliver this information in forms that are functional for instructional management and planning purposes and perhaps for program evaluation and accountability.

Assessment of Cross-Curricular Extensions

In addition to the focus on complex problem solving and fluency, the Jasper adventures provide a context for helping students appreciate the relevance and interrelatedness of various curriculum areas. Rather than provide these links in a textbooklike fashion, we decided to create conditions that would motivate students to provide them. In an earlier section of this chapter, we referred to our HyperCard "Publisher" environment and noted that, unlike traditional report formats that present information in a linear order, hypermedia allows for "many branching" links among concepts. The "Jasper Publisher" is a tool to be used by the students. Using this software, students produce relational databases instead of 10- or 20-page papers. This activity should help them learn to notice relevant issues to be explored, learn how to find information to explore the issues, and learn to communicate the results of their findings. The Jasper Publisher program also allows students to create multimedia presentations to show others about the results of their research (CTGV, 1991b).

There are many questions with respect to the assessment and evaluation of student-generated multimedia projects. We have considered several possibilities for the skills and processes we might evaluate. We might look at (a) the skill of posing interesting questions, (b) how individuals frame issues, and (c) the effectiveness and efficiency of information search and retrieval skills. The technology itself may facilitate certain forms of assessment of the aforementioned skills. For example, graph theory might be used to analyze the relational databases that students produce in terms of the number and nature of the links among different entries. We might also track the production process by analysis of "dribble" files or traces of the students' production process. Alternatively, we might assume that the act of generating the database is a sufficient performance index. These products could comprise student portfolios. The quality of the projects should improve over time and should show evidence of students' increasing familiarity with multimedia publishing. Familiarity with this new media should affect how students think about new reports that they choose or are asked to write.

A number of guidelines for other forms of assessment of the aforementioned skills and processes come from the "Young Sherlock" program that has been studied by members of our center (e.g., Bransford et al., 1989; CTGV, 1990; Kinzer, Hasselbring, Schmidt, & Meltzer, 1990; Risko, Kinzer, Vye, & Rowe, 1990; Rowe, Goodman, Moore, & McLarty, 1990). The Sherlock project used the videodisc "The Young Sherlock Holmes" as an anchor for literacy instruction but its use also involved many cross-curricular links to history, geography, and science. Thus, it has a number of overlaps with respect to the cross-curricular extensions of Jasper.

Classroom ethnography revealed that one important effect of the Sherlock program was an extremely high number of student generated questions (e.g., see Rowe et al., 1990). A major reason for this high rate of student-initiated questions was that all students shared an interesting macrocontext yet all were allowed to choose their own specific points to query and explore further. Students quickly began to notice many features of the videos they wanted more information about, and this frequently led to lively discussions and searches for relevant information. We expect similar types of activities with Jasper and could observe this through ethnographic studies such as those used in the Sherlock project. Needless to say, however, this is expensive and time-consuming research to perform.

Another approach to assessment is to show groups of students new sets of videos and ask them to state what they noticed in these videos and why it might be important to explore these issues in more detail. In research in the Sherlock project we found evidence that students in the experimental group did better at this task than those in a control group (e.g., Vye, Rowe, Kinzer, & Risko, 1990). A related assessment task is to provide students with a topic to explore and ask them to show how they would search for relevant information. The more that students have had to search (e.g., through the library, through national databases) in order to retrieve relevant information, the better they should be at information search.

A potential danger of database production is that the database produced by one student can very easily become the decontextualized and inert knowledge of another. To forestall this outcome, we encourage students (and teachers) who create multimedia presentations to pose interesting questions and challenge other students to accept the challenges. The ability of students to pose interesting "challenge" questions given an assigned topic provides valuable information about what they have learned. Challenge questions also become a way of closely linking instruction and assessment, an issue we turn to by way of concluding this chapter.

New Arenas for Assessment

Among the problems we noted in our discussion of traditional assessment was that students develop increasingly negative attitudes toward tests as they progress through school. This problem does not go away even when the material on which students are being tested is interesting and challenging. In the context of our Jasper series, students developed an intense dislike for the paper-and-pencil tests we devised. So intense were these negative emotions that a few children said they would give up Jasper rather than continue with the testing program (for details see CTGV, 1992c, 1992d). In our thinking, a key to new approaches to assessment is how to make students *want to* self-assess and improve their performances. By defining new arenas for assessment we think we can alter the negative view of assessment. Challenge questions play a key role in these new arenas.

We call our approach Scientific and Mathematical Arenas for Refining Thinking (SMART) assessments. They combine the strengths of "systemic" models of assessment (e.g., Frederiksen & Collins, 1989) with those of "dynamic" assessment models that focus directly on potentials for learning (e.g., Bransford, Delclos, Vye, Burns, & Hasselbring, 1987; Campione & Brown, 1987; Feuerstein, Rand, Jensen, Kaniel, & Tzuriel, 1987; Lidz, 1987; Vye, Burns, Delclos, & Bransford, 1987). In addition, SMART assessments further increase the strengths of the systemic and dynamic models by using technology for teleconferencing to create frequent, intrinsically motivating assessment arenas. These arenas provide cost-effective opportunities for students, teachers, administrators, and communities to more effectively evaluate their own work because they have the opportunity to (a) see the products and performances of others around the country, (b) receive new information about ways to improve their learning and understanding of particular issues, and (c) test their abilities to adapt following an opportunity to assimilate new information.

SMART assessments can be designed to provide an opportunity to collect system-level "accountability" data while also assessing complex thinking and learning rather than just the ability to remember discrete skills and factual content. The SMART approach makes use of information about assessment to drive teaching and learning. Our SMART assessments include opportunities for students to learn and to then evaluate their responses to those learning activities. If the assessment involved making a presentation on a topic, for example, students would prepare for and then make a presentation, receive feedback about performance plus be given material that includes suggestions for doing it better, and then receive a second chance for a similar presentation that would include additional feedback. This provides students and teachers with an opportunity to assess the kinds of affective and cognitive "responsivity to instruction" that proponents of dynamic assessment emphasize.

Components of a SMART Assessment Model

At a general descriptive level there are five "stages" in our SMART assessment approach. We describe them from the perspective of a pilot test we conducted in spring 1991. The pilot test used a teleconferencing format, a highly motivating format for students and teachers.[1] Nevertheless, SMART assessments could be implemented in other formats as well. The five components of SMART assessments are:

1. Completion of a substantive unit of instruction.
2. Presentation and solution of problems to prepare for the teleconference Challenge.
3. Participation in Challenge I; for example, by observing and evaluating challenge-based answers and arguments made by people featured in the teleconference.
4. Immediate feedback followed by the presentation and solution of new preparation problems (for Challenge II) plus information about strategies for enhancing learning of everyone in the classroom, including strategies for collaborating more effectively (e.g., through "jigsaw" teaching).
5. Participation in Challenge II followed by feedback.

Stage 1: The first stage presupposes the completion of some substantive unit of instruction. For our pilot, students had completed the Jasper episode "Rescue at Boone's Meadow" (RBM). Our "Challenge" questions were based on analogs to the RBM problem.

Stage 2: In the second stage, the "Preparatory" stage, students are presented a new set of problems to be solved in order to prepare for the Challenge. These problems are nontrivial extensions of the preceding unit; they represent substantive variations that should require generalization and extension of the knowledge previously acquired. Examples might include simple or complex analogs of problems previously posed and solved. A fixed time period is allotted for student work on the problems. Student work can be done individually, in small collaborative groups, via whole class, or any combination thereof, and this will vary with the needs and general instructional philosophy of the target classroom. Thus, the assessment procedures do not presuppose a particular organizational format for the classroom. In fact, the procedures permit an evaluation of the effectiveness of different instructional arrangements in such a dynamic assessment situation. Within this stage it is possible for the teacher to monitor student behavior and progress.

For our pilot, teachers received our Challenge Preparation tape. The announcer on the tape (Larry Peterson, the students' favorite character) announced

---

Members of our center who scripted and produced the teleconference game show were Ron Kanter, director; David Edyburn, Ben Ferron, Laura Goin, Seth Goldman, Allison Heath, Dan Hickey, Kirsten Rewey, Seth Strauss and Susan Warren. Video support was provided by Leigh Kahan and the media group at Northern Telecom, and studio time was provided by Jim Owens Studios, Nashville, Tennessee.

the upcoming teleconference and, in order to help students prepare, taught the students something about the effects of headwinds and tailwinds on groundspeed. The tape then posed problems that asked students to reconsider how the original solution to "Rescue at Boone's Meadow" would be affected by various changes in headwinds and tailwinds and by using planes with different types of characteristics from the one used in the original adventure. Students solved these problems, usually in groups.

Stage 3: In the third stage, students and teachers participate in a teleconference where they are presented the answers and arguments of various individuals for questions that relate directly to the content of the challenge problems. Thus, rather than directly assess student solutions to problems, the goal is to assess their understanding and knowledge by their ability to evaluate the quality of the answers provided by others. The answers to be evaluated are designed to reflect correct content and logic as well as systematic deviations from the correct answer. One goal in developing such responses is to create the opportunity for diagnosticity in the response patterns in the event that students positively evaluate flawed or incomplete answers and arguments. This third stage can be designed so that several options are available for quantitative and qualitative assessment. These variations include absolute judgments as well as paired or multiple comparison procedures. In all cases students can make choices and can be required to justify their reasons for doing so. Furthermore, the procedure can be designed so that students respond individually as well as in small groups or whole classes An interesting variation is to move through these successive levels of responding, that is, as an individual, as a member of a small group, as a whole class, as part of producing a "consensus" or majority response. Our expectation is that students would then be forced to deal with differences underlying their responses and thereby become more aware of both the content and process of their reasoning and that of others.

For the pilot, on the day of the teleconference, we used a "Pick the Expert" game show format. Students had to decide which of three college-age contestants knew what they were talking about when asked questions about the effects of headwinds and tailwinds and about the trip time of different types of aircraft with different fuel capacities, consumption rates, and so on. All three contestants answered the first several questions appropriately. By the third and fourth round of questions, two of the contestants made mistakes so that only one possible expert was left.

Following the game show portion of the teleconference, a representative of each class called in the number of students in that class who had voted for each contestant.

Stage 4: The third stage directly transitions to the fourth stage. Feedback is quickly provided to the students and teachers so that a self-assessment and evaluation can be conducted in the classroom. During the pilot, results were compiled on the air and broadcast to the students, hence they received very rapid feedback on who was the true expert. Eighty-five percent of the students voted for the correct expert. Reports from our teachers indicated that students discussed the pros and cons of various votes long after the teleconference went off the air. Teachers also reported that the students were very motivated to work on the Challenge Preparation problems. One of the reasons was that they were learning something new that interested them; that is, about headwinds and tailwinds. Another was the opportunity to participate in a teleconference with sites from a number of different states.

As we envision it, the feedback from SMART assessments involves much more than mere knowledge of results. For example, feedback for "Rescue at Boone's Meadow" and its related problems could continue by providing information about strategies for improving the overall score of one's class. This could be done either through telecommunications or by using text or video that is sent to each class. The feedback could include information about strategies for improving the group score—strategies such as analyzing the class data to find overall areas of weakness and concentrating on them (such analyses would not require that one make public the scores of individual students), articulating reasons for various decisions about arguments rather than simply learning that particular ones are right versus wrong, using jigsaw teaching to have different students help one another, and so forth. The goal of this feedback would be to help students prepare for Challenge II.

For future SMART assessments, we envision a situation in which the "errors in reasoning" are discussed and explained on the video thereby modeling monitoring and evaluation processes. Thus, students would have the opportunity to see the difference between good and less good performance models. The feedback could also include strategies for how to improve one's performance on the next set of problems. These problems provide a second opportunity for students to apply what they have learned. In this case, however, the application includes not only the original content of the instructional unit but what they have learned from the process of responding to the original challenge problems together with the answer evaluation activity. As in Stage 2, students would be given a fixed period of time to respond to the new challenges, for example, a week. The manner in which they work on this can vary depending on the classroom arrangements and teacher models in place. It is expected that students would keep a journal of their activities that includes their reflections on what they have learned to date and how they are attempting to adapt based on the feedback from the first cycle.

Stage 5: In the fifth stage, students are again presented the answers and arguments of various individuals for questions that relate directly to the content of the second set of challenge problems. The same task structure and logic are involved in this stage as was the case for Stage 3. The principal goal of this stage is to provide students a new opportunity to apply what they have learned with a new self-assessment and evaluation cycle. As before, students would get feedback and would then reflect on changes in their performance, including what they have learned from the entire instructional and assessment process. Both Challenge II (Phase 5) and the preparation problems for it (Phase 4) would include problems analogous in content and difficulty to Preparation and Challenge I. Challenge II would also include feedback to students. This type of format would provide an opportunity for classes to see their improvement from Challenge I to II. By systematically helping classes develop strategies for learning, plus helping them develop relevant content knowledge that builds on previous Challenge experiences, the SMART assessments that take place during a year can each build upon one another.

It is important to point out that all five phases are seen as critical components in order to have an assessment model that meets criteria of being both systemic and dynamic. For example, Frederiksen and Collins (1989) identified a number of principles and criteria as critical for a systemic assessment plan. These include components of the system, standards to be sought, and methods by which the system encourages learning. In order to design to meet such criteria there must be multiple problems and learning opportunities with clearly specified models of performance and feedback. By providing two complete challenge–answer evaluation cycles in SMART assessment designs, we also provide the conditions necessary for a dynamic assessment environment (e.g., Lidz, 1987) where a person's performance can change in response to prompting, support, and feedback and where there is opportunity for all individuals involved to see the nature of the progress that has been made.

Within this general model there are multiple opportunities for both quantitative and qualitative assessment. This includes student self-assessment as well as teacher assessment of student outcomes and processes. For example, the choices that students make during the answer evaluation stages can be quantified if that is a desired goal, error patterns can be discerned and interpreted for diagnostic use, and rationales can be evaluated for correct and incorrect conceptions of content. Student learning processes and metacognitive functioning can be monitored during different phases of the assessment model. These assessment strategies can be carried out multiple times, that is, applied across multiple units of instruction, to determine cumulative gain.

There are many variations on this model that we expect to explore and one very important one that we will pursue is the use of two-way video conferencing as a means for delivery of the challenge and/or answer evaluation components of the process. (In contrast, our pilot challenges involved one-way video and two-way audio conferencing.) There are several reasons for pursuing this delivery strategy. First, this delivery vehicle increases students' level of motivation by giving them an opportunity to visually interact with people from throughout the country. Students (and teachers) perceive themselves as part of an extended network with the possibility for both healthy competition as well as perspective sharing. We have seen this work very effectively with one-way video and hope to exploit such technologies to create more dynamic assessment environments.

A second reason for using teleconferencing is to aid teachers in better understanding both the instructional and assessment issues that come with constructivist learning environments. We envision an expanded assessment design in which teachers share feedback about their students' individual and group performance. They then have an opportunity to discuss, as professionals, their judgments and the implications for instructional activities that would enhance student understanding and subsequent responding. Thus, the teleconference format allows for knowledge sharing among the very professionals who must oversee the larger instructional and assessment enterprise. It gives them a stake in the enterprise that might otherwise be difficult to achieve. Another virtue of such a design is that it incorporates mechanisms for professional development with respect to dissemination of new theories and methods of assessment.

SUMMARY AND CONCLUSIONS

In this chapter we have focused on assessment issues that arise in the context of learning environments that emphasize complex thinking and problem solving. We used the video-based mathematical problem-solving series "The Adventures of Jasper Woodbury" as an example of an environment that affords students the opportunity to engage in generating solutions to authentic and meaningful problems. Such problem solving involves important skills such as problem formulation and subgoal generation; information search, retrieval, and organization processes; and communication and reasoning about mathematics.

We described seven design principles for these environments, and we noted that different aspects of the series pose different assessment challenges. For example, one can assess students' gains in abilities to solve problems analogous to the Jasper adventures but the series also extends far beyond complex mathematics problem solving. The Jasper series also functions (a) as a motivator for students who need to develop fluency with mathematical concepts and operations; and (b) as a rich environment for connecting to other areas such as other aspects of mathematics, science, and social studies.

We discussed the assessment issues surrounding each of these functions and provided some ideas regarding new approaches to assessment of complex mathematical problem solving by individuals and by groups. We also discussed the importance of finding ways to integrate fluency on basic concepts with curricula and assessment of higher order skills. We noted that the episodes in the Jasper series provide a rich context for illustrating the importance of basic fact and procedural fluency. We proposed a set of questions regarding extensions into other areas of the curriculum, and stressed that the skill of posing interesting and challenging questions was a key to effective assessment.

Our emphasis on generating challenging questions, coupled with our experience in dealing with negative reactions to traditional-looking tests, led us to propose new arenas for assessment in mathematics and science. The basis of SMART assessment is the observation that students learn to study differently depending on the test and that teachers tend to teach to the tests. Many educators argue that the problem of "teaching to the test" is not a problem if the tests demand important sets of skills and knowledge. (e.g., Fredericksen & Collins, 1989; L. B. Resnick & D. P. Resnick, 1991). If the tests demand rigorous problem solving, for example, they seem to be worth teaching to. It is when tests demand only the rote memory of isolated facts or procedures that it seems harmful for teaches to teach to them. Many educators also argue that the creation of new and more challenging tests may be the most efficient and effective way to spark a change in the kinds of teaching that typically takes place in classrooms.

SMART assessments involve five component phases that provide opportunities for receiving feedback, for learning from one's mistakes (and successes), and for making a second assessment of performance. These phases were instantiated in the context of the Jasper series and the use of teleconferencing and satellite transmission were mentioned as ways to implement such SMART assessments.

In summary, we have argued for the need for new learning environments as well as for new forms of assessment. Environments such as the Jasper series create authentic and meaningful problems that students enjoy solving. To do so requires students to use traditional basic skills plus new generative skills, such as subgoal formulation, planning, search strategies, and information coordination and evaluation techniques. We also argued that SMART assessments developed around interesting, project-based curricula such as the Jasper series are one possible answer to the challenge of how to create tests that are worth teaching to and are administrable on a large scale.

ACKNOWLEDGMENTS

Preparation of this chapter and the research reported herein was supported, in part, by grants from the James S. McDonnell Foundation (No. 87-39) and the National Science Foundation (No. NSF-MDR 9050191), and in part by a contract from the Defense Advanced Research Projects Agency (DARPA), administered by the Office of Naval Research (ONR), to the UCLA Center for the Study of Evaluation/Center for Technology Assessment. However, the opinions expressed do not necessarily reflect the positions of these agencies, and no official endorsement should be inferred.

REFERENCES

American Association for the Advancement of Science (1989). *Science for all Americans: A project 2061 report on literacy goals in science, mathematics, and technology.* Washington, DC: Author.

Bank Street College of Education (1984). *Voyage of the Mimi.* Scotts Valley, CA: Wings for Learning, Inc., Sunburst Co.

Barron, B.J.S. (1991). *Collaborative problem solving: Is team performance greater than what is expected from the most competent member?* Unpublished doctoral dissertation, Vanderbilt University, Nashville, TN.

Belli, R., Soraci, S., & Purdon, S. (1989). *The generation effect in learning and memory: Implications for theory and practice.* Unpublished manuscript, Vanderbilt University, Learning Technology Center, TN.

Bransford, J. D., Delclos, V. R., Vye, N. J., Burns, M. S., & Hasselbring, T. S. (1987). State of the art and future directions. In C. S. Lidz (Ed.), *Dynamic assessment: An interactional approach to evaluating learning potential* (pp. 479–496). New York: Guilford Press.

Bransford, J. D., Franks, J. J., Vye, N. J., & Sherwood, R. D. (1989). New approaches to instruction: Because wisdom can't be told. In S. Vosniadou & A. Ortony (Eds.), *Similarity and analogical reasoning* (pp. 470–497). New York: Cambridge University Press.

Bransford, J. D., Goldman, S. R., & Vye, N. J. (1991). Making a difference in peoples' abilities to think: Reflections on a decade of work and some hopes for the future. In L. Okagaki & R. J. Sternberg (Eds.), *Directors of development: Influences on children* (pp. 147–180). Hillsdale, NJ: Lawrence Erlbaum Associates.

Bransford, J., Hasselbring, T., Barron, B., Kulewicz, S., Littlefield, J., & Goin, L. (1988). Uses of macro-contexts to facilitate mathematical thinking. In R. Charles & E. A. Silver (Eds.), *The teaching and assessing of mathematical problem solving* (pp. 125–147). Hillsdale, NJ: Lawrence Erlbaum Associates.

Bransford, J. D., & Nitsch, K. E. (1978). Coming to understand things we could not previously understand. In J. F. Kavanaugh & W. Strange (Eds.), *Speech and language in the laboratory, school, and clinic* (pp. 267–307). Cambridge, MA: MIT Press.

Bransford, J., Sherwood, R., & Hasselbring, T. (1988). The video revolution and its effects on development: Some initial thoughts. In G. Foreman & P. Pufall (Eds.), *Constructivism in the computer age* (pp. 173–201). Hillsdale, NJ: Lawrence Erlbaum Associates.

Bransford, J. D., Sherwood, R. S., Vye, N. J., & Rieser, J. (1986). Teaching thinking and problem solving: Research foundations. *American Psychologist, 41,* 1078–1089.

Bransford, J. D., & Stein, B. S. (1984). *The IDEAL problem solver.* New York: W. H. Freeman.

Bransford, J. D., & Vye, N. J. (1989). A perspective on cognitive research and its implications for instruction. In L. Resnick & L. E. Klopfer (Eds.), *Toward the thinking curriculum: Current cognitive research* (pp. 173–205). Alexandria, VA: ASCD.

Brown, A. L., Bransford, J. D., Ferrara, R. A., & Campione, J. C. (1983). Learning, remembering and understanding. In J. H. Flavell & E. M. Markman (Eds.), *Carmichael's manual of child psychology* (Vol. 1, pp. 77–166). New York: Wiley.

Brown, J. S., Collins, A., & Duguid, P. (1989). Situated cognition and the culture of learning. *Educational Researcher, 18*(1), 32–41.

Brown, S. I., & Walter, M. I. (1990). *The art of problem posing* (2nd ed.). Philadelphia: Franklin Institute Press.

Campione, J. C., & Brown, A. L. (1987). Linking dynamic assessment with school achievement. In C. S. Lidz (Ed.), *Dynamic assessment: An interactional approach to evaluating learning potential* (pp. 82–114). New York: Guilford Press.

Charles, R., & Silver, E. A. (Eds.). (1988). *The teaching and assessing of mathematical problem solving.* Hillsdale, NJ: Lawrence Erlbaum Associates & National Council for Teachers of Mathematics.

Chi, M. T., Bassok, M., Lewis, P. J., & Glaser, R. (1989). Self-explanations: How students study and use examples in learning to solve problems. *Cognitive Science, 13,* 145–182.

Cognition and Technology Group at Vanderbilt (CTGV) (1990). Anchored instruction and its relationship to situated cognition. *Educational Researcher, 19*(6), 2–10.

Cognition and Technology Group at Vanderbilt (1991a, May). Integrated media: Toward a theoretical framework for utilizing their potential. In *Proceedings of the multimedia technology seminar* (pp. 3–27), Washington, DC: Council for Exceptional Children.

Cognition and Technology Group at Vanderbilt (1991b). Technology and the design of generative learning environments, *Educational Technology, 31*(5), 34–40.

Cognition and Technology Group at Vanderbilt (1991c). *Video environments for connecting mathematics, science and other disciplines.* Paper presented at the Wingspread Conference on Integrated Science and Mathematics Teaching and Learning, Racine, WI.

Cognition and Technology Group at Vanderbilt. (1992a). Anchored instruction in science and mathematics: Theoretical basis, developmental projects, and initial research findings. In R. A. Duschl & R. J. Hamilton (Eds.), *Philosophy of science, cognitive psychology, and educational theory and practice* (pp. 244–273). New York: SUNY Press.

Cognition and Technology Group at Vanderbilt. (1992b). The Jasper experiment: An exploration of issues in learning and instructional design. *Educational Technology Research and Development, 40,* 65–80.

Cognition and Technology Group at Vanderbilt. (1992c). The Jasper series: A generative approach to mathematical thinking. In K. Sheingold, L. G. Roberts, & S. M. Malcolm (Eds.), *This year in science series 1991: Technology for teaching and learning* (pp. 108–140). Washington, DC: American Association for the Advancement of Science.

Cognition and Technology Group at Vanderbilt. (1992d). The Jasper series as an example of anchored instruction: Theory, program description and assessment data. *Educational Psychologist, 27,* 291–315.

Cognition and Technology Group at Vanderbilt. (1993). Toward integrated curricula: Possibilities from anchored instruction. In M. Rabinowitz (Ed.), *Cognitive science foundations of instruction* (pp. 33–55). Hillsdale, NJ: Lawrence Erlbaum Associates.

Dossey, J. A., Mullis, I.V.S., Lindquist, M. M., & Chambers, D. L. (1988). *The mathematics report card: Are we measuring up?* Princeton, NJ: Educational Testing Service.

Frederiksen, J. R., & Collins, A. (1989). A systems approach to educational testing. *Educational Researcher, 18*(9), 27–32.

Feuerstein, R., Rand, Y., Jensen, M. R., Kaniel, S., & Tzuriel, D. (1987). Prerequisites for assessment of learning potential: The LPAD model. In C. S. Lidz (Ed.), *Dynamic assessment: An interactional approach to evaluating learning potential* (pp. 35–51). New York: Guilford Press.

Gick, M. L., & Holyoak, K. J. (1980). Analogical problem solving. *Cognitive Psychology, 12,* 306–365.

Goldman, S. R., et al. (in preparation). *Grounding mathematical problem solving in complex and meaningful situations.* Vanderbilt University, Nashville, TN.

Goldman, S. R., & the Cognition and Technology Group at Vanderbilt. (1991, August). *Meaningful learning environments for mathematical problem solving: The Jasper problem solving series.* Paper presented at the Fourth European Conference for Research on Learning and Instruction, Turku, Finland.

Goldman, S. R., Mertz, D. L., & Pellegrino, J. W. (1989). Individual differences in extended practice functions and solution strategies for basic addition facts. *Journal of Educational Psychology, 81,* 481–496.

Goldman, S. R., & Pellegrino, J. W. (1991). Cognitive development perspectives on intelligence. In H. Rowe & J. Biggs (Eds.), *Intelligence: Reconceptualization and measurement* (pp. 77–95). Melbourne, Australia: ACER.

Goldman, S. R., Pellegrino, J. W., & Mertz, D. L. (1988). Extended practice of basic addition facts: Strategy changes in learning disabled students. *Cognition and Instruction, 5,* 223–265.

Goldman, S. R., Vye, N. J., Williams, S. M., Rewey, K., & Pellegrino, J. W. (1991, April). *Problem space analyses of the Jasper problems and students' attempts to solve them.* Paper presented at the American Educational Research Association, Chicago.

Hasselbring, T. S., Goin, L. I., Alcantara, P., & Bransford, J. D. (1990, April). *Developing mathematical fluency in children with learning handicaps.* Paper presented at the annual meeting of the American Educational Research Association, Boston.

Hasselbring, T., Goin, L., & Bransford, J. D. (1988). Developing math automaticity in learning handicapped children: The role of computerized drill and practice. *Focus on Exceptional Children, 20*(6), 1–7.

Johnson, D., Maruyama, G., Johnson, R., Nelson, C., & Skon, L. (1981). The effects of cooperative, competitive, and individualistic goal structures on achievement: A meta-analysis. *Psychological Bulletin, 89,* 47–62.

Kaye, D. B. (1986). The development of mathematical cognition. *Cognitive Development, 1,* 157–170.

Kinzer, C., Hasselbring, T., Schmidt, C., & Meltzer, L. (1990, April). *Effects of multimedia to enhance writing ability.* Paper presented at the annual meeting of the American Educational Research Association, Boston.

Kouba, V. L., Brown, C. A., Carpenter, T. P., Lindquist, M. M., Silver, E. A., & Swafford, J. O. (1988). Results of the fourth NAEP assessment of mathematics: Number, operations, and word problems. *Arithmetic Teacher, 35*(8), 14–19.

LaBerge, D., & Samuels, S. J. (1974). Toward a theory of automatic information processing in reading. *Cognitive Psychology, 6,* 293–323.

Larson, C. O., Dansereau, D. F., O'Donnell, A. M., Hythecker, V. I., Lambiotte, J. G., & Rocklin, T. R. (1985). Effects of metacognitive and elaborative activity on cooperative learning and transfer. *Contemporary Educational Psychology, 10,* 342–348.

Lesh, R. (1981). Applied mathematical problem solving. *Educational Studies in Mathematics, 12,* 235–264.

Lidz, C. S. (1987). *Dynamic assessment: An interactional approach to evaluating learning potential.* New York: Guilford Press.

Lipman, M. (1985). Thinking skills fostered by Philosophy for Children. In J. Segal, S. Chipman, & R. Glaser (Eds.), *Thinking and learning skills: Relating instruction to basic research* (Vol. 1, pp. 83–108). Hillsdale, NJ: Lawrence Erlbaum Associates.

McKnight, C. C., Crosswhite, F. J., Dossey, J. A., Kifer, E., Swafford, J. O., Travers, K. J., & Cooney, T. J. (1987). *The underachieving curriculum: Assessing U.S. school mathematics from an international perspective.* Champaign, IL: Stipes Publishing.

McLarty, K., Goodman, J., Risko, V., Kinzer, C. K., Vye, N., Rowe, D., & Carson, J. (1990). Implementing anchored instruction: Guiding principles for curriculum development. In J. Zutell & S. McCormick (Eds.), *Literacy theory and research: Analyses from multiple paradigms* (pp. 109–120). Chicago: National Reading Conference.

McNamara, T. P., Miller, D. L., & Bransford, J. D. (1991). Mental models and reading comprehension. In R. Barr, M. L. Kamil, P. B. Mosenthal, & P. D. Pearson, (Eds.), *Handbook of reading research* (Vol. 2, pp. 490–511). New York: Longman.

Mokros, J. (1991). Meeting the challenge of mathematics assessment. *Hands On!, 14*(2), 1, 18–19.

National Assessment of Educational Progress (NAEP). (1983). *The third national mathematics assessment: Results, trends and issues* (Rep. No. 13-MA-01). Denver: Educational Commission of the States.

National Council of Teachers of Mathematics (1989). *Curriculum and evaluation standards for school mathematics.* Reston, VA: Author.

National Research Council (1989). *Everybody counts: A report to the nation of on the future of mathematics education*. Washington, DC: National Academy Press.

Newmann, F. M. (1991, February). Linking restructuring to authentic student achievement. *Phi Delta Kappan, 72*, 458–463.

Papert, S. (1980). *Mindstorms: Children, computers, and powerful ideas*. New York: Basic Books.

Paris, S. G., Lawton, T. A., Turner, J. C., & Roth, J. L. (1991). A developmental perspective on standardized achievement testing. *Educational Researcher, 20*(5), 12–20.

Pellegrino, J. W., Heath, A., Warren, S., with the Cognition and Technology Group at Vanderbilt (1991, April). *Collaboration at a distance: A Jasper implementation experiment in nine states*. Paper presented at the annual meeting of the American Educational Research Association, Chicago.

Piaget, J. (1952). *The origins of intelligence in children*. (M. Cook, Trans.). New York: International Universities Press.

Porter, A. (1989). A curriculum out of balance: The case of elementary school mathematics. *Educational Researcher, 18*(5), 9–15.

Resnick, L. B., & Klopfer, L. E. (Eds.). (1989). *Toward the thinking curriculum: Current cognitive research*. Alexandria, VA: ASCD.

Resnick, L. B., & Resnick, D. P. (1991). Assessing the thinking curriculum: New tools for educational reform. In B. R. Gifford & M. C. O'Connor (Eds.), *New approaches to testing: Rethinking aptitude, achievement and assessment* (pp. 37–76). New York: National Committee on Testing and Public Policy.

Rewey, K. L. (in preparation). *Small group problem solving in the Jasper environment*. Vanderbilt University, Nashville, TN.

Risko, V. J., Kinzer, C., Vye, N. J., & Rowe, D. (1990, April). *Effects of videodisc macrocontexts on comprehension and composition of causally-coherent stories*. Paper presentation at the American Educational Research Association meetings, Boston.

Rowe, D., Goodman, J., Moore, P., & McLarty, K. (1990, April). *Effects of videodisc macrocontexts on classroom interaction and student questioning during literacy lessons*. Paper presented at the annual meeting of the American Educational Research Association, Boston.

Salomon, G., & Perkins, D.N.B. (1989). Rocky road to transfer: Rethinking mechanisms of a neglected phenomenon. *Educational Psychologist, 24*(2), 113–142.

Scardamalia, M., & Bereiter, C. (1991). Higher levels of agency for children in knowledge building: A challenge for the design of new knowledge media. *Journal of the Learning Sciences, 1*, 37–68.

Schoenfeld, A. (1985). *Mathematical problem solving*. Orlando, FL: Academic Press.

Schoenfeld, A. H. (1989). Teaching mathematical thinking and problem solving. In L. B. Resnick & L. E. Klopfer (Eds.), *Toward the thinking curriculum: Current cognitive research* (pp. 83–103). Alexandria, VA: ASCD.

Shakhashiri, B. Z. (1989). NSF education makes risky bid. *Science, 246*(4928), 317–319.

Sharp, D.L.M., Bransford, J. D., Vye, N., Goldman, S. R., Kinzer, C., & Soraci, S., Jr. (1992). Literacy in an age of integrated-media. In M. J. Dreher & W. H. Slater (Eds.), *Elementary school literacy: Critical issues* (pp. 183–210). Norwood, MA: Christopher-Gorden Publishers, Inc.

Shavelson, R. J., Baxter, G. P., Pine, J., Yuré, J., Goldman, S. R., & Smith, B. (1991). Alternative technologies for large scale science assessment: Instrument of education reform. *School Effectiveness and School Improvement, 2*, 97–114.

Sherwood, R. D., Hasselbring, T. S., Marsh, E. J., & Mertz, J. C. (1990, April). *Using videodisc-based instruction to develop computational and conceptual understanding in elementary school mathematics*. Paper presented at the annual meeting of the American Educational Research Association, Boston.

Sherwood, R. D., Kinzer, C. K., Bransford, J. D., & Franks, J. J. (1987a). Some benefits of creating macro-contexts for science instruction: Initial findings. *Journal of Research in Science Teaching, 24*(5), 417–435.

Sherwood, R., Kinzer, C., Hasselbring, T., & Bransford, J. D. (1987b). Macro-contexts for learning: Initial findings and issues. *Applied Cognitive Psychology, 1,* 93–108.

Sherwood, R. D., Kinzer, C. K., Hasselbring, T., Bransford, J. D., Williams, S. M., & Goin, L. I. (1987c). New directions for videodiscs. *Computing Teachers, 14*(6), 10–13.

Silver, E. A. (1986). Using conceptual and procedural knowledge: A focus on relationships. In J. Hiebert (Ed.), *Conceptual and procedural knowledge: The case of mathematics* (pp. 181–189). Hillsdale, NJ: Lawrence Erlbaum Associates.

Simon, H. A. (1980). Problem solving and education. In D. T. Tuma & R. Reif (Eds.), *Problem solving and education: Issues in teaching and research* (pp. 81–96). Hillsdale, NJ: Lawrence Erlbaum Associates.

Slamecka, N. J., & Graf, P. (1978). The generation effect: Delineation of a phenomenon. *Journal of Experimental Psychology: Human Learning and Memory, 4,* 592–604.

Slavin, R. (1984). When does cooperative learning increase student achievement? *Psychological Bulletin, 94,* 429–445.

Soraci, S. A., Jr., Franks, J. J., Bransford, J. D., Chechile, R. A., Belli, R. F., Carr, M., & Carlin, M. T. (1994). Incongruous item generation effects: A multiple-cue perspective. *Journal of Experimental Psychology: Learning, Memory, and Cognition, 20,* 1–12.

Stein, N. L., & Trabasso, T. (1982). What's in a story: An approach to comprehension and instruction. In R. Glaser (Ed.), *Advances in instructional psychology* (Vol. 2, pp. 213–267). Hillsdale, NJ: Lawrence Erlbaum Associates.

Sternberg, R. J. (1986). *Intelligence applied.* San Diego, CA: Harcourt Brace Jovanovich.

Systems Impact, Inc. (1985). *Core concepts in math and science: A series of educational videodiscs.* Washington, DC: Systems Impact, Inc.

Van Haneghan, J. P., & Baker, L. (1989). Cognitive monitoring in mathematics. In C. B. McCormick, G. Miller, & M. Pressley (Eds.), *Cognitive strategy research: From basic research to educational applications* (pp. 215–238). New York: Springer-Verlag.

Van Haneghan, J. P., Barron, L., Young, M. F., Williams, S. M., Vye, N. J., & Bransford, J. D. (1992). The Jasper series: An experiment with new ways to enhance mathematical thinking. In D. F. Halpern (Ed.), *Enhancing thinking skills in the sciences and mathematics* (pp. 15–38). Hillsdale, NJ: Lawrence Erlbaum Associates.

Vye, N. J., Burns, M. S., Delclos, V. R., & Bransford, J. D. (1987). A comprehensive approach to assessing intellectually handicapped children. In C. S. Lidz (Ed.), *Dynamic assessment: An interactional approach to evaluating learning potential* (pp. 327–359). New York: Guilford Press.

Vye, N., Rowe, D., Kinzer, C., & Risko, V. (1990, April). *Effects and anchored instruction for teaching social studies: Enhancing comprehension of setting information.* Paper presented at the annual meeting of the American Educational Research Association, Boston.

Webb, N., Ender, P., & Lewis, S. (1986). Problem solving strategies and groups processes in small group learning computer programming. *American Educational Research Journal, 23,* 245–261.

Young, M., Van Haneghan, J., Barron, L., Williams, S., Vye, N., & Bransford, J. (1989). A problem solving approach to mathematics instruction using an embedded data videodisc. *Technology and Learning, 3*(4), 1–4.

Young, M., Vye, N. J., Williams, S., Van Haneghan, J., Bransford, J., & Barron, L. (1990, April). *Research on videodisc macrocontexts to enhance problem-solving instruction for middle school students.* Paper presented at the annual meeting of the American Educational Research Association, Boston.

11 Assessing Technology in Assessment

Henry Braun
Educational Testing Service, Princeton, NJ

Powerful tools of modern technology, such as personal computers, often seem to take on a life of their own, overshadowing the tasks to which they are applied. For this reason alone, it is useful to step back occasionally and reflect both on the actual contributions of the technology and on the costs associated with its use. In so doing we may hope to learn better how to harness technology for our purposes.

This chapter considers the role of computer-based technology in assessment, particularly for the licensing and certification of professionals such as architects, engineers, and physicians. It should be noted at the outset that whatever the contribution of this chapter, it rests on informed speculation rather than on a completed formal evaluation. The case study that underlies the presentation concerns the development of computer-based simulations of architectural practice. As of July 1992, 4 years of work have been completed and 4 more are planned. The prototyping phase is nearly complete and preparations for operational implementation are being finalized. Despite the somewhat fragmentary nature of the results, there has been some opportunity to consider the impact of technology. Hopefully, our thoughts and reflections will prove useful to others.

TECHNOLOGY IN THE ASSESSMENT OF PROFESSIONALS

Perhaps the first contribution of the new technology has been to stimulate many professions and licensing agencies to reexamine their assessment procedures. The advent of relatively inexpensive personal computers connected through local area networks, as well as peripherals such as videodisc players, promises both enhanced efficiency and greater comprehensiveness of domain coverage. Concurrently, the testing industry sees an opportunity to introduce new kinds of questions that can be organized in novel ways, making it feasible both to validly assess a broader range of competencies and to provide useful feedback to the candidate. Moreover, computer technology may well facilitate more efficient test development, better security, and quicker reporting.

However, there are potential problems with the application of technology to assessment. These problems include cost, delivery, program maintenance, and equity. Each point is examined in turn. At the same time, it is important to take an ecological perspective. It may be that the introduction of technology can have systemic effects, both positive and negative, that are not captured by a more reductive analysis. In a later section, we discuss a particular benefit that appears to result from one technological innovation. Other areas in psychological testing have recognized the issues posed by the new technology (Conoley, Plake, & Kemmerer, 1991).

THE ARCHITECTURAL REGISTRATION EXAMINATION

A case study in the use of technology in assessment involves work underway at Educational Testing Service (ETS) on the use of computer-based simulations of architectural practice. The goal is to facilitate performance assessment of aspiring architects by creating on the computer a version of a natural work setting. By using technology, it is possible to create a dynamic environment in which candidates can work much as they would in a modern architectural office. (Although most architects do not regularly work with computers, there is a clear trend toward increased usage, particularly among younger practitioners.) Moreover, advances in artificial intelligence make possible automated scoring of complex constructed responses (Bejar, 1991; Braun, Bennett, Frye, & Soloway, 1990).

Inasmuch as testing and computer technology are relatively new bedfellows, it seems safer to reason from the specific to the general, rather than the other way around. Accordingly, let's begin with a brief discussion of the context in which the Architect Registration Examination (ARE) operates.

Architects, like physicians, cannot simply hang up a shingle once they have completed their academic training. In most states, they must enter into an internship program and, after 3 to 4 years, are eligible to take a series of examinations, the ARE, sponsored by the National Council of Architectural Registration Boards (NCARB). Each member board represents a different state or other legal jurisdiction. The purpose of the examination is to protect the public's health, safety, and welfare. Consequently, the tests focus on essential elements of competent practice, rather than on areas like the aesthetics of design. Nonetheless, candidates have the opportunity to produce creative solutions that integrate design principles and the constraints imposed by the building program.

The current test battery is composed of nine examinations, seven employing paper-and-pencil-based multiple choice testing and two employing an open-ended graphical response modality requiring the demonstration of design skills. Student solutions in the latter two examinations are scored by trained pairs of architects randomly drawn from juries specially convened for this task.

In 1987 NCARB asked ETS to develop a computer-delivered test of the multiple choice examinations. That project is effectively complete and some small-scale operational testing has been carried out. Moreover, a new form of test administration, called computerized mastery testing (CMT), has been developed (Lewis & Sheehan, 1989).

Under computerized mastery testing, the item pool for each of the seven multiple choice divisions is organized into sets of items called *testlets* (Wainer & Kiely, 1987), which are constructed to be roughly equivalent in content and in psychometric characteristics. Each testlet contains 10 to 25 items, depending on the particular test. Each candidate begins by taking two testlets. On the basis of the responses obtained, a determination is made as to whether the candidate has passed, failed, or whether there is insufficient information to determine the outcome. In the latter case, additional testlets are administered until sufficient information to make a decision has been obtained, or a predetermined maximum number of testlets has been administered. Overall, a considerable saving in testing time can be realized.

THE GRAPHIC DESIGN TEST

NCARB also asked ETS to develop a new computer-based simulation of architectural practice. Whereas the proposed role of this new test has changed somewhat over time, its present purpose is to replace one of the open-ended examinations, a 12-hour graphic design test. The current test poses to the candidate the task of designing a two-story building (such as a school) while imposing certain requirements and restrictions on potential solutions (such as the number of classrooms, volume of student traffic, climatic conditions, etc.). The candidate must produce four drawings: two floor plans, a building elevation, and a building section.

Early on it was decided that the new test would not simply be a computer-based version of the old. Rather, it would take a somewhat different approach to assessing graphic design skills. This approach was based on considerations of both validity and feasibility and is discussed later. As presently conceived, the new test will consist of four simulations, each based on a different architectural project. A simulation, in turn, will be composed of up to four problems, called *vignettes,* that arise in the course of an architectural project. Each vignette presents the candidate with a number of related tasks and the candidate must produce a solution.

A number of important issues confronted the team charged with implementing the simulation test. These include authoring, delivery, scoring, and security. To give the reader a flavor of the test, we begin with a brief description of the delivery component. The other issues are addressed in subsequent sections.

The delivery mechanism must provide a computer-based version of the architect's work setting, including the resources and design tools typically available in that setting. The environment should permit all candidates, even those with no previous experience with the computer, to develop and modify solutions easily.

The system we have developed employs two monitors. A high-resolution monitor is used as a model office. It contains icons reflecting three types of resources: a "bookshelf," a "drafting table," and a "file cabinet." The bookshelf contains excerpts from standard architectural references and codes. The drafting table contains blueprints and other drawings relevant to the particular project at hand and, similarly, the filing cabinet contains written materials that are specific to the project. Using a mouse, the candidate may access any of the resources at any time, may page through either reference volumes or project materials, may record copies of those materials in an on-screen notebook, and may access the notebook directly at any time during the simulation.

The other monitor, called the *work screen,* has a lower resolution at the moment and represents the work space. Here candidates carry out their design activities in response to the tasks posed in the vignette. Each vignette displays a set of icons representing different functional capabilities. The icons are activated by the click of a mouse. A few icons, such as "HELP" or "START OVER," are common to all vignettes. Together, the tools available to the candidate constitute a simple system for computer-aided design. It is worth mentioning that, using the mouse, the candidate can move smoothly from one monitor to the other; hence it is very easy for the candidate to employ the resources in the model office whenever they are needed.

In one vignette, the task is to design a block diagram (a kind of preliminary floor plan) for a particular building, say a library. The candidate is provided with a set of design elements that must be arranged on a particular site in a way that is responsive to the demands of the building program. The spaces comprising the building are initially represented by squares whose areas are proportionally scaled to the areas described in the program. The introductory screen is illustrated in Fig. 11.1. The design elements are initially placed in a horizontal strip along the top edge. For example, the largest element (denoted A) represents the adult study area, whereas the next largest (denoted MR) represents the meeting room. The central portion of the screen displays the site, including relevant information such as contour lines, existing streets and trees, and the perimeter of the buildable area. Along the left edge are the icons representing the different functionalities.

For example, one icon allows the candidate to move ("drag") the design elements onto the site. A second icon permits the height and width of the element to be adjusted while keeping the area constant. A third causes the design ele-

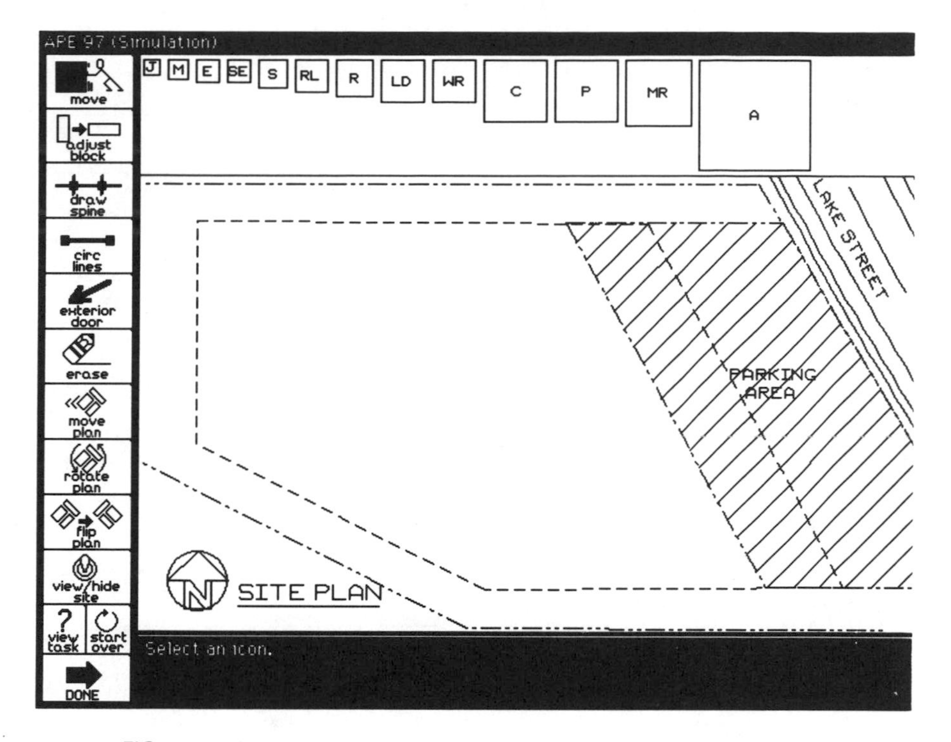

FIG. 11.1. Introductory screen for vignette for designing a block diagram.

ments to be rotated on the site in order to achieve certain requirements (i.e., to create views or to avoid removing nearby trees). Another allows the candidate to indicate how the circulation in the building will occur, either between spaces or along public corridors. Obviously, the number of potential solutions, even for a relatively small number of design elements, is very large, making scoring a nontrivial task. One possible solution is presented in Fig. 11.2.

Another vignette requires production of a structural schematic drawing. In this vignette, candidates must indicate how they would lay out the structural frame for a building or a particular section of a building. The building program provides information on live loads and dead loads to be supported as well as other structural requirements such as clear span areas. The introductory screen for this vignette is presented in Fig. 11.3. In this case, there is not a fixed number of design elements to be manipulated. Instead, the candidate must call on different icons depicting load-bearing walls, columns, beams, and joists, in order to construct a viable and economical structural frame. One solution for the adult study area is displayed in Fig. 11.4. Again, even for a relatively small problem, the number of potential solutions is very large.

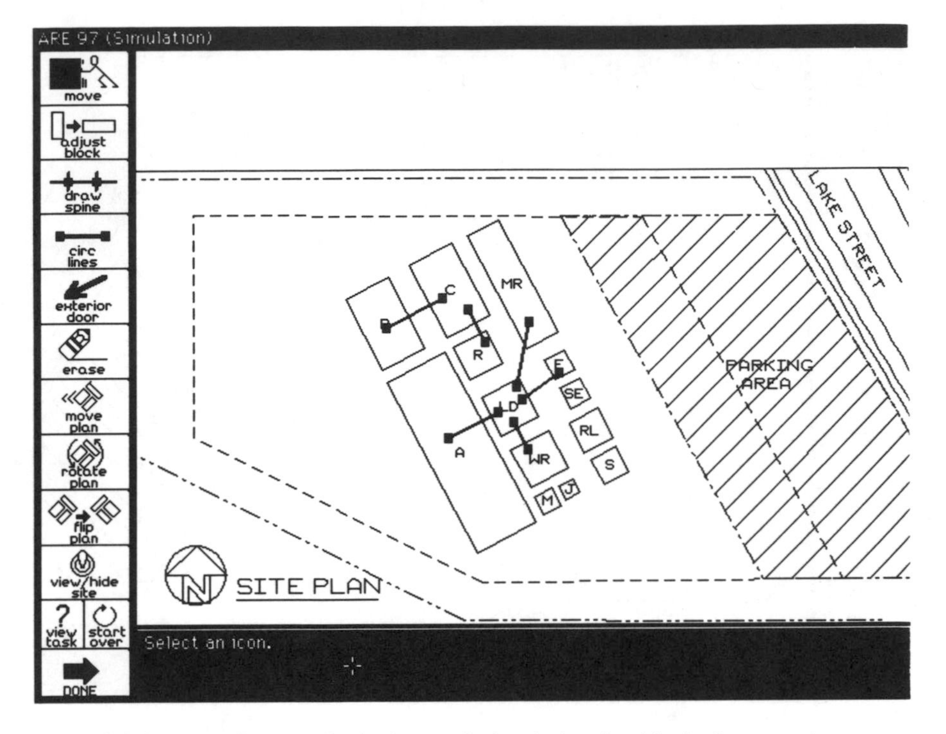

FIG. 11.2. Screen displaying typical solution for block diagram vignette.

ASSESSING THE ROLE OF TECHNOLOGY

The usual purpose of a licensing program for a profession is to assure the public that practitioners meet certain qualifications deemed essential for competent performance. The assessment component of the program usually provides critical data to inform the licensing decision. In considering the role of technology, we must focus on two sets of questions. The first set concerns the impact of technology on the validity, reliability, comparability, and fairness of the examination. The second set revolves around the technical, psychometric, and economic feasibility of a computer-based examination. It is important to note that both feasibility and validity must be considered from the start but, naturally, the empirical evidence on feasibility usually precedes validity evidence.

Let us begin by reviewing the conception underlying the structure of the simulation test. The test is construct driven in the sense that it is thought of as a vehicle for assessing the skills and abilities essential for competent practice. This approach stands in contrast to a task-centered one in which ultimate interest

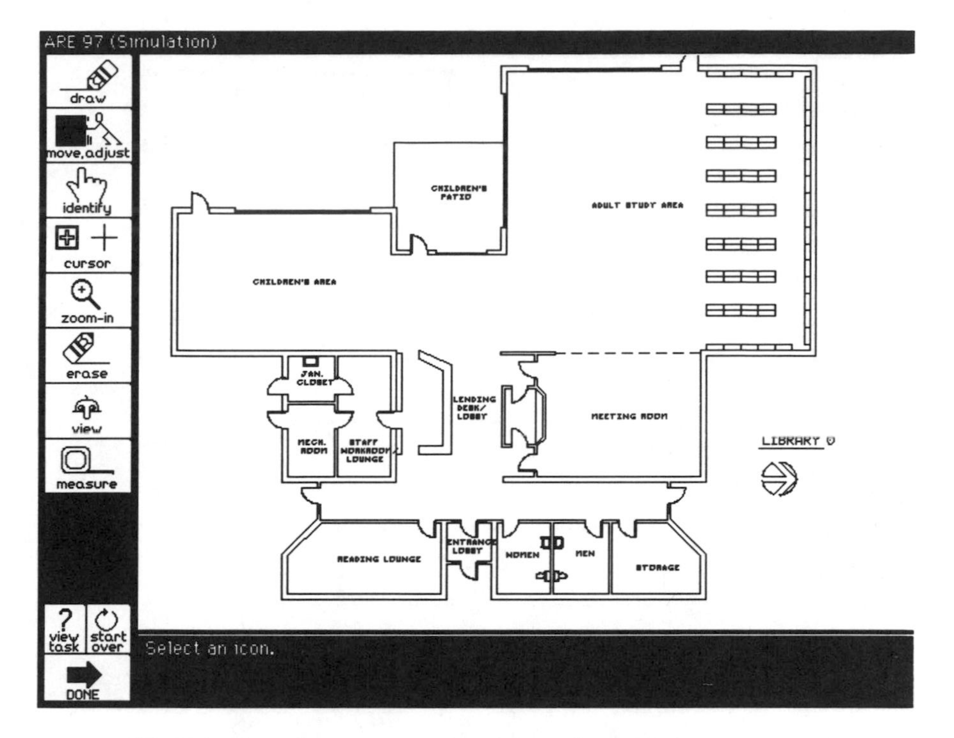

FIG. 11.3. Introductory screen for vignette for designing a structural schematic diagram.

focuses on the specific behaviors elicited by the tasks presented. As Messick (1994) argued, the latter approach is deficient when the purpose of the test is to make inferences about future performances in a broad range of settings.

The operational implication of a construct-driven strategy is that vignettes are primarily designed to provide useful information about the underlying constructs of interest—such as the candidate's ability to solve design problems under the conditions and requirements typical of architectural practice. Aspects of real-world tasks that do not contribute materially to this end are eliminated or simplified, particularly if this would contribute to the practicality of the enterprise.

For example, in practice, projects may call for designs with 20 or more elements. It is not unreasonable to speculate that as the number of elements increase, the difficulty and the required time to complete the task also increases. Beyond some point, however, the increase in difficulty may be due to implementation issues rather than conceptual factors. That is, as with any other measure, the identification of relevant and irrelevant sources of response difficulty is essential.

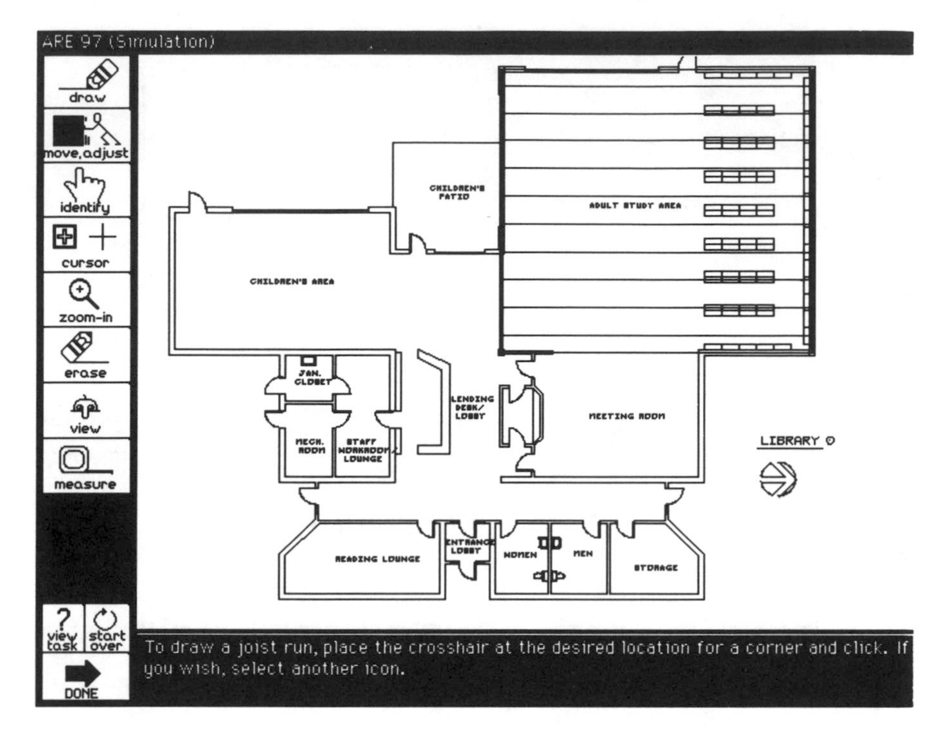

FIG. 11.4. Screen displaying typical solution for structural schematic diagram vignette.

Once the examination is operational, tests for individual candidates will be constructed by sampling four simulations from a large library of simulations. (This library will remain relatively stable over time with some small percentage of elements replaced each year.) Again, a problem is how to select the four simulations so that together they provide maximum information about the candidate's skills. These test design issues at different levels lead us naturally into a discussion of feasibility.

FEASIBILITY

Feasibility is concerned with whether the examination can be developed, delivered, and maintained at a reasonable cost. Achieving feasibility requires constant tradeoffs between goals and resources available. An ostensible goal of any simulation is to achieve high fidelity (Fitzpatrick & Morrison, 1971). In an examination of architectural skills, realism—in both the resources available to the candidate and the nature of the exercises presented—is desirable. The challenge is to maximize fidelity without incurring prohibitive developmental and operational costs.

For example, providing an extensive set of design tools will increase development costs, as will constructing complex vignettes involving many design elements. There are hidden costs as well. Increased complexity necessitates the need for more elaborate tutorials and longer practice time to prepare candidates to take the examination. One solution lies in identifying those features of the real-life setting that are essential to the assessment of the desired constructs and to making appropriate distinctions between candidates. The simulation should then be designed to be as simple as possible while capturing those critical features. Thus, practical assessment through simulations will depend as much on a talent for knowing what to leave out as what to put in. Research currently underway at ETS in support of this project should provide answers to these questions. One research project, for example, is investigating the nature of response difficulty and covariation among design tasks.

Computer-based tests also necessitate extended administrations due to the lack of a sufficient number of computer terminals with which to test the candidate population at one time. Whereas candidates benefit from more flexible testing schedules, security is more complicated than simply hiring a number of proctors to make sure examinees do not cheat. The security issue revolves around the fact that if the examination is given repeatedly over a period of time, those taking it later will have the advantage of talking to friends who took it earlier. Presumably, the exam will be easier for the candidates tested later in the administration period. One way of countering this scenario is to create an extensive library of simulations so that it is very unlikely that two people will take exactly the same set of simulations. This, in turn, requires that a very large number of vignettes be available.

Another technical issue concerns the generation and maintenance of scoring programs. As mentioned earlier, for vignettes that result in complex constructed responses, the number of potential solutions is usually so large that it is not possible to score a response by simply comparing it to templates of model solutions at different levels. In fact, there may be many classes of ideal solutions (or, for that matter, many classes of solutions meriting partial credit), each class having many members. Consequently, an acceptable scoring program must be able to decompose and reason about the candidate's solution and then place each solution at the appropriate point on a score scale.

These desiderata pose several challenges. First, building such programs requires extensive knowledge engineering as well as substantial empirical testing to assure accuracy and comprehensiveness. Because both activities are labor intensive and time consuming, each program must be designed so that it can accommodate an entire class of vignettes. The effort needed to construct a new program for each specific vignette would be prohibitive.

Interestingly, building algorithms for assigning partial credit scores to solutions also involves considerable effort in setting and validating standards. Although there has been some work in the psychometric literature (Andrich, 1978; Wilson, 1990) on developing relevant models, there has been comparatively little reported on systematically eliciting experts' judgments for such purposes (though some organizations, like ETS, have considerable practical experience in this area). Accordingly, there are a number of issues to be resolved. Among them are (a) determining the optimal number of score categories, (b) generating usable descriptions of each category to facilitate the establishment of specific scoring guidelines, and (c) developing methods for monitoring the alignment of scoring standards among different vignettes. Each problem requires both analytic and empirical contributions for its resolution.

The introduction of tasks requiring complex constructed responses also raises many interesting questions for the measurement community. Because candidates need more time to respond, it is essential that the maximum amount of information be extracted from the solution. Yet logic suggests that the task of developing appropriate psychometric models will be simplified if the number of features retained is kept as small as possible. Resolving the tension between these two demands will be critical.

It is also generally accepted that current psychometric theory does not adequately address the needs of simulation tests. Most likely, we need to rethink classical notions like reliability, rather than engage in simple modifications of existing measures. Moreover, a new framework for making pass–fail decisions must be developed. Having completed the exam, the candidate presents a profile of vignette scores. A defensible decision-theoretic framework for mapping profiles into the pass or fail categories is essential. Developing such a framework is now underway at ETS and involves close collaboration between psychometricians and expert architects.

The difficulty is due to the fact that different vignettes may well test different constellations of skills, mastery of which is considered essential to competent practice. If the public's health, safety, and welfare is to be protected, a strong performance in one area should not be allowed to compensate for a poor performance in another area. Thus, adding the vignette scores and locating a convenient cut point on the resulting scale would not be a desirable procedure. More refined methods are needed.

Economic feasibility has two major aspects. The first concerns the costs associated with developing and maintaining the infrastructure required by a national testing program. The second is related to the cost of delivering the examination, the principal factor being the charge back for an appropriate workstation.

With each passing year, the latter expense appears to be increasingly less significant. As hardware costs decline and testing volume expands, unit costs for computer-based testing are being reduced rapidly. Although such testing cannot compete directly with traditional paper-and-pencil testing, savings realized through automated scoring of candidate productions (in contrast to human scoring) may offset much of the cost differential.

Certainly, the initial outlays in developing new computer-based tests are large and often represent a substantial barrier to the client. For example, the development of a large library of simulations can be extremely costly, though efficient test development procedures, including the use of computer-based authoring tools, can be quite effective. Annual maintenance costs, though, should be no greater—and perhaps less—than the current cost of developing an entirely new exam each year.

The price of the computer-delivered test is likely to be greater than that of the paper-and-pencil test it replaces, so two points are worth noting: Candidates who are working professionals will appreciate the freedom to schedule the examination at a convenient time. Moreover, if computer tests are considerably shorter than their paper-and-pencil counterparts, the time saved may well result in increased earnings. It is projected, for example, that the computerized battery for architects will require some 12 fewer hours than the current battery.

VALIDITY

The notion of validity has undergone substantial evolution over the last 40 years (Angoff, 1988). The current view (Messick, 1989) emphasizes construct validity as the central conception and declares that validity concerns the appropriateness of the inferences and decisions that are made on the basis of the test. In the present setting, this suggests the following questions: Are we measuring the appropriate constructs of architectural practice with the use of this test? Are these constructs measured reliably (with sufficient replication) and accurately (with effective scoring programs)? Are the decisions made appropriate and defensible?

Leaving aside for the moment these core issues, let us first consider the impact of the computer-based test on reliability, comparability, and fairness. The combination of more disciplined test development procedures, the new test structure (multiple simulations composed of linked vignettes), and automated scoring should yield improvements on all three dimensions.

Under the current examination system, a new design problem is produced each year. Whereas the requirements remain the same over time, the overall difficulty of the problem, as well as the difficulty of the particular segments, may vary considerably. The new test will be built from a fixed number of vignette types, expressed through different projects in a carefully determined manner to control difficulty. Moreover, each test will offer a better sampling of building types than is now the case through the use of multiple simulations.

Consequently, two forms of the new test taken by a candidate are more likely to be parallel in the psychometric sense (Lord & Novick, 1968) than two of the annual versions now available. Reliability should be further enhanced through the use of automated scoring, eliminating the rater-to-rater variability that bedevils current performance assessments. Thus the new test addresses both sources of unreliability: form-to-form differences and between-rater disagreements.

The situation is somewhat more complex when we turn our attention to comparability. Candidates who take the current test in the same year are given exactly the same form, whereas candidates who take the current test in different years are given quite different forms. With the new test, all candidates receive essentially different forms so that there is no uniformity within an administration as at present. On the other hand, as we have argued, comparability between administrations should be greatly improved.

Improved reliability and comparability clearly contribute to greater fairness for the candidate. The effects of differences in drawing skills is eliminated with computer delivery, though degree of comfort with computers may prove to be a factor. It remains to be seen whether there will be any significant differences in performance among the various subgroups in the population.

Certainly reliability, comparability, and fairness are important components of the validation argument. But establishing the construct validity of any examination is an arduous and ongoing task. One approach (Messick, 1994) is to examine the evidence for "the two major threats to construct validity—namely construct underrepresentation and construct-irrelevant variance." Development of the simulation exam is ongoing, thus this exercise has more of a formative than a summative flavor.

Over the years, NCARB has commissioned a number of job analyses to determine the critical tasks in current architectural practice, as well as the knowledge, skills, and abilities required for competent performance. Updates are carried out at 5-year intervals. The test development committees, composed of expert architects and testing specialists, work with these task analyses in the construction of vignettes. Beyond coverage of the generic tasks appropriate to a building design examination, a critical concern is that the activities embedded in the vignettes in fact tap into various aspects of the underlying constructs of interest.

As prototype vignettes take shape, we have begun preliminary field trials to collect data that will enable us to build the evidential bases for construct validity. This will include process data obtained through various protocol studies and psychometric analyses that compare performance on different vignettes as well as with performance on multiple choice components of the ARE battery.

It is important that the construct representation argument be carried though the scoring phase. That is, the design of the scoring rubrics that are at the heart of the automated scoring systems must be consistent with the structure of the domain as expressed in the design of the test. Here, too, we have initiated some studies to examine consistency in the scoring rubrics developed by different groups and the comparability of experts' holistic judgments of candidate productions with those obtained through the analytical approach of expert systems.

With respect to construct-irrelevant variance, there are a number of obvious issues. Prior familiarity with computers, or with computer-aided design, should not confer an advantage (or disadvantage!) in test performance. The system interface has been designed to be relatively transparent and easy to master after a short trial period. Moreover, we need to assure ourselves that the structure of the tasks and the power of the interface do not permit students to employ inappropriate strategies in problem solving. Again, pilot studies and further field trials will provide empirical evidence on these two issues.

We have already noted that fully automated scoring eliminates one important source of construct-irrelevant variance, rater viability. However, lacunae in the design logic of these scoring systems may introduce other forms of unwanted variance and this possibility must be checked through the analysis of large number of solutions.

Perhaps the most natural approach to validating a licensing examination would be to demonstrate high correlations between test scores and some reliable measures of job performance. Unfortunately, this seems to be impractical and it has been argued (Kane, 1982) that it is nearly impossible to develop suitable criteria with which to conduct classical predictive validity studies in professional settings. Although such studies, in any case, would not have been sufficient to establish full construct validity, their absence places a greater burden on the remaining validation strategies.

ECOLOGICAL APPROACH TO ASSESSING TECHNOLOGY

It is important that any attempt to assess the contribution of technology to the practice of testing take account of potential system effects that might not be captured by a series of focused questions formulated a priori. An analogous situation arises in the classroom, where the introduction of computers may change the nature of the teacher–student dynamic as well as specific student-centered learning behaviors.

The systemic validity argument (Frederiksen & Collins, 1989) declares that good tests will force the school system to adapt in educationally sound ways in order to meet the new goals. There may well be such an effect on schools of architecture when the simulation test becomes operational, although the gap between the end of schooling and the taking of the test is rather substantial. I would like to argue that it is more certain that the new technology will have profound effects on the organization that produces the test!

As we gain experience with computer-based testing, it becomes clearer that a new partnership must be forged among test developers, cognitive scientists, computer scientists, and psychometricians. Successful development of performance assessments (sometimes referred to as "authentic assessments"), will require close collaboration of these different specialties in order to ensure that a viable examination emerges. For example, rather small differences in the presentation of a vignette can have substantial implications for the complexity of scoring. Consequently, an efficient iterative process must be worked out so that the finished product reflects the best attainable compromise between say, fidelity and feasibility.

Perhaps the most exciting (unanticipated) benefits arising from the introduction of technology lie in the consequences of developing programs for carrying out automated scoring. By virtue of having to create computer programs to score complex constructed responses, test developers are forced to rationalize and stabilize a set of test specifications which in the past may have been vague and ambiguous. A clear definition of the vocabulary and universe examined by the test will be essential in building an operational scoring system. Once the test specifications are developed in a way that can support automatic scoring, there exists the basis for creating a system that provides greater stability of test vignettes from one administration to the other. We have already argued that such achievements should contribute to the construct validity of the test.

Equally important is the fact that by developing such systems, approximately 90% of the work required for diagnostic feedback will have been done. That is, once automated scoring is on line, useful diagnostic feedback can be provided to the candidate with little extra effort. This innovation can then be transferred to both the school and workplace. A number of related issues are treated by O'Neil and Baker (1991) in their discussion of intelligent computer-assisted instruction (ICAI). In particular, they pointed out that the use of expert systems can help make the test development process more rigorous. Moreover, provision of diagnostic feedback from tests can clearly benefit from the more ambitious work in ICAI.

CONCLUSIONS

The preceding analysis has suggested some of the ways in which the introduction of technology can aid assessment. Of course, not all of the innovations discussed depend on technology. In principle, a vignette-based examination could be introduced with paper-and-pencil delivery. However, the cumulative impact of the introduction of technology and the accompanying changes in test design, delivery, and scoring is likely to be enormous. It is essential, however, that the use of technology be shaped by the needs of the assessment program and not driven solely by the potential of the technology.

This balance will be difficult to maintain as new innovations, such as virtual reality, become more widely available. At the same time, it is important that simulations for assessment be clearly distinguished from simulations for training. When training is the major purpose, the balance between fidelity on the one hand and cost or feasibility on the other may well shift toward the former.

Although the discussion has focused on the example of architecture, most of the points raised should be relevant to other professions as well. Naturally, though, each profession will require certain specialized features in the assessment program. In medicine, for example, time pressure is often a critical element in medical decision making. A proper simulation should recreate the temporal character of medical practice. In fact, the simulations now under development by the National Board of Medical Examiners (S. G. Clyman, D. E. Melnick, E. R. Julian, N. A. Orr, & K. E. Cotton 1991) incorporate this aspect of practice.

By stimulating fresh thinking about the assessment enterprise, the new technology has already made positive contributions. In particular, simulations incorporating computer technology provide an exciting and practical means of assessment. The testing profession must hope that by developing assessment instruments embodying the precepts of systemic validity, it can begin to change the attitudes of the public, as well as segments of the educational community, toward the concept of standardized testing as a fair way of generating information for decisions.

ACKNOWLEDGMENTS

I would like to thank Isaac Bejar, Randy Bennett, Richard Devore, and William Ward for their helpful comments on earlier drafts of this chapter. I also want to take this opportunity to express my appreciation to my co-workers at ETS, members of the staff of the National Council of Architectural Registration Boards (NCARB), as well as the practicing architects who have volunteered their time to the Architectural Simulations Project for providing such a stimulating, collegial environment within which to carry out the work described herein. The research reported here has been jointly supported by NCARB and ETS.

The writing of this chapter was supported in part by a contract from the Defense Advanced Research Projects Agency (DARPA), administered by the Office of Naval Research (ONR), to the UCLA Center for the Study of Evaluation/Center for Technology Assessment. However, the opinions expressed do not necessarily reflect the positions of DARPA or ONR, and no official endorsement by either organization should be inferred.

REFERENCES

Andrich, D. (1978). A rating formulation for ordered response categories. *Psychometrika, 43*, 561–573.

Angoff, W. (1988). Validity: An evolving concept. In H. Wainer & H. I. Braun (Eds.), *Test validity* (pp. 19–30). Hillsdale, NJ: Lawrence Erlbaum Associates.

Bejar, I. I. (1991). A methodology for scoring open-ended architectural design problems. *Journal of Applied Psychology, 76,* 522–532.

Braun, H. I., Bennett, R. E., Frye, D., & Soloway, E. (1990). Scoring constructed responses using expert systems. *Journal of Educational Measurement, 27,* 93–108.

Clyman, S. G., Melnick, D. E., Julian, E. R., Orr, N. A., & Cotton, K. E. (1991). *The National Board of Medical Examiners' Computer-based Examination Clinical Simulation* (*CBX*). Philadelphia: National Board of Medical Examiners.

Conoley, C. W., Plake, B. S., & Kemmerer, B. E. (1991). Issues in Computer-Based Test Interpretive Systems. *Computers in Human Behavior, 7,* 97–101.

Fitzpatrick, R., & Morrison, E. (1971). Performance and product evaluation. In R. L. Thorndike (Ed.), *Educational measurement* (2nd ed., pp. 237–279). Washington, DC: American Council on Education.

Frederiksen, J., & Collins, A. (1989). A systems approach to educational testing. *Educational Researcher, 18,* 27–32

Kane, M. (1982). The validity of licensure examinations. *American Psychologist, 37,* 911–918.

Lewis, C., & Sheehan, K. (1989). Using Bayesian decision theory to design a computerized mastery test. *Applied Psychological Measurement, 14,* 367–386.

Lord, F. M., & Novick, M. R. (1968). *Statistical theories of mental test scores.* Reading, MA: Addison-Wesley.

Messick, S. M. (1989). Validity. In R. L. Linn (Ed.), *Educational Measurement* (pp. 13–103). New York: American Council on Education and Macmillan Publishing.

Messick, S. M. (1994). The interplay of evidence and consequences in the validation of performance assessments. *Educational Researcher.*

O'Neill, H. F. Jr., & Baker, E. L. (1991). Issues in intelligent computer-assisted instruction: Evaluation and Measurement In. T. Gutkin and S. Wise (Eds.), *The Computer and the Decision-Making Process.* Hillsdale, NJ: Lawrence Erlbaum Associates.

Wainer, H., & Kiely, G. (1987). Item clusters and computerized adaptive testing: A case for testlets. *Journal of Educational Measurement, 24,* 185–201.

Wilson, M. (1990). *An extension of the partial credit model to incorporate diagnostic information.* Berkeley: University of California Press.

Author Index

K

L

M

Subject Index